AIRWORLD

Vitra Design Museum

AIRWORLD

DESIGN AND ARCHITECTURE FOR AIR TRAVEL

Catalogue

Editors: Alexander von Vegesack, Jochen Eisenbrand
Picture Editor: Elgin Schultz
Graphic Design: Thorsten Romanus
Copy Editors: Brian Currid and Wilhelm Werthern
Translations: Brian Currid, Barbara Hauß, Robyn de Jong,
and Julia Thorson
Lithography & Printing: GZD, Ditzingen
Production Management: Roman Passarge

Exhibition

Curator: Jochen Eisenbrand
Assistant: Elgin Schultz
Exhibition Design: Dieter Thiel
Graphic Design: Thorsten Romanus
Technical Planning: Thierry Hodel, Stefani Fricker,
and Michael Simolka
Financial Planning: Roman Passarge
Model construction: Marc Gehde, Patrick Maier,
and Oswald Dillier
Press and Publicity: Gabriella Gianoli, Alexa Tepen
Tour Organisation: Reiner Packeiser and Sandra Bachmann

The Deutsche Bibliothek has registered this publication
in the Deutsche Nationalbibliografie; detailed
bibliographical information can be found on the Internet at
http://dnb.ddb.de

ISBN 3-931936-49-X
Printed in Germany

©2004 Vitra Design Stiftung gGmbH,
the authors, and translators.
Charles-Eames-Str. 1
D-79576 Weil am Rhein
Second edition, 2006

The copyright owners for images used are named in the
list of illustrations credits.
If individual rights have not been recognised, we ask for
your understanding and will correct this immediately.

Airworld: Design and Architecture for Air Travel is a project
of Vitra Design Museum.

We thank the following lenders
for their support:

Albrecht Bangert
Hans Theo Baumann
Bluequest
Boeing
Design Council Archive, University of Brighton
Deutsches Museum, Munich
EADS, Deutschland GmbH
Foster and Partners
Hector Cabezas, Luftfahrthistorische Sammlung Frankfurt
Hochschule für Angewandte Wissenschaften, Hamburg
Lothar Grim
GSA Facilitaire Diensten Schiphol-Oost
Pieke Hooghoff
Ross Lovegrove
Musée de l'Air et de l'Espace, Le Bourget
Centre national d'art et de culture Georges Pompidou
Die Neue Sammlung, Staatliches Museum für Angewandte
Kunst, Design in der Pinakothek der Moderne, Munich
Nick Roericht
Swiss International Air Lines
Teague
Verkehrshaus der Schweiz
Wilhelm Wagenfeld Stiftung

The publication and exhibition were made possible
in part by the support of:

8   Preface

12   Hasso Spode, 'Let Us Fly You Where the Sun Is':
Air Travel and Tourism in Historical Perspective

36   Koos Bosma, In Search of the Perfect Airport

82   Barbara Fitton Hauß, A Trip Through Time
in the Aircraft Cabin

124   Jochen Eisenbrand, 'More Legroom Please':
A Historical Survey of the Aircraft Seat

144   Jochen Eisenbrand, Airlines and
Corporate Design

176   Joanne Entwistle, Fashion Takes Flight:
The Air Stewardess and Her Uniform

212   Jochen Eisenbrand, Dining Aloft

230   Mathias Remmele, An Invitation to Fly:
Poster Art in the Service of Civilian Air Travel

264   Christoph Asendorf, The Inspiration of Flight:
Developments in Art, Design, and Architecture
since the 1930s

291   Authors

292   Illustration Credits

295   Index

Preface

Of course, air travel also has its disadvantages, that cannot be denied, but it is nonetheless quite the right thing for people of my sort. For the stays on barren empty airfields [...] only last quarters of an hour, and everything else is quite pretty and agreeable [...] [T]he noise [of the propellers] is bearable, one plugs one's ears, and while the ear was mistreated, the eye luxuriated [...] the bodily feeling, sense of touch, the sense of balance — in floating through the air, the corporeality of which was clearly noticeable, there were many fine, sensual sensations.[1]

Today, it is certainly the rare exception that a trip in an aeroplane causes feelings like those had by Hermann Hesse in 1928 when he flew from Berlin to Stuttgart. Flying, once the adventurous and exclusive pleasure of a select few, has long become part of everyday life, with an annual 1.6 billion passengers world-wide travelling by air. The development from the first regular airline flights in 1919 to today's mass air transport is more dramatic than in any other means of transportation during the twentieth century. The Junkers F 13 from the early days of regular air travel, which with its all-metal body and cantilever wings was considered the first modern passenger aircraft, offered only room for four passengers in its cabin, and at speeds of 170 km/h it could fly non-stop over a distance of 1,000 km. Fifty years later, the Boeing 747 took its first flight: this immense jumbo jet could fit almost 500 passengers in its body, and fly them five times as fast and ten times as far.

The rapid development of passenger air travel has up until now hardly been studied from the perspective of design history. Aviation museums usually concentrate in their exhibitions more on the pioneering years of flight, as well as military and private aviation, rather than commercial air travel. Above all, they usually narrate the history of aviation from a technological perspective: the impressive outer appearance of the original aeroplanes is central. The technological aspects of aircraft also play a central role in the histories of aeroplane manufacturers. The airlines usually narrate their corporate history as a succession of 'firsts'. We read of routes first flown, the aeroplane types an airline was the first to use, or speeds and distances that they were the first to achieve. Until now, the work of prominent industrial designers, graphic artists, and fashion designers for the air travel industry has only received marginal attention. Even if technological progress was the fundamental precondition for the rapid development and enormous spread of air travel, it is also thanks to the designers that the experience of air travel has changed so dramatically since its beginnings. Thus, as the artist Martha Rosler observed, one can today speak of a 'totalized, industrialized representation of air travel and its associated spaces as a "world apart" [...] different from that of any form of mass transport'.[2] In his 2001 novel *Up in the Air*, Walter Kirn describes the world of passenger flight in somewhat more exaggerated terms, indeed as a closed aesthetic system: 'I call it airworld; the scene, the place, the style. Airworld is a nation within a nation, with its own language, architecture, mood and even its own currency – the token economy of airline bonus miles that I've come to value more than dollars.'[3] The historical transformation of this 'airworld' is the subject of the exhibition and catalogue: airport architecture, airline corporate design, aeroplane seats and interiors, flight attendant uniforms, and finally the design of in-flight tableware.

Airports, in a sense the metropolises of this airworld, mark the beginning and end of each flight.[4] A long time has passed since the age of 'barren, empty airfields' at which one spends 'quarters of an hour'. At the latest with the arrival of the jet plane around 1960, the airports saw themselves confronted with an explosion in passenger volume that required increasingly complex logistics to keep the streams of arrivals and departures, transit passengers, luggage, and freight flowing in a relatively smooth fashion. At the same time, distances for the passengers inside the airport had to be kept to a minimum and quick and simple orientation had to be guaranteed. In part for this purpose, the first comprehensive signage systems and pictograms were developed for airports in the 1960s. Over the decades, various basic types of airport came to crystallise: the simple, rectangular passenger terminals of the early years of flight, buildings that hug the landing field in an arc, terminals with fingers or satellites, or decentrally organised airports with individual terminals that can be accessed directly with ground transportation. Convincing architectural models provide more than merely a well-functioning machine for passenger transfer. They plan for expansion from the very beginning and succeed in offering something of the fascination that flying, despite everything, can still evoke.

Passenger aviation poses special challenges not only for architects, but also for designers. Space on the aeroplane is limited, every excess gram on board raises the costs to operate the aircraft, and all materials used are subject to the strictest safety regulations. This would seem to leave little room for creative freedom.

Nonetheless, an astonishing number of prominent designers have worked for the air travel industry. Some, like Henry Dreyfuss and especially Walter Dorwin Teague, specialised already early in working with aeroplane manufacturers and airlines, setting new standards in cabin design. For many others, the work with the airlines was something new and an exception. Today almost inconceivable, in the 1920s artists were entrusted with aviation design, and through the 1960s aeroplane manufacturers and airlines sometimes commissioned furniture designers and architects to develop aeroplane interiors or a corporate image. One reason for this might be that the air travel industry emerged at about the same time in which the profession of the industrial designers and the commercial graphic artists began to take on clear contours. Today, in contrast, transportation design and aviation design have long become their own highly specialised disciplines.

Many fashion designers have also worked with airlines. Airline uniforms are changed about every five years, making the airlines lucrative customers, in turn only too happy to use the resonant name of a fashion designer to enhance their own prestige. In the 1960s, when the 'jet set' came to epitomise the cosmopolitan and glamourous life, the airlines' cooperation with the fashion industry produced the most exciting results: uniforms that also would have made a good

1 Hermann Hesse, 'Luftreise', first published under the title 'Spazierenfliegen', *Berliner Tagblat*, 21 April 1928, reprinted in: Volker Michels, ed., *Herman Hesse. Luftreisen*, Frankfurt am Main and Leipzig, 1994, pp. 50 and 53. Previously, Hesse had flown in 1911 with the airship *Schwaben* across Lake Boden and in 1913 with Oskar Bider, the Swiss pioneer of flight, over Bern.
2 Martha Rosler, *In the Place of the Public: Observations of a Frequent Flyer*, Ostfildern, 1998, p. 28.
3 Walter Kirn, Up in the Air, New York, 2001, p. 7. *Airworld* is also the name of an Internet art project initiated in 1999 by Jennifer and Kevin McCoy. See www.airworld.net.
4 The airport is one of the most important new building types of the twentieth century, and deserves its own exhibition. See John Zukowsky, ed., *Building for Air Travel. Design and Architecture for Commercial Aviation*, New York, 1996; Steven Bode, Jeremy Millar, ed., *Airport*, Amsterdam, 1997; Ingeborg Flagge, ed., *World Airports*, Frankfurt am Main, 2002.

5 See Hugh Pearman, 'The Invention of Flight', *Domus*, 865 (December 2003), p. 52. The long-troubled TWA was taken over by American Airlines in 2001.

figure on the catwalk. The sober business-like uniforms that today again dominate, testify not only to the transformation of the self-understanding of the flight attendant, but also that of the whole industry, which offers affordable services to so many.

In recent years, air travel has found itself in a process of transformation. Some airlines that could look back at decades of history, like Swissair or Sabena, had to close operations. Others were taken over by larger airlines – as KLM was by Air France – and others, like SAS, now see themselves forced to undertake fundamental restructuring. Cheap airlines increasingly provide competition for the established airlines, which in turn are moving part of their traffic volume to small local airports. In this light, the plans of the airline JetBlue to use that icon of air travel architecture, Eero Saarinen's TWA terminal, seem almost symbolic. With this, a cheap airline occupies the 'trademark building' of one of the great pioneer airlines, which disappeared from the scene in 2001.[5]

In aeroplane construction, the last truly decisive innovations – the Boeing 747 in terms of size, the Concorde in terms of speed – lie thirty years back. When the elegant supersonic jet took off for the last time in 2003, exactly one hundred years after the memorable flight of the Wright Brothers, this was nothing but the first regressive step in the history of passenger aviation, which had always been dominated by a spirit of 'larger, faster, further, higher'. The anonymous buyer who in a subsequent auction at Christie's and Air France acquired the famous nose of the Concorde for 320,000 British pounds was clearly aware of the significance of this event.

Today, however, there are new developments on the horizon. Airbus has already begun construction of the A380, which in terms of size with place all prior passenger airliners in the shadows. Boeing is developing entirely new concepts for the 7E7, and in research and development centres scientists are experimenting with so-called blended wing bodies. The shape of these aircraft is intended to provide additional thrust, and would also allow them to hold more passengers than any other aircraft. In this way, the researchers hope to achieve significantly lower costs per mile and passenger. If such blended wing bodies come to dominate air travel in twenty or thirty years, this could mark the end of the aeroplane as we know it.

During the more than two years of preparing this exhibition, numerous persons have contributed to its success, and we would like to take this opportunity to thank them all. First of all, our thanks to those people and institutions who have lent us exponents for the exhibition; without their friendly support and assistance, this exhibition could not have been realised: Albrecht Bangert, Hans Theo Baumann, Katja Gerdes (Bluequest), Jeffrey Haber (Boeing), Catherine Moriarty (Design Council Archive, University of Brighton), Hans Holzer (Deutsches Museum, Munich), Robert Heitmeier (Deutsches Museum), Karin Aulinger (Deutsches Museum), Marc Velten (EADS, Munich), Katy Harris (Foster and Partners, London), Hector Cabezas (Luftfahrthistorische Sammlung Frankfurt), Werner Granzeier (Hochschule für Angewandte Wissenschaften, Hamburg), Lothar Grim, Jeroen Elshof (GSA Facilitaire Diensten), Pieke Hooghoff, Ross Lovegrove, Gilbert Mas (Musée de l'Air et de l'Espace, Le Bourget), Alfred Pacquement (Centre national d'art et de culture Georges Pompidou), Jean Claude Boulet

(Centre Georges Pompidou), Liliana Dragasev (Centre Georges Pompidou), Josef Strasser, Tim Bechthold (Neue Sammlung, Munich), Hans (Nick) Roericht, Michaela Grossmann (Swiss International Air Lines), Kenneth Dowd (Teague), Christine Bösiger (Verkehrshaus der Schweiz), Beate Manske (Wilhelm Wagenfeld Stiftung), Kathrin Hager (Wilhelm Wagenfeld Stiftung), and Michael Wette.

Our thanks also to all those who supplied us with archive materials and supported our research with valuable information and references: Rudolf Bircher, Robin Day, Martin Darbyshire (Tangerine), Anne Klein (Swiss International Air Lines), Caroline Lilja (Stockholm Design Lab), Carina Diamant (SAS), Marianne Hjertquist (SAS), Ebba Rappe (SAS), Kevin Roche, Karl H. Sandberg (DNL/SAS Historical Society), Sophie Lecorre (Marc Newson Ltd), Amélie Gastaut (Musée de la Publicité, Paris), Diane Charbonneau (Musée des beaux-arts de Montréal), Claudio Castellacci, Oliver Class, Etjen van der Heyden (Dester), Gerhard Büsch (Deutscher Modellfliegerverband), Laurence Loewy (Raymond Loewy Foundation), David Hagerman (Raymond Loewy Foundation), Marietta Georgia (Raymond Loewy Foundation), Lisa House (Raymond Loewy Foundation), Søren Daugbjerg (Vilhelm Lauritzen AS), Daniel Lehmann, Mirjam Gelfer-Jørgensen (Kunstindustrimuseet, Copenhagen), Edith Lorensen (Wilhelm Hansen Fonden), Nel Verschuuren (Kho Liang le Associates), Barbara Visser (Kho Liang le Associates), Bente Kornbo (Copenhagen Airport Kastrup), Charles E. Inman, Marie Donatello (Estate of Edith Lutyens Bel Geddes), Marianne Blom (Lexel Electric), Martti Hannula (Lexel Electric), Matti Koskinen (Lexel Electric), Ludo van Halem, Beate Dannhorn (Deutsches Filmmuseum Frankfurt), Hetta Huitinnen (Finnair), Sophie Bellé (Fonds Régional d'Art Contemporain du Centre, Orléans), René Grüninger PR, Erica Stoller (Esto), Christine Cordazzo (Esto), Eames Demetrios (Eames Office, Santa Monica), Heidi Dörner (Classicon), Eva Mayring (Deutsches Museum, Munich), Cilla Robach (Nationalmuseum Stockholm), Dagmar Rinker (HfG Ulm Archiv), Philippe Gras (Musée de l'air et de l'espace, Le Bourget), Craig Likness (Otto G. Richter Library, University of Miami), Johanna Luhtala (Designmuseo Helsinki), Gees-Ineke Smit (KLM Art and Historical Collections), Stephen van Dyk (Cooper-Hewitt, National Design Museum, Smithsonian Institution), Jill Bloomer (Cooper-Hewitt), Rolf Thalmann (Plakatsammlung Basel), Alessia Contin, (Plakatsammlung, Museum für Gestaltung, Zurich), Bettina Richter, (Plakatsammlung, Museum für Gestaltung), Tuija Toivanen (Plakatsammlung, Museum für Gestaltung), Myrtha Steiner (Grafische Sammlung, Museum für Gestaltung), Ignazia Favata (Studio Joe Colombo), Teresa Bocchi Galassini (Studio Joe Colombo), Cathy Leff (The Wolfsonian–Florida International University), Debbie Kirschtel-Taylor (The Wolfsonian–FIU), Werner Zingg, Achim Möller, Delphine Daniels (Achim Moeller Fine Art Ltd.), Latanne Steel (C. R. Smith Museum), Claudia Matthes (British Airways Pressestelle Deutschland), Pressestelle Fraport AG, Gonni Christine Engel (Gerkan, Marg und Partner), Hellmuth, Obata + Kassabaum, Inc., Wallace A. Peltola (Tola Design), Toyo Ito & Associates, Kikutake Architects, Rolf Loepfe (Lantal Textiles), Martha Rosler, Timm Bauer (Singapore Airlines), Linda Rutherford (Southwest Airlines), Barbara Hanson (United

Airlines Archives), Virgin Atlantic Airways Ltd., Tupolev Joint Stock Company, Alan Janus (National Air and Space Museum, Smithsonian Institution), Alex Spencer (National Air and Space Museum), Marilyn Graskowiak (National Air and Space Museum), Mark Taylor (National Air and Space Museum), as well as Werner Bittner, Rolf Bewersdorf, Rolf Köllejan, Ralf Rudorf, Ulrich Vossnacke, and many others at Deutsche Lufthansa AG Cologne.

John Zukowsky's *Building for Air Travel: Design and Architecture for Commercial Aviation* was the first comprehensive scholarly study on this issue, and served as a catalogue for a 1996 exhibition held at The Art Institute of Chicago. We are greatly indebted to this informative volume, which served as an important starting point for our own research.

We would especially like to thank the following, who took that extra step in helping us assemble this exhibition: Sonia Ountzian (Musée Air France), Rick Watson (Harry Ransom Humanities Research Center, University of Texas at Austin), Melissa Keiser (National Air and Space Museum, Smithsonisan Institution), Patricia Casse (Paul Andreu Architecte), Nicholas Brown, Richard Szary (Manuscripts and Archives, Yale University), Danelle Moon (Manuscripts and Archives, Yale University), Ilse Ludewig, Carola Kapitza (Deutsche Lufthansa AG, PR Bildstelle), Lynn Catanese (Hagley Museum), Michael Hughes (The Wolfsonian–FIU), Kenneth Dowd (Teague), and Cliff Muskiet.

We would like to also thank the authors of the catalogue, who shared their knowledge with us. Barbara Fitton Hauß offered with her extensive research vital contributions to the preparation of the exhibition and the catalogue. Finally, our thanks to the translators who participated in this multi-lingual project, and to Brian Currid and Wilhelm Werthern who undertook the copyediting of the English catalogue with extreme care.

At Vitra Design Museum, many colleagues have accompanied the project with their interest – and the always vital pep talks: Mathias Remmele, Mateo Kries, and Isabel Serbeto gave helpful tips, Andreas Nutz provided many informative references in the literature, Sixta Quassdorf helped with Internet research and correspondence. Britt Angelis researched important archive material in Berlin and Frank Ubik organised the shipping of borrowed materials.

Dieter Thiel expressed the theme of the exhibition in an ingenious way in its design. Stefani Fricker, Thierry Hodel, and Michael Simolka were responsible for the perfect execution of his ideas and plans. Thorsten Romanus found with his graphic design for the catalogue and its large volume of illustrations the right form. Marc Gehde and Oswald Dillier mastered with their fabulous models the organic architecture of Eero Saarinen, Patrick Maier allowed for the resurrection of Norman Bel Geddes' Airliner N°4, and Franz Nadhesi completed true-to-the-original replicas of the cushions of a historic aeroplane seat. Our thanks to all for their support and productive collaboration.

A very special thanks is due finally to Elgin Schultz for her collaboration in the project. Without her untiring research and careful administration of the illustrations, neither the exhibition nor the catalogue could have been realised in this way.

Alexander von Vegesack, Jochen Eisenbrand

The pictogram ✈ indicates illustrations that can be found in other contributions to the catalogue

'LET US FLY YOU WHERE THE SUN IS': AIR TRAVEL AND TOURISM IN HISTORICAL PERSPECTIVE

HASSO SPODE

Translation by Brian Currid

Today, 700 million international arrivals are registered around the world, two thirds of these arrivals for 'purposeless' tourist travel. Europe's Mediterranean beaches alone attract around 100 million sun worshippers.[1] This gigantic migration is only conceivable on the basis of an industrialisation of travel: organisation, lodging, and transportation require elaborate logistical planning and technology. It is commonly thought that aviation was the cause of the victorious march of mass tourism.[2] The aeroplane did in fact make it possible for us to reach almost any point on the globe in a few hours: put more critically, 'Man has reached the limits of his cage'.[3]

However, this conclusion was already reached by the French geographer Jean Brunhes in 1909. Although mass air travel was still unimaginable, and holiday vacations were still a privilege limited to the upper echelons of society, this was the dawn of mass tourism. In Great Britain, the beaches of Blackpool and Brighton thus drew hundreds of thousands on good days, and German seaside resorts claimed almost one million vacationers and visitors; Switzerland registered a total of over 20 million foreign overnight stays. The transportation required for this was achieved with the railroad. In terms of the relation between tourism and aviation, two precisely opposite causal links are conceivable: either the aeroplane helped mass tourism to achieve its breakthrough – or mass tourism guaranteed the breakthrough for the aeroplane.

The 'Heroic' Age of Aviation

It would be an entirely different question to explore the relations between aviation and war. For our purposes, we must be satisfied with the remark that World War I brought an enormous push of innovation in flight technology and also instigated an awareness of the strategic importance of the air. The popularity of air travel was promoted by the so-called 'ace pilots', those flyers who during the war were able to down more than four planes, like the 'Red Baron', Manfred von Richthofen.

The Daredevil Years of Air Travel

Although the Treaty of Versailles not only forced Germany to make very high retribution payments, but also forbade an air force and limited aeroplane construction, it ultimately served to promote entrepreneurial endeavours in the area of aeronautics. Numerous pilots bought military planes in order to try their luck as stunt airmen or to begin a flight service. Around 30 companies specialising in flight were active in post-war Germany. The airline industry began to blossom, even if until 1926 most aeroplanes had to be manufactured abroad. The first airline in Germany was opened in 1919.[4] The Deutsche Luft-Reederei (001) transported politicians (like President Ebert) and files from Berlin to the National Assembly in Weimar, where the deputies negotiated the constitution and were to ratify the Treaty of Versailles. The two-hour adventure cost the substantial sum of 700 Reichsmarks, approximately half the annual income of a bricklayer.

Air travel was nothing for people with weak nerves. As one set of passenger guidelines explained, 'Special clothing will be distributed at the airport. In case of warmer weather, only a cap and protective glasses are required'. Regarding the most precarious moment of flight, the passenger was merely told, 'On take-off, after 100–200m of rolling the machine elevates – almost unnoticeably – from the ground'. Photography was allowed, but: 'When holding the camera out of the plane, strong air pressure should be expected'.[5] This referred to the F 13, developed by Junkers in 1919. The all-metal cabin aeroplane became the prototype of all civilian planes. With windows that could be opened, heating, and cushioned seats, it was more comfortable for the four passengers than the open military planes (002). Since then, the experience of flight became increasingly marked by a cabin interior cut off from the outside world. The second 'revolution' after the F 13 in this light was the Boeing 307 in 1938, with its own climate-controlled pressurised cabin in which the passengers floated restfully above the clouds (005). Of course, even today the ambivalent psychic state between euphoria and panic caused by overcoming gravity has still not entirely dissipated.[6]

The queasiness felt by passengers was at first due to quite real risks. As late as 1930, around every tenth flight in Germany ended with an 'unforeseen landing', one of every 150 ended in human injury. Although such

1 Source: Voyage 1 ff. (1997 ff.)
2 See for example Peter J. Lyth and Marc L. J. Dierikx, 'From Privilege to Popularity: The Growth of Leisure Air Travel since 1945', Journal of Transport History, 15 (1994).
3 Quoted in Daniela Trom, 'Natur und nationale Identität. Der Streit um den Schutz der Natur um die Jahrhundertwende in Deutschland und Frankreich', Nation und Emotion. Deutschland und Frankreich im Vergleich. 19. und 20. Jahrhundert, eds. Etienne Francois et al., Göttingen, 1995, p. 147. On tourism's phase of expansion see: Hasso Spode, Wie die Deutschen Reiseweltmeister wurden. Eine Einführung in die Tourismusgeschichte, Erfurt, 2003. The sources used in this essay come primarily from the Historisches Archiv zum Tourismus (HAT) at the Willy-Scharnow-Institut für Tourismus der Freie Universität Berlin.
4 On this, see Joachim Wachtel, 'Gebucht nach Berlin', Die Reise nach Berlin, eds. Dieter Vorsteher, et al., Berlin, 1987, pp. 145 f. Already during the years 1910–14 a flight service was operated by the Deutschen Luftschiffahrts-AG. The take-off of the German aeronautics industry could not be stopped by the Versailles treaty. In 1925, for example, planes from the Dessau's Junkers plant would make up 40 percent of all aeroplanes used. See Walter Scheiffele, Bauhaus, Junkers, Sozialdemokratie: Ein Kraftfeld der Moderne, Berlin, 2003, p. 77.
5 Wachtel, 'Gebucht nach Berlin'.
6 This was shown by the applause on the landing of charter aeroplanes. See Rainer Schönhammer, In Bewegung. Zur Psychologie der Fortbewegung, Munich, 1991. The fact that present day aeroplanes still have windows is primarily thanks to the fear of flying and claustrophobia. See Rudolf Metzler, Zukunft unbegrenzt. Die fantastischen Aussichten des Flugverkehrs jetzt und in den nächsten Jahren, Munich, 1967, p. 106.

001 From an advertising brochure for Deutsche Luft Reederei, c. 1920.

002 With its all-metal body and cantilever wings, the Junkers F 13 (1919) was the first modern airliner.

001

002

003 The trimotor Junkers Ju 52 was first used by Lufthansa for regular air travel in 1932, initially for flights within Europe, later also to Asia and South America, as far as Santiago de Chile.

004 A poster advertising Deutsche Luft Hansa, c. 1928–29.

003

004

7 See Christoph Asendorf, *Super Constellation. Flugzeug und Raumrevolution. Die Wirkung der Luftfahrt auf Kunst und Kultur der Moderne*, Vienna and New York, 1997. Until 1940, the number of deaths sank to around 3 for every 100 million passenger kilometres flown: the improvement around 1930 is shown by the decrease in both fatal and non-fatal accidents from one in every 0.4 million km in 1926 to one in every 2.9 million km in 1931. Sources: Wulf Bley, *Deutsche Luft Hansa A.G.*, Berlin, 1932, p. 62; Heinz Schamp, *Luftverkehrsgeographie. Deutschlands Lage im Weltluftverkehr*, Wiesbaden, 1957, p. 11, and footnote 10.
8 Friedrich A. Fischer von Poturzyn, *Luft Hansa. Luftpolitische Möglichkeiten*, Leipzig, 1925, p. 24; see also *Die Luftreise*, October 1932, pp. 55 ff.
9 This in turn encompassed further airlines. On the following see Deutsche Lufthansa (DLH), Firmenfestschriften, 1929, 1975 and 1980; Karl-Dieter Seifert, *Der deutsche Luftverkehr*, Volume 1, Bonn, 1999; Albert Fischer, *Luftverkehr zwischen Markt und Macht, 1919–1937. Lufthansa, Verkehrsflug und der Kampf ums Monopol*, Stuttgart, 2003; and Wachtel, 'Gebucht nach Berlin'.
10 Martin Wronsky, *Deutscher Luftverkehr. Sonderdr. WGL-Jahrbuch*, Munich and Berlin, 1927, p. 11. Wronsky was here referring to Hans Grimm's bestseller, which played a fateful role in the development of Hitler's thinking.
11 Seifert, *Der deutsche Luftverkehr*, pp. 344 f., *Brockhaus Edition 15*, Volume 9, 1928, pp. 652 f. On the USA, see: Joseph Corn, *The Winged Gospel: America's Romance with Aviation*, New York, 1983; Roger E. Bilstein, *Flight in America. 1900–1983*, Baltimore and London, 1984; Blistein, 'Travel by Air: The American Context', *Archiv für Sozialgeschichte*, 33 (1993); Robert J. Serling, *Eagle – The Story of American Airlines*, New York, 1985.

'hard' landings usually went well, around the world there were an estimated 10 deaths per 100 million passenger kilometres of flight. Suspiciously, one listened to the unsteady rattle of the motor – and prayed that the interruptions might only last a few seconds! But soon, the passengers were more able to relax: the trend towards creating 'artificial environments' also made flying safer.[7] The gyroscopic compass, flight indicator, direction finder, and automatic pilot made it possible to fly by instrument. Together with more robust motors, multiple-motor planes, fixed inspection schedules, professional pilot training, and stricter state regulation, it was possible to lower the number of accidents markedly.

Air Policy

Despite the risks, as early as 1920 air routes dedicated solely to tourist travel began operation in Germany and in the US (from Miami to sinful Havana or from Berlin to the seaside resort Usedom). Germany, highly interested in a civilian 'air policy' that helped to mitigate the limitations entailed by the Versailles treaty, was also one of the initiators of the IATA, the International Air Traffic Association, founded in 1919. The first international connection, however, was established in 1920 by the Koninklijke Luchtvaart Maatschappij voor Nederland en Kolonien (KLM) between Amsterdam and London. But air travel strategists were already thinking far into the future. Since England, France, Holland and other colonial powers had to pursue primarily the establishment of air connections to their distant colonies, Germany was left with the strategic goal of constructing long distant routes to the gaps in the geopolitical system: the Far East and America. At the same time, the goal was also to develop intra-European travel. While many countries, like Hungary, kept their air space closed except for a few 'flight corridors', some stretches were already jointly operated by numerous companies in a pool or in joint ventures.

The Junkers press spokesman Friedrich A. Fischer von Poturzyn, a pioneer of 'the possibilities of air policy', set the tone in 1925: '[A]ir travel is either international – or it is nothing at all!'[8] But the first task at hand was to put an end to the destructive competition on the national level. Subsidies were cut, and, bowing to pressure from the national government, the two largest carriers firms in Germany, Deutsche Aero Lloyd and Junkers Luftverkehr,[9] fused in 1926, and the Deutsche Luft Hansa AG was born. The name was Fischer von Poturzyn's creation, and Aero Lloyd's crane was chosen as the emblem. With stock holdings of 26 percent and re-instituted subsidies, the national government was the most important owner of this new company, which was now to be operated strictly in accordance with 'business principles'.

Air policy was of course more than keeping the books; flight symbolised the future. 'One needn't be a Jules Verne or a Wells to see how soon mutli-motored large aeroplanes [...] will carry travellers and goods to all countries of the planet, across the blue world of our globe, which has become so small', the Luft-Hansa director Martin Wronksy effused, and added a prognosis that fatefully would soon be fulfiled: the Germans 'have recently been described in a brilliant book as a "people without space". Air travel shows us ways to new space'.[10]

But a quite 'unheroic' tourism was also to play a crucial role in the operations of the new company; especially the *Bäderdienst*, or 'seaside service', to the North Sea and the Baltic was expanded. The entire network of air routes was 20,000 km; 56,000 passengers were flown on these routes with 162 aeroplanes, two-thirds of all German airline traffic.[11] Foreign destinations included London, Paris, and Malmö. In 1929, the initial dramatic growth in passenger numbers was again on the decline, due to the outbreak of the Depression. Nonetheless, Luft Hansa was still able to invest.

Around 1930, with just over 100,000 passengers German airline travel exceeded the English and the French by three times. Although an airline had already opened in 1914 in Florida, the air craze in America first began in 1927 with Lindbergh's ingeniously marketed transatlantic flight. The kilometres flown per year were barely higher than those in smaller Germany, the approximately 40,000 km route network only half that of Europe. Now, however, the rapid expansion of the air routes began to take off in the United States. United, Transworld, Eastern, American, and Pan American engaged in a brutal competitive struggle. Preferred by the government, Pan Am took on the leading role in foreign business, especially with Latin America. Around

005

005 The Boeing B 307 Stratoliner (1938) was the first passenger airliner with a pressurised cabin.

006 A Fokker F-32 on the cover of a flight plan from 1930.

007 United Airlines advertisement, focusing on the luxurious service offered in the Douglas DC-3, c. 1937.

008 A Douglas DC-3 from Swissair.

009 A Douglas DC-2 on the flight plan for KLM's Summer Service, 1936.

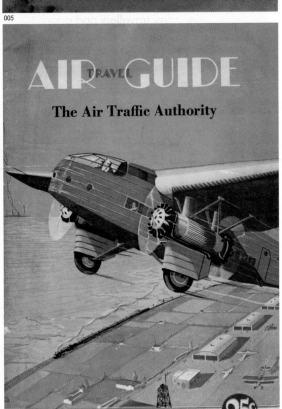

006

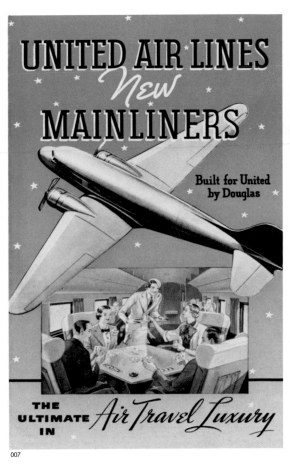

007

008

009

12 Deutsche Lufthansa, Firmenfestschrift 1936, p. 50.

13 Ibid., pp. 53 f. and p. 89. Görings famous dictum, 'I decide who's a Jew!', was applied to Milch – who was of 'mixed' descent. Milch, a former fighter pilot, prepared the integration of DLH into the Nazi system; in 1938 he was made General Inspector of the Air Force, in 1940 General Field Marshal, in 1942 President of the DLH and in addition was delegated to the Speer's 'Office of Central Planning', where one of his tasks involved the atomic bomb program. In 1944, he fell out of favour with Göring. On the following, as in footnote 8 and Bibliographisches Institut, ed., *Schlag nach! Wissenswerte Tatsachen aus allen Gebieten*, Leipzig, 1941, pp. 395 ff.

14 See Friedrich A. Fischer von Poturzyn, *Luftmacht. Gegenwart und Zukunft im Urteil des Auslands*, Heidelberg, 1938; the subsidies of the DLH sank from 62.8 percent in 1932 to 40.6 percent in 1938. On this, see Fischer, *Luftverkehr zwischen Markt und Macht*, p. 315.

15 Seifert, *Der deutsche Luftverkehr*, p. 345.

16 'Blitz' was a fashionable word of a fast time, which would soon culminate in the *Blitzkrieg*. As early as 1936–37, DLH flew part of the Legion Condor to Spain – the 'Condor' was also a word of the new time.

17 Between 1931–1937, the LZ 127 transported also passengers on a total of 65 flights to South America – with a menu at the Captain's Table, and amazing views ('endless palm forests along the coast') (*Die Luftreise*, August 1932, pp. 12 ff).

the world, the more economical all-metal planes began to dominate airline fleets: the Junkers Ju 52 (1932) (003) and the streamlined Douglas DC-3 (1935), which would become the most frequently built aeroplane in the world (007, 008). In Germany, Lufthansa (the one word spelling was introduced in 1933–34) consolidated its position still further. Almost every European country now had its own airline, from the French Air Union (which in 1933 was absorbed by Air France), to British Imperial Airways, the Italian airline SISA, the Belgian state carrier Sabena, Swissair, or the tiny Danish Luftfartselskab. Not least the Soviet Union, on the basis of its own air travel industry, greatly expanded its Aeroflot (which in 1937 also took over the German-Russian Deruluft); in 1935 it possessed a network of air routes that stretched over 47,000 km.

The Crane and the Swastika

Like Stalin, Hitler was thrilled by technology and air travel. A sensation in 1932 were the five election campaign tours, on which he flew 35,000 km – high above Germany – while his competitors took the train on the ground. In 1936, Lufthansa proudly advertised its part in helping Hitler to become chancellor with a celebratory publication. In 1932, as it was put it retrospect, 'the number of special flights grew dramatically, since Lufthansa repeatedly provided the Führer […] the fastest, multi-motor aeroplanes of the time. Through this, it became possible for the Führer and his fellow fighters to carry the National Socialist idea to all regions [*Gaue*] of the Fatherland'.[12]

The connection to the National Socialists paid off for Lufthansa. When Hermann Göring, once an ace pilot in the First World War and a civilian pilot in Sweden, was named Minister for Aviation, he made Erhard Milch, a member of Lufthansa's board of directors, his 'closest associate'.[13] Little changed in terms of strategy: already before 1933, Lufthansa had been following the 'same goals in traffic policy and technology'. Able to harvest the foreign political and economic crop that had been sown by the democratic governments in the Weimar Republic, the Nazi regime was not only able to begin building up an air force in 1935, but also encouraged Lufthansa's policy of expansion. The economy

recovered, and the 'chains of Versailles' were 'burst'. In 1934, Hitler held the opening speech at the IATA convention. 'Flight is victory', Lufthansa proclaimed.

By this point, all major European cities were connected by airlines, and in North America as well the network became even tighter. After the United States, the 'Third Reich' finally achieved the status of an air power,[14] and in German civil aviation only Lufthansa could profit from this development. In 1935 it could for the first time cover half of the operating costs through ticket sales: after the elimination of the remaining competitor, the Deutsche Verkehrsflug AG, it held a practical monopoly on the German market with 94 percent of all passengers (1938).[15] Lufthansa nonetheless remained highly innovative. Thus, fast domestic connections were established with the small Heinkel He 70 (010), which flew speeds of up to 360 km.[16] For long distance routes, however, regular passenger service could only operate over land or with stops on islands. Beginning in 1938, Lufthansa served the route Berlin–Athens–Bagdad–Teheran–Kabul. It took four days to get to Afghanistan, the price of 1300 Reichsmarks included room and board, feeder service, and tips. This geopolitical prestige object would in the following year also fly to Bangkok, but the extension to the ally Japan did not come about due to the outbreak of war. Similar long distance routes were operated by Air France (Paris–Hanoi), Pan Am (San Francisco–Manila), or KLM (Amsterdam–Batavia, now Jakarta) (✈ 393). Lufthansa succeeded in establishing a regular connection to South America in 1934 – in cooperation with Air France, and to the annoyance of the United States. The ocean between Gambia and Brazil was bridged with seaplanes and 'swimming airports', a complicated system only suited for postal service.[17] (011, 012) This was also attempted for longer stretches over the North Atlantic, but never came into use.

Instead, Lufthansa bought into the Zeppelin company to establish a direct connection to New York. The airships LZ 127 (like Jules Vernes' *Robur the Conqueror*, it had circumnavigated the world in 1929) and LZ 129 (013) (248 m in length, the largest airship in the world) now connected Europe and America with regular service. The giants floated across the Atlantic at a leisurely pace of 130 km/h. The impressive technology was matched

010 A Lufthansa Heinkel He 70 at Berlin Tempelhof Airport.

011 A Dornier Wal on take-off from the motor boat *Schwabenland*, c. 1934. The ship served as a stop en route to South America.

012 Poster advertising air service to South America, a joint venture undertaken by Lufthansa, Air France, and Syndicato Condor.

010

011

012

013 The 248 metre long *Hindenburg* (LZ 129) connected Europe and the USA for a brief period in regular service – until the accident in Lakehurst, May 1937.

014 Interior of the Zeppelin LZ 129, with aluminium chairs by Fritz Breuhaus de Groot.

013

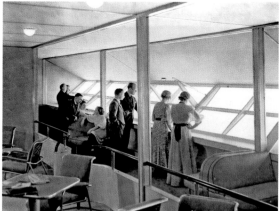

014

by the futuristic interior design, with Bauhaus inspired aluminium furniture in the smoking room (014). The route became a symbol of progress, but soon it would come to symbolise the risks of progress as well. The cool luxury and the peace offered by a 50 hour flight for 1000 RM veiled the carelessness of the operators, that already in the second year of operation – in May 1937 resulted in catastrophe: LZ 129, the *Hindenburg*, exploded while docking in Lakehurst, New Jersey.[18] Not only the 36 deaths – airship accidents had already resulted in up to 73 deaths – but more the media presence of the accident, the visual power of the fire ball and the dramatic radio reportage, made the *Hindenburg* into a symbol of technological risks.

Civil Aviation before Take Off

But even without the debacle of Lakehurst, the zeppelin would probably have remained only a brief episode in the history of air travel. A new generation of four-motor land aeroplanes allowed new achievements: the Focke-Wulf Fw 200 Condor, the Boeing 307 Stratoliner and the Junkers Ju 90 (015) (as well as the Douglas DC-4 and Lockheed Constellation, completed during the war). In 1938, the Condor, which could fly at speeds of 430 km/h, achieved the non-stop flight from Berlin to New York. On the eve of the war, in technological terms the aeroplane was already able to compete with railroad and ship lines. Like this a complex network of means of transportation, routes, trans-shipment centres, security systems, provisions, and information, civil aviation was ready for 'take off'.

The airport, just like train stations in the nineteenth century, now served as the imposing entryway to this system; instead of provisional solutions, now modern logistical and aesthetic solutions were to provide worldly elegance. Pioneering here was the reconstruction of the Zentralflughafen Berlin Tempelhof, begun in 1936. The complex, opened in 1923, was already Germany's largest airport.[19] The location had an additional invaluable advantage: its central urban location. Ernst Sagebiel was commissioned to build the airport; once an associate of Erich Mendelsohn, who had emigrated to America, he was later Göring's architect for Berlin's monumental

Ministry of Aviation, now the Federal Ministry of Finance. The hangars and the area for arrivals and departures are placed along a 1.2 km long arc; the planes can role directly into the hangars, making it an airport of short distances (017, 018). In the centre, attached to the main hangar on the city side is a spacious terminal hall, which opens onto an impressive plaza. The side facing the city is in a monumental neo-classicist style, whereas from the runway side the building appears as an elegant steel and glass construction. On the roof, spectator stands were planned to hold 80,000 – a truly impressive gateway to the planned European capital 'Germania'. But like Prora, a structurally similar gigantic Nazi seaside resort on the island of Rügen, the almost completed building was not opened during the Nazi era: it instead served the air force. But even if the architectural style might run contrary to current tastes,[20] Tempelhof remains an ingenious solution, the 'mother of all modern airports', as Norman Foster put it.[21]

Not only did airports become more impressive, passenger comfort also began to come into its own. Already in 1928, Lufthansa introduced 'flying dining cars', and an experiment was even made with film screenings during flight. In 1938, the first 20 stewardesses took up service on the Condor; following American models outfitted with a uniform and with sassy sailor's caps, these first German stewardesses were selected from among 2000 applicants.[22] The great interest in this position reflects the prestige of flight. But the everyday life of flying was sobering: long approaches, delays for hours or even days, on board the deafening roar of the engines, headaches and an up and down which made the vomit bag an absolute requirement.[23] All of this compounded the already prevalent fear of flying. In fact, the relative risk of death was incomparably higher than that on trains – but the absolute risk was certainly low.[24]

After a series of accidents in 1936–37, a broad campaign was launched in the United States to make America 'air-minded':[25] from newspaper ads ('Afraid to Fly?') and free flights for wives (it was known that they were afraid when their husbands used the aeroplane) to 'Air Babies' toys, intent to make even the little ones excited about flight. The United States had long overtaken Europe in terms of air travel,[26] counting in 1937 almost

18 Although the danger of explosion was known, the zeppelins were filled with hydrogen, since helium was rare and expensive. (LZ 129 would have required almost half of the annual production of Helium in the United States.) In 1938, Lakehurst was still served (Weltreise-Zeitung, 24.4 [1938], p. 22), but on Göring's order the almost complete LZ 130 and the LZ 131 – waiting in the dockyard – were demolished. Since also the British R 101 burned and a number of other airships crashed, the fate of these aircraft were sealed.

19 Approximately 100,000 departures, around 50,000 in Frankfurt, Munich, and Hamburg. See Werner Treibel, *Geschichte der deutschen Verkehrsflughäfen. Eine Dokumentation von 1909–1989*, Bonn, 1992, p. 17.

20 Thus, Asendorf makes the critical observation that the construction 'allows nothing of the function to be recognised' (Asendorf, *Super Constellation. Flugzeug und Raumrevolution*, p. 152). On the debate about so-called 'Nazi architecture', see my article on 'Mass Tourism, Fordism, and the Third Reich', *Journal of Social History* (in press).

21 Quoted by Asendorf, *Super Constellation. Flugzeug und Raumrevolution*; see also Matthias Heisig and Michael Thiele, *Landing at Tempelhof*, Berlin, 1998.

22 Wachtel, 'Gebucht nach Berlin', pp. 154 and 161.

23 See Bilstein, 'Travel by Air: The American Context', pp. 276 f. and note. 10.

24 In fact, the relative risk of death in air travel was around 100 times that of train travel. The estimates are taken from Schamp, *Luftverkehrsgeographie*; Brockhaus, Fifteenth Edition, Volume 7, 1928; Statitisches Bundesamt: Bevölkerung und Wirtschaft 1872–1972, Stuttgart and Mainz, 1972. In Germany, 460 people died in air accidents in 1937, compared to 1027 in train accidents; the first with 120 million, the latter 51 billion passenger kilometres, which even results in a 200 times greater risk. However, the highest number of traffic fatalities were due to automobile: 9700, or 86 percent of all traffic fatalities (Bibliographisches Institut, Schlag nach!, p. 345).

25 See *Scribner's Magazine*, Nr. 104/3. Sept. 1938, S. 7 ff., also Bilstein, *Flight in America* and Bilstein, 'Travel by Air: The American Context'.

26 Bibliographisches Institut, Schlag nach!, p. 398; Schamp, *Luftverkehrsgeographie*, p. 9; see also Seifert, *Der deutsche Luftverkehr*, pp. 344 f. Around the world, 2–4 million passengers were flown.

015 The Junkers Ju 90, which seated 40 passengers, was part of Lufthansa's fleet from 1939 to 1944.

016 Focke-Wulf FW 200 Condor after its Atlantic flight from Berlin to New York on August 11, 1938.

017 Berlin Tempelhof Airport in the 1940s. A view from the airport restaurant onto the gates.

018 Airport Berlin Tempelhof, designed by Ernst Sagebiel, 1936–39. Aerial photograph, 1960s.

015

017

016

018

1.3 million passengers, in Germany around 0.3 million, in Great Britain 0.2 and Italy and France around 100,000. This meant that on annual average a mere 1 percent of the US population flew, while in Germany only 0.5 percent took to the skies.[27] Price was not responsible: 'It's fear not fare that keeps the public on the ground', as one American magazine put it. This was also true of Germany, where Lufthansa fares had now come below the price of a first class rail ticket.[28]

The choice between 'fast and prestigious or comfortable and safe' was not decided in favour of the aeroplane, at least in Europe, where the distances were shorter and the rail system was more tightly woven. The aeroplane was used by prominent figures from business, politics, and culture – their flights had little to do with vacations. In affluent circles, it was much more the car that was increasingly used as a tourist mode of travel. There was however no lack of attempts to open up the leisure market. Thus, Lufthansa offered beside the beach service also flights to Heidelberg and to the mountains, and Air France maintained a route from London to the Riviera, while Swissair served Swiss resorts. As a whole, the portion of tourist travel in European civilian air travel might have been approximately 10 percent.[29]

The role of air travel was thus accordingly modest in German tourism. In 1937, there were 8 million registrations of guests at vacation sites but only a total of 323,000 airline passengers. While perhaps 30,000 tourists booked flights on Lufthansa, over 1.5 million *Volksgenossen* ['national comrades'] had gone on holiday with the Nazi leisure organisation *Kraft durch Freude* [Strength through Joy, or KdF].[30] Similarly marginal was Lufthansa's spectacular seaside resort service. In the summer of 1938 the resorts at the Baltic and the North Sea counted 1.3 million arrivals, but only six thousand of those arriving had come by water plane to the eight landing sites. (✈ 373)[31] Thus, just as tourism – despite KdF and the English holiday camps – remained primarily a phenomenon of the upper and middle classes, the aeroplane remained something reserved for the 'upper ten'.

However, the psychological effect was entirely the opposite. The sporty exclusive allure that exuded from the fascinating new technology allowed a few passengers to fly into the future. Into a future of streamlined progress, luxury, and fashion, into a global society without borders. In May 1939, an English magazine put it: 'In these days of international tension and alarm it is really quite heartening to read the summer timetables of the regular air services. Most companies might easily have used "Forget the Frontiers" as a slogan.'[32]

Technologically quite advanced, air travel served as a screen onto which more sweeping social fantasies were projected. Airmindedness was neither only a phenomenon of the post-war period, nor was it limited to certain countries.[33] Even if in reality many still avoided the aeroplane, it had long conquered the souls. Fischer von Poturzyn had announced the new age, an age of 'three dimensional politics'.[34] In his view, early humanity had only known one dimensional 'street routes', a thousand years ago the two-dimensional 'area' was added; today, however, with the 'ocean of the air', a further quantum leap had been made. This notion of a 'spatial revolution'[35] was by no means new. One hundred years prior, the poet and journalist Ludwig Rellstab had celebrated the destruction of 'all spaces and times' by the steam locomotive. The railroad pioneer Friedrich List saw in it a 'Hercules in the crib that will redeem the peoples of the world from the plague of war'. The railroad would overcome the 'hate of nations' and take even the 'lowest' to 'far-away beaches'.[36] Those were precisely the same hopes and expectations that now were tied to the aeroplane.

With the attack on Poland on 1 September 1939, these hopes were burst: aviation was placed in the service of war. A fundamental innovation was the jet engine, which in 1939 was tested in the Heinkel He 178, and in 1944 came to be used in the Messerschmitt fighter jet Me 262. But such 'miracle weapons' were not decisive for the war. Although the German aviation industry remained technologically more advanced in many ways, its capacities remained limited. While in 1944, 41,000 planes were built, in the United States alone 96,000 were produced. Ignoring all warnings, the production was long suppressed on orders from Hitler and Göring; a devastating bombing war was not part of their scenarios. On the wings of the success of his Stukas on the fronts, air force chief Göring in 1940 emphasised that 'you could call me Jones' if ever an

27 This is true considering that the actual percentage was lower, since many passengers flew a number of times. In the United States domestic travel, the aeroplane achieved between 5 and 8 percent of the 16 million passengers of the Pullman trains. See Bilstein, 'Travel by Air: The American Context', p. 279; *Scribner's Magazine*, 1938, p. 8.
28 A one hour flight from Berlin-Hamburg cost 25 RM, the two and a half hour journey in the 'Fliegenden Hamburger' train around 30 RM (Bibliographisches Institut, *Schlag nach!*, pp. 379 f. and 399).
29 Lyth and Dierikx, 'From Privilege to Popularity: The Growth of Leisure Air Travel since 1945', p. 98. Tourist travel in Europe made up 9 percent of all flights in 1932.
30 Hasso Spode, 'Arbeiterurlaub im Dritten Reich', Timothy W. Mason, et al., *Angst, Belohnung, Zucht und Ordnung*, Opladen, 1982, p. 298.
31 Of the 7069 passengers, some even were intending to continue their travels. See *Vierteljahreshefte Stat. Dt. Reichs*, 47 (1938), p. IV.52 und *Statistisches Jahrbuch des Deutschen Reichs*, 58 (1939–40), p. 252.
32 *The Bystander*, 5.3 (1939), p. 196.
33 Asendorf attributes 'airmindedness' to the United States (see *Super Constellation. Flugzeug und Raumrevolution*, p. 269) and Lyth and Dierikx to Great Britain ('From Privilege to Popularity', p. 102).
34 Fischer von Poturzyn 1925, pp. 1 f. Twenty-five years later, R. Buckminster Fuller developed a similar notion. Fuller suggested that for 500,000 years, the world was only made of isolated points, while the railroad had created lines, and now the three-dimensional era had begun. See Asendorf, *Super Constellation. Flugzeug und Raumrevolution*, p.267.
35 An excellent source on images of flight is Asendorf, *Super Constellation. Flugzeug und Raumrevolution*, 1997; on the train as a space destroying time machine, see Spode, *Wie die Deutschen Reiseweltmeister wurden* 2003, Chapter 2.
36 Ibid., pp. 58 and 61 f.

37 In 1917–18, a few individual bombing raids were flown. But it took until the 1930s for bomber fleets to be built up, and Italian, Japanese, and German military targeted them against the civilian population. With the outbreak of World War II, they declared that they would restrain from such attacks. Trusting in the success of the 'Blitzkrieg', Germany neglected to develop a long-range bomber, and only undertook a modification of the Condor for this purpose. The air war against the German civilian population became a doctrine with the British cabinet decision in February 1942 that bombing be directed primarily against German working-class areas. 'Area bombing' was however not able to break the 'morale of the enemy', as Arthur Harris later admitted, instead producing a defiant 'will to endure'. In 1944, when 1.2 billion tons of bombs rained down, arms production reached its highest levels. Nonetheless, only with the debacle of the Napalm bombs in Vietnam was the doctrine of 'area bombing' called into question. See Erhard Klöss, ed., Der Luftkrieg über Deutschland 1939–1945, Munich, 1963; Jörg Friedrich, Der Brand. Deutschland im Bombenkrieg 1940–1945, Berlin, 2002.

38 Those responsible for 'area bombing' (and the two atomic bombs afterward) were not convicted as war criminals, but celebrated as heroes. But the Germans also quickly wanted to forget: on the one hand, as a psychological mechanism, on the other, due to the lacking legitimacy of such a complaint. In Brockhaus, a German encyclopaedia, one looks in vain for an entry on 'Bomber-Harris', whose work left such lasting traces – but there is mention made of a number of 'ace pilots' from World War I.

39 See Asendorf, Super Constellation. Flugzeug und Raumrevolution, Part 4, as well as note 10.

40 1952: 0.9 deaths per 100 Million passenger kilometres; 1962: 0.6 per million; 1967: 0.3 per million (Brockhaus Sixteenth Edition, Volume IV, 1953, p. 159; Brockhaus, Volume VII, 1953, pp. 366 ff.; Brockhaus, Seventeenth Edition, Volume 11, 1966, pp. 665 ff; Meyers Neues Lexikon, First Edition, Volume 5, Leipzig, 1961, p. 500; Schamp, Luftverkehrsgeographie, pp. 9 ff.; Bilstein, 'Travel by Air: The American Context', p. 286). On the history of Aeroflot, see Flieger-Jahrbuch 1964, pp. 47 ff.

41 John B. Lansing and Ernest Lilienstein, The Travel Market 1955, Ann Arbor, 1957, pp. 31, 65 ff. The (holiday) travel intensity, defined in slightly different ways, measures the share of the population that travels per year: see Voyage.

enemy plane would fly over the borders of Germany. Two years later, the 'Third Reich' sank in ash and rubble: the horror had returned to its originators.[37]

The Golden Age of Air Travel

While in the aftermath of World War I, the so-called chivalrous age of air jousts could flow into a sporty image of flying, now Anglo-American area bombing had robbed flying of all its optimistic, progressive innocence. Nonetheless, a rapid and fundamental suppression of the destructive side of flight set in after World War II.[38] The next two decades thus became the golden age of civil aviation, directly picking up on the heroic phase from the inter-war period and ultimately culminating in the normalisation of flight.

This era was also the beginning of the 'American century' (H. R. Luce) – of course countered by the Soviet Union, the only power that had spread its colonial realm as a consequence of the war. But the charm of the red flags remained limited in comparison to the 'American way of life'. Besides Coca-Cola, rock and roll, chewing gum, and filtered cigarettes, it was Boeing and Pan Am that symbolised the new age.[39] If World War I finally made the United States a great power, they were now the unquestioned leading power of the West and thus the aeronautics industry as well. This military industrial complex now sought to conquer the civilian market.

To the extent that the safety of passenger planes increased, the fear of flying decreased, and enthusiasm for the newest means of transportation grew.[40] Already in 1945, the number of worldwide passengers had more than doubled in comparison to pre-war years. According to the vague estimates available, in 1949 over 20 million people seem to have used the aeroplane. By 1955 it was almost 70 million. The Hercules nurtured during the interwar period now could leave its crib. The largest airline with around 8 million passengers was the Soviet Aeroflot, but in national terms the United States dominated. Leading the market was American Airlines with 5.8 million passengers, followed by Eastern with 4.8 million, and United with 3.9 million in 1953, the long distance companies TWA and Pan Am (PAA) reached a passenger volume of 3.1 and 1.6 million, respectively. In

Europe, only the British BEA, founded in 1946, and Air France could compete (1.6 and 1.3 million passengers, respectively); traditional carriers like KLM with 0.6 million passengers were distant followers up, and Lufthansa no longer existed.

The largest growth market was that the domestic American airline industry. In 1951, the number of flight passengers exceeded that of the Pullman long distance trains. According to a survey, a little more than half of all flights were undertaken for non-business reasons, but this is not necessarily the same thing as tourism. On the one hand, compared to many European countries, holiday travel intensity was low in the United States, on the other, flying remained something reserved for the upper middle classes; by far the most import means of transportation was the automobile.[41] While airlines worked with travel agencies and hotels on the tourist market, they were slow to start offering tourist and second class or economy seats, following the model of the railroad. Both were introduced in 1952 and 1958, respectively, also on transatlantic flights. This market grew in leaps and bounds, despite the still high prices. The normal fare for the direct flight Berlin–New York was thus 484.50 DM, in the tourist class 329.80 DM.[42] This was certainly not more expensive than the ship, since one also saved a week of travel. In 1956–57, aeroplane passenger volume exceeded that of ship travel on the North Atlantic routes: here, the number of passengers soon reached the two million mark.

It was the era of the Lockheed Super Constellation. Since its first flight in 1948, the elegant propeller plane with its spacious accommodations and ultimately with speeds of up to 540 km/h dominated the IATA routes:[43] passengers were spoiled with extravagant menus and drinks, during the day passengers were free to smoke, and at night the beds were pulled out. Since the prices were fixed, the airlines attempted to outdo each other in terms of service. The price system – supported domestically by the national regulation authorities, internationally by the IATA – was still entirely kept within a bourgeois-elite model of tourism, which still gave flying an exclusive, polyglot character.

Airline offices, located at the best city addresses, exuded the cool elegance of the most modern interior

019 The routes flown by American Airlines and American Overseas Airlines (AOA). Founded in 1945, American Airlines was the majority shareholder in the new airline, which beginning in October 1945 was the first airline that offered regular air service over the North Atlantic.

020 The domestic route network of American Airlines in 1945. American was then the largest airline of the Untied States.

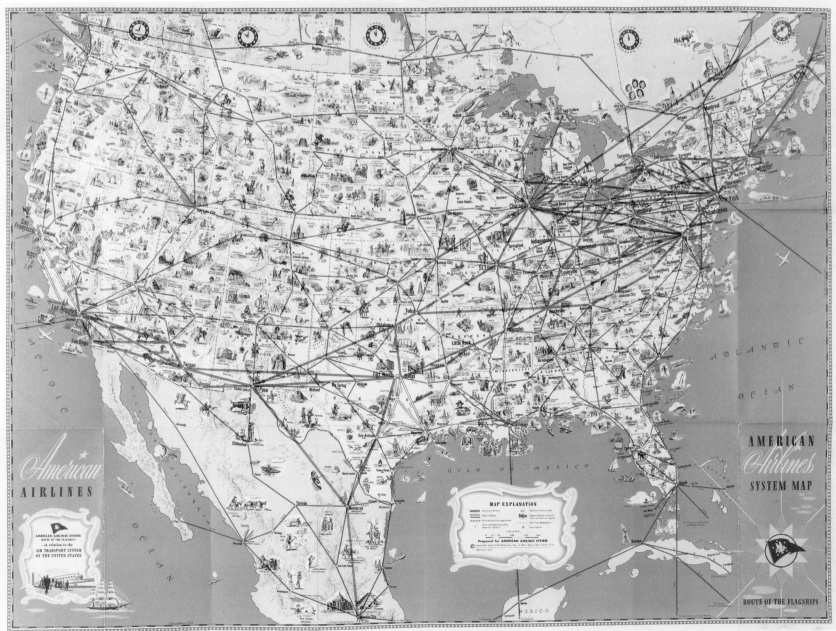

42 This was about equivalent to a worker's average monthly salary. See *Hapag-Lloyd Luftkursbuch,* Winter 1952–53.

43 In 1945, the association of airlines was reformed as the International Air Transport Association; in addition there was the International Civilian Aviation Organsation (ICAO). See *Lufthansa-Jahrbuch 1990,* pp. 48 ff.

44 See Robert A. M. Stern et al., *New York 1960. Architecture and Urbanism between the Second World War and the Bicenntenial,* New York, 1995, pp. 381 ff.; *Das Deutsche Luftkursbuch 1,* 1953.

45 In addition, the French and English expanded their airfields at Tegel and Gatow. In 278,000 flights, 2.1 million tons were flown to West Berlin: see Wachtel, 'Gebucht nach Berlin', pp. 162 ff.

46 Erhard Milch also profited from the new tolerance: convicted in 1947 to a life sentence, he was freed in 1954.

47 On this and the following, see Hans M. Bongers, *Deutscher Luftverkehr. Entwicklung – Politik – Wirtschaft – Organisation. Versuch einer Analyse der Lufthansa,* Bad Godesberg, 1967; Karl-Dieter Seifert, *Der deutsche Luftverkehr,* Volume 2, Bonn, 2001; DLH-Firmenfestschriften 1975 and 1980.

48 *Meyers Lexikon,* First Edition, Volume 2, Leipzig, 1961, pp. 489 f. On Interflug, see: Karl-Dieter Seifert, *Weg und Absturz der Interflug. Der Luftverkehr der DDR,* Bonn, 1994.

49 Even here, Adenauer was faster: a week before, he had flown with the DLH to Moscow to negotiate the return of German POWs.

design: clear lines with much glass and steel. The foreign offices of the (half) state-run airlines were also to propagate a positive image of the country in question.[44] Thus Japan Airlines, El Al, KLM, and Alitalia maintained exquisite offices on New York's Fifth Avenue (✈209, ✈210); on Berlin's Kurfürstendamm not only PAA or BEA had offices, but also airlines that could not even serve the half city, like Air India, KLM, Sabena, and later of course Lufthansa. Essential in these offices were the blinking world maps and aeroplane models (201). The children pressed their noses flat on the showcase windows, the fathers smoked Peter Stuyvesant cigarettes, the 'flavour of the great wide world', and on the weekend one visited the airport to be able to experience a feeling of worldly elegance.

The Crane Rises from the Ashes

The 'great wide world' was still divided in two. In 1946, the first American civilians landed at Berlin's Zentralflughafen, which lay well preserved in the bombed out US sector; beginning in January 1948, Germans were also allowed to use Tempelhof. In June, however, for ten months the airport had to be left to the cargo planes that supplied the three western sectors with coal and food.[45] With Stalin's dilettantish attempt to force West Berlin into the Soviet occupied zone by blocking the access routes, the Cold War had broken out. For the West Germans, there was a pleasant side to this: wartime enemies became allies. The Berliners standing up to the Soviets caused a well of sympathy in the USA: the beginning of a long friendship that would remain almost entirely unclouded until 1968 – a friendship underwritten by the aeroplane. Instead of punishing the Germans,[46] they were given funds from the Marshall Plan, and Allied terror bombers were transformed by the Berlin Airlift into friendly 'Raisin Bombers'.

On one point, however, the friendship reached its limits: the Americans did not once again want to have their hegemony in air travel challenged by the Germans. While the Japanese were already allowed to found an airline in 1951, the Federal Republic was still forbidden to own and operate aeroplanes (this stipulation was even more strict than the Treaty of Versailles, which otherwise

was not supposed to be repeated). Nonetheless, the Federal government prepared to begin the reconstruction of Lufthansa, which had been dissolved in 1945. The company was finally registered in 1953, with the Federal government as main owner; as a precaution, the company was named Aktiengesellschaft für Luftverkehrsbedarf [Air Travel Services Corporation, or LUFTAG][47] A provocative step, but the US aeronautics industry was grateful for new customers, and an agreement was reached on the delivery of Super Constellations and Convairs. When it began to become clear that the USSR was going to allow East Germany to operate and build aeroplanes, the end of the ban had come. In 1954, Luftag again became Deutsche Lufthansa (DLH). However, negotiations with the Western powers allowed only for a special permission for the import of the planes ordered: at first only for training purposes. But for better or worse, the Paris Treaties guaranteed the Federal Republic air sovereignty in 1955, and Lufthansa took up operations (024). The first flight abroad brought a proud Chancellor Adenauer to Paris. At the same time, two new charter airlines also came onto the scene: LTU and the Deutsche Flugdienst, which later became the Lufthansa subsidiary Condor.

On the other side of the Iron Curtain, airline operations also began with the Deutsche Lufthansa, the 'socialist traffic company of the GDR' (025)– not to be confused with the Deutsche Lufthansa AG, 'the air traffic company dependent on monopolies and closely woven together with German militarism and fascism'.[48] In September 1955, a half year after Adenauer's visit to Paris, Prime Minister Grotewohl flew with the GDR Lufthansa to Moscow.[49] The socialist 'crane' served a number of necessarily quite short domestic flights (in 1980 these were ended) as well as the most important cities of the Eastern bloc. The disagreement over the names brewed under the surface, bursting out into the open when the two airlines attempted to fly to the same place: Belgrade. When in 1963 the matter came before the Yugoslavian courts, the GDR ended the comedy: by transferring their Lufthansa to Interflug (026), which just in case had already been founded in 1958.

Like all state airlines, the East German Lufthansa and later Interflug served to promote the country. But

021 Lufthansa's first city office was opened in 1955 in Dusseldorf.

022 A Lufthansa Lockheed Super Constellation at Frankfurt Airport, 1958.

023 Frankfurt Airport in the late 1950s.

024 The first Lufthansa flight plan, beginning April 1, 1955.

025 A Douglas DC-4 of the East German Deutsche Lufthansa at Berlin Schönefeld Airport.

026 Baggage sticker for Interflug, the airline of the German Democratic Republic.

021

022

023

024

025

026

50 Departing passengers in 1950 from Berlin and Frankfurt in 1960: 0.8 every 1 million; 1970: 2.8 to 4.4 million. See Treibel, *Geschichte der deutschen Verkehrsflughäfen*, p. 36.

51 Wolfgang A. Kittel, 'Die Deutsche Lufthansa als Förderer des Fremdenverkehrs nach Deutschland' (lecture), 1962.

52 Passenger numbers grew from 0.7 million In 1955 to 5.5 million in 1971, but sank as a result of the Berlin Treaty, to then around 1989 again reach 4.5 million. The percentage of air travel in Berlin in domestic travel was up through the 1960s two thirds, to 1973 over 50 percent, and in 1989 still more than one third. Seifert, *Der deutsche Luftverkehr*, p. 2.

53 See Spode, *Wie die Deutschen Reiseweltmeister wurden*.

54 See Peter J. Lyth, 'History of Commercial Air Transport', *Journal of Transport History*, 14 (1993) and Lyth and Dierikx 1994; Lyth strongly emphasises the special role of the British. On Germany, see Spode, 'Wie die Deutschen Reiseweltmeister wurden', *Goldstrand und Teutonengrill. Kultur- und Sozialgeschichte des Tourismus in Deutschland, 1945–1989*, ed. Spode, Berlin, 1996.

55 Frankfurt counted in 1961 only 20,000 charter passengers, in 1967 already 0.6 million. See *Flughafennachrichten*, 4 (1968), p. 41.

the West German Lufthansa was much more successful in this: it acquired a good reputation, and soon was counted as one of the leading European airlines. In the long distance routes, pre-war plans were realised by 1960: the airline now served North and South America as well as the Near and Far East, flying as far as Bangkok. In 1964, Lufthansa achieved profits for the first time. Frankfurt Airport was built up as an international hub, replacing politically isolated Berlin (023).[50] Lufthansa understood itself as the most important 'supporter' of incoming tourism. As a member of the board of directors pointed out, even the name alone developed a 'general promotional effect'[51], further supported by the on-board service: the passengers enjoyed 'German hospitality, be it through serving beer and wine from kegs, be it through typically German meals, of which the Lufthansa soup pot already enjoys great popularity among the American guests'. In 1962, DLH operated 95 city offices abroad, 40 of these in North America alone – in comparison with four official government tourism centres. The Public Relations Division also launched exhibitions, congresses, and festive events. These activities were not solely motivated by economic interests, but also political ones: 'The most promotion should be done for Berlin, even if Lufthansa cannot serve Berlin'.

Here, the GDR airline had a significant advantage: it could – using Schönefeld Airport, located on the outskirts of Berlin – serve its capital city. The three air corridors to the island of West Berlin in contrast remained restricted to the airlines of the Western powers until reunification. A most profitable business, since a large portion of domestic air traffic went to Berlin.[52] In addition, the air routes, and thus Pan Am, BEA, and Air France, had to be subsidised by the West German federal government. Even the Eastern side profited from this relic of the Occupation Statute: Interflug, which like all Eastern bloc airlines was not a member of IATA, could establish itself among West German tourists and so-called 'guest workers' as an affordable, but also excellent, high quality alternative. In 1963, for these purposes a border crossing connecting West Berlin to Schönefeld was set up along the Berlin Wall, which had been built two years prior. Thus, some holiday travellers flew form Hanover to Tempelhof, where they took the transit bus to Schönefeld, where there would then check into their flights to Tunis.

Up, Up, and Away

Interflug increasingly became a charter airline serving the West, and thus relied on an expanding market segment: mass tourism. The social opening of air travel was thus driven from two sides: a sales and a technological aspect. The price policy of the IATA could be circumvented when a tour operator ordered whole ticket contingents from a charter airline along with the hotel beds at the holiday destination. Due to the guaranteed full booking (the IATA airlines were only about 60 percent booked), the charter carriers could fly more cheaply. This principle of the inclusive tour (IT) or 'all inclusive holiday' was almost as old as the railroad. In 1841 Thomas Cook had rented his first special train, and with special trains and busses the Nazi organisation *Kraft durch Freude* had brought serial production in holiday travelling to full blossom.[53]

The Rise of Charter Tourism

Charter flights first became popular in Great Britain, Scandinavia, and West Germany. Now even those with a moderate income in search of relaxation could head for Costa Brava or Majorca. In late 1960s England, the portion of all-inclusive among vacationers had reached around 8 percent.[54] The same share was achieved by the aeroplane as a means of transport in West Germany; here as well, charter flights had grown over-proportionally.[55] Majorca trips – by train and ship – were already offered by Dr Tigges in 1934; starting in 1956, the island was served by charter airlines – at this time, still an expensive pleasure. At the beginning of the 1970s, however, the boom of all-inclusive air holidays began in many countries. In West Germany, the great demand for foreign travel allowed this market to expand especially dramatically: in 1968, for the first time over 50 percent of all holiday journeys went abroad (in Great Britain, as in the GDR, it was only 15 percent). But the car was still the dominant mode of transportation to Austria and Italy. However, with the large tour operators

Come aboard THE **707**

027 A Boeing brochure on the introduction of the 707, issuing in the jet age.

028 The British De Havilland Comet began service in 1952, and was thus the first jet used in airline service. Due to a number of serious accidents due to material defects, it was not able to establish itself in the long term.

028

027

let us fly you where the sun is
OVERSEAS NATIONAL AIRWAYS

A U.S. Certificated Supplemental Air Carrier   **Headquarters:** JFK International Airport, New York

030 The SE 210 Caravelle was the first jet for short routes. It began service on inner European flights in 1959.

031 A Soviet Tupolev 104.

032 A Boeing 747-130, Lufthansa. As the jumbo jets became established in airline fleets at the start of the 1970s, the aeroplane finally had finally become accessible to the masses.

033 The Airbus A-300, a jet for short and mid-length routes, was first used in regular service in 1974.

030

032

031

033

56 This number includes all arrivals, departures, and transit passengers. *Fischer Weltalmanach 2000*, Frankfurt am Main, 1999, p. 1246.

57 See Metzler, *Zukunft unbegrenzt*, pp. 133 ff. In contrast, the project of a European airline failed.

58 Jet plane also displaced the turbo prop planes. In 1959, jet planes made for 8 percent of world air traffic in terms of tons/km, in 1969 89 percent; the number of world passengers grew from 100 to 200 million (around 2000 around 2.5 billion). See *Brockhaus*, Seventeenth Edition, Volume 9, pp. 665 f.; see also *Meyers Lexikon*, First Edition, Volume 2, p. 307; *Flieger-Jahrbuch 1964*, pp. 38 ff. Die German aviation industry, in contrast to Lufthansa, had been destroyed over the long term, and had nothing from this boom. In West Germany, it was forced to produce small cars until in 1959 the licensed construction of military aircraft began (it then however also became a driving force behind Airbus). East Germany was far more advanced here: not only was a Soviet turbo prop plane manufactured in the GDR (IL 14 P), but the East Germans also developed their own jet airliner. Since the '152' crashed just as it was to be presented to Khrushchev in 1959, and then hardly found any buyers, aeroplane construction was stopped (www.flughafen-dresden.de).

entering the market in the early 1960s – 'Neckermann macht's möglich' ['Neckermann makes it possible'] was one of the advertising slogans of the time, referring to one of the main charter companies – the foundations for a mass use of air travel for tourism had been laid. By 1970, over half of all German all-inclusive tourists landed in Palma de Mallorca – the picturesque insider's tip became a 'cleaning ladies island'. At the same time, the good flight connections guaranteed that the wealthy and beautiful settled here as well.

Lufthansa also participated in the business of offering cheap seats with its subsidiary Condor and contracts with non-IATA airlines, like Aeroflot. Not only the airlines of the Eastern bloc countries undermined the IATA system, but also smaller Western state-owned lines, like Loftleidir (now Icelandair), and especially British entrepreneurs, in particular Freddy Laker, whose Skytrain even regularly flew to New York as of 1977. Cheap carriers like Court Line and People's Express did go bankrupt, but at the same time the trick had become established to issue a fictitious hotel voucher with the ticket, thus legally exempting an IATA flight from the fixed price system. For this the IATA airlines even themselves opened up seats (ITX tickets). At the same time driven and profiting from this loosening of the fixed price system, IATA introduced special fares (like the APEX ticket of 1975).

But the system of price regulation could no longer be maintained. In the Western capitals, the neo-liberal credo gained the upper hand. At the latest, deregulation in the United States in 1978 marked the beginning of the end of the state airlines with their role as agents of national promotion (airport construction and kerosene of course remained subsidised.) One of the first to go bankrupt was the once proud Pan Am, and just recently even Swissair was hit by this fate. But the expansion of air travel proved the policy of liberalisation right – London, the world's busiest air hub, counted over 85 million passengers at the turn of the millennium, Chicago-O'Hare, which since the 1970s has been the world's largest airport, over 70 million, and Frankfurt over 40 million.[56] The 'flavour of the great wide world' that had earlier been effused by Stuyvesant cigarettes has long been lost in the endless corridors and security

checks – not only because smoking is prohibited, and since the 1970s terror attacks have required increasingly more complex security measures, but also because this is the unavoidable price of the democratisation of flying. The ecological costs of this rise in air travel, and whether the retreat of the state from 'air policy' is actually in the national interest, are different questions altogether.

Europe, at any rate, was well advised to build up an aeronautics industry under state direction in the 1960s.[57] Today, after the collapse of the Russian aeronautics industry, only Airbus Industries keeps the Boeing-McDonnell-Douglas group from holding a world-monopoly. We thus come to the technological side of mass tourist air travel. Since the Messerschmitt fighter had shown the superiority of the jet propulsion, the British introduced the first passenger jet in 1949, the two-engine Comet (**028**). Spectacular crashes caused it to fail on the market, but other jet airliners had success beginning in 1954–55, in particular the 900 km/h fast Boeing 707 (**027**), but also the French Caravelle (**030**) and the Soviet Tupolev 104 (**031**). In the 1960s the more efficient jet planes finally pushed out the propeller planes, which went back to the pre-war period.[58] When Lufthansa retired its last Super Constellation from service in 1967, the next generation of jet airliners was already in development, taking off in 1969 and 1972 on their first flights: the Boeing 747 Jumbo Jet (**032**) for large numbers of passengers and long distances, and the Airbus (**033**) for medium numbers of passengers and distances. At comparable costs these 'wide-bodied jets' could carry twice as many passengers as the jet planes in use up until then. The dam preventing the mass use of air transport for tourist purposes was thus finally broken. At first, the plan had been to use the extra space for luxury: reclining seats, clubrooms, bars, game rooms, etc. But the premonition had by a pessimist already before the first jumbo was in the air would become reality: 490 passengers would be 'herded in' like a pack of sheep and all comforts that initially were installed in the early period of enthusiasm would later be removed. Instead of menus cooked in the on-board galleys, there would be 'soft rolls in plastic foil', and the rows of seats would be placed as close together as possible.[59]

034

59 On airbus and jumbo jet plans, see Metzler, *Zukunft unbegrenzt*, p. 115.

60 With approximately 75 percent, travel intensity in 1989 was around 10 percent higher than in West Germany. See on the GDR: Spode, 'Wie die Deutschen Reiseweltmeister wurden'; on West Germany: Cord Pagenstecher, 'Der touristische Blick', Diss., Freie Universität Berlin 2003. West Germans flew five times as much as the East Germans. See Gesamtdt. Institut: *Zahlenspiegel. BRD–DDR*, Third Edition, Bonn 1988, S. 67.

61 'The perfumes of the tropics…have been corrupted …[by a busyness that] mortifies our desires' (Claude Lévi-Strauss: *Triste Tropiques*, trans. John Weightman and Doreen Weightman, New York, 1973, pp. 23–24). The critique of tourism is almost as old as tourism itself – but it is not (only) an elitist complaint, but also indicates the deep ambivalence of modernity. On this and the de-localisation of travel, see Spode, *Wie die Deutschen Reiseweltmeister wurden*; for more on the problem of delocalisation, see Pagenstecher, 'Der touristische Blick'.

Conclusion: Interchangeable Destinations

The generation of aeroplanes from around 1970 still dominates the skies today. The supersonic prestige projects of the period, like the Tupolev (034) and the Concord (✈264), long remained a towering leftover from the golden age of flying, well into the time when the aeroplane had already become a 'normal' means of transportation. With the last flight of the Concorde in 2003, the superplane that permanently ran at a loss, this proud relic of 'airmindedness' was also sent to its grave. Symbolic for both the golden and the 'normal' age of air traffic are its most prominent fossils: once the elegant Super Constellation, with its strangely elite sounding name, futurist and global in its reach. Now, the fat and comfy jumbo jet, which allows families to take off for their beach holidays with the greatest ease in its confidence inspiring mammoth tummy.

Today, civil aviation is to a large part dependent on tourism, but mass tourism was by no means a result of air travel. The technological watershed in the history of tourism is much more fundamental: the replacement of muscle power with motors. Steam-driven boats and railroads introduced the truly epochal 'space revolution' which caused mobility to cease being a social privilege. Already Thomas Cook demanded successfully: 'We must have railways for the millions!' The aeroplane has not increased the number of travellers, but only the distances involved.

Nothing demonstrates this more clearly than the comparison between East and West Germany. The travel destinations of GDR citizens were geographically quite limited, while for West Germans the world was open, if the money was available. But the basic structures of tourist travel differed little in the two states. Thanks to state-organised social tourism and the increase in purchasing power, the GDR achieved even a higher intensity of travel than the FRG in the late 1980s – the East Germans had become 'world champions of travel'.[60] But they hardly used the aeroplane, travelling instead by car and train.

The aeroplane did not create any entirely new practices of tourism: the repertoire of holiday travelling was basically set before World War II, with city trips on the one hand and the three S's – sun, sand, and sex – in the de-localised 'south' of the beach holiday on the other. While holiday travellers and advertisers emphasise the 'distinctions' between destinations, in a broader historical framework the shared characteristics are far more revealing. From this perspective it makes no difference whether the trip – as was true already around 1900 – reached Usedom, 'Berlin's bathtub', in two and one half hours, or, as is the case today, in the same time reached Majorca. The *Kraft durch Freude* project of a mass resort for 20,000 'national comrades' on Rügen was an anticipation of what was realised in the 1960s in Benidorm on the Costa Blanca. By now countless such holiday factories have long been in existence. Already in the 1920s, Siegfried Kracauer spoke of a 'the growing interchangeability of the destination' ['Vergleichgültigung des Reiseziels']; today, what Karlheinz Wöhler calls 'tourism without distance' has become a reality. The aeroplane has indeed played a decisive part in this, making possible the globalisation of the South, from Thailand to the Dominican Republic. For such countries, tourism has in the meantime become an important economic factor. The loser is in any case the environment due to the increase in transportation, perhaps in the end also travel itself.

The aeroplane as a 'normal' means of mass transportation cannot fulfil its promise of the 'somewhere else' – instead it causes the 'somewhere else' increasingly to disappear. Man has not only 'reached the limits of his cage', but also increasingly designs this cage as a homogenous space, at best marked by differences of a carefully maintained local colour. Already in 1955, Claude Lévi-Strauss darkly noted this: 'Journeys, those magic caskets full of dreamlike promises, will never again yield up their treasures untarnished'.[61] In its heroic and its golden age, the aeroplane was an emissary of the future; it opened the magic caskets wide, only then to fill them with cheap factory products.

IN SEARCH OF THE PERFECT AIRPORT

KOOS BOSMA

Translation from the Dutch by Robyn de Jong

The airplane is a new kind of carrier, keyed to a new type of world, a world lighter and more fluid than the world of the nineteenth century. And with the recession of that century, characterized by the heavy movement of raw materials from place to place, the laying down of roads and rails and keels, the airplane comes forward as the true vehicle of twentieth century man, moving swiftly upon a universal highway of air, fashioned to carry the lighter commerce of a new era.[1]

The New Task of Design

During World War II, it became obvious that the flying machine was capable of having a decisive impact on human civilisation. However, the happy-go-lucky heroism of the pre-war pioneering age had come to an end. While most European airfields (with the exception of those in Great Britain) were systematically made unusable by target bombing, in the US the number of aircraft and airfields increased exponentially. In 1941, the country boasted 72 large airports; two years later this number had risen to 865,[2] and it became apparent that the United States would overtake Europe in the conceptual development of the modern airport during and after the Second World War. While in 1941 terminal facilities catered to a mere 330 commercial aircraft, by the year 1955 they were expected to deal with 5,000.[3] In light of this growth and rapid advances in aviation technology, it was assumed that all buildings at existing airports would have to be demolished in order to be able to start afresh. How to avoid constructing white elephants that were already out of date on the day of their opening? What logistical growth concept would best serve the booming airport?

The implications of the 'Air Age' were abstractly understood: 'The relation of space and time, the re-study of physical geography, the re-analysis of commercial geography, and the capabilities of the aeroplane',[4] in short, the shrinking of space and the prolongation of time. It was also clear that there was a real need to assemble technical and logistical knowledge concerning the construction and development of airports and that a competent architect could deliver satisfactory building plans.[5] It was even recognised that civil aviation requires good connections with urban transportation networks. The days of barnstorming were well and truly over now that aircraft were suddenly carrying eighty to a hundred passengers. In the new era – the era of the untiring search for the perfect airport – planners and designers pondered over the ideal runway configuration, landing facilities, passenger and freight accommodation, the design of the building complex, and the links between the airport and the urban surroundings. American publications of the 1940s displayed a recognition that the airport was going to be of prime importance for every large city as the site for the transfer from urban to air transport. Yet despite the early realisation that the airport as transfer machine represented a major regional infrastructural task, it would take decades before bus, train, subway, or road networks were properly linked up to the terminal.[6]

The airport as a whole demanded 'a program based on the needs of aircraft operations, maintenance and storage, as well as those of cargo, mail, passenger, private flyer and spectator potential'.[7] Questions of architectural style, construction techniques, materials, specifications and building regulations had to be combined with civic pride, flow, alarm systems, fuel storage, air-conditioning, signage, and acoustics; on top of all this, the airport was also to be integrated into the surrounding landscape. In the switch from one type of highway to the other, the architectural design of the terminal buildings was required to serve three functions: the processing of passengers, baggage, and freight, control and transfer rituals, and protection against external influences. Ultimately, the public would judge an airport's success on the efficiency, ease, and speed with which the switch from land to air transportation was made.

The Allies' victory heralded the advent not only of large American and British commercial aircraft, but also of new marketing techniques. Whereas air travellers

1 'The Air of a Trade Route', *Fortune* (March 1941). Quoted in: *Luchthaven Schiphol. Plan voor uitbreiding*, Amsterdam, 1949, p. 1.
2 Kenneth Reid, 'Aviation is a Client', *New Pencil Points* (November 1943), p. 1.
3 Marc Thompson, 'What's Wrong with Our Air Terminals?', *The Architectural Forum* (January 1946).
4 Francis R. Meisch, 'Architecture and Air Transportation', *New Pencil Points* (November 1943), p. 38.
5 Henry A. Wallace and T.P. Wright, *Airport Buildings*, Washington, 1946.
6 See: Koos Bosma, 'European Airports, 1945–1995: Typology, Psychology, and Infrastructure', John Zukowsky (ed.), *Building for Air Travel. Architecture and Design for Commercial Aviation*, Munich and New York, 1996, pp. 62–65.
7 Smith, Hinchman and Grylls, Inc., 'An Airport Planning Program', *Architectural Record* (October 1947), p. 91.

035 According to the original plan for the runways at London Central (today Heathrow), the runways were to form a star. The three runways in the North were never built.

036 The first terminal building of London Central Airport, today Terminal 2 at London Heathrow, designed by Frederick Gibberd, 1955.

037 The main hall of the passenger terminal at London Central Airport.

038 Interior, Terminal 1, London Heathrow Airport. Designed by Conran Design Group, 1969.

039 Seating system for Terminal 1, London Heathrow Airport, Conran Design Group, 1969.

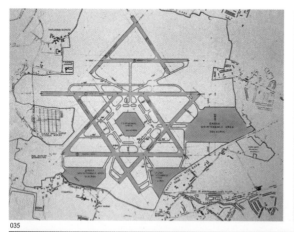

035

036

037

038

039

040 Zurich Airport, Alfred and Heinrich Oeschger, 1951–53. (Photograph: 1957).

041 Runways at Zurich Airport, 1957.

041

040

042 Early, unrealised plan for Idlewild Airport (April 1945). The later airport (now called John F. Kennedy International Airport) did place the terminal building in the centre of the runways, as proposed by this early plan.

043 View of New York's Idlewild Airport in 1961, showing Terminal City, in construction. Already recognisable is Eero Saarinen's TWA Terminal on the upper left.

044 Airport architecture that communicates something of the fascination of flight: Eero Saarinen's TWA Terminal (1956–62).

042

043

044

045 The TWA Terminal, seen from the landing field. On the left, one of originally two planned concrete tubes leading to a satellite building from which the passengers board the aeroplane.

046 Saarinen's TWA Terminal unites all design elements using one fluid style.

045

046

41

8 'Red Carpet Service' was introduced by United Airlines in September 1956. See William Garvey and David Fisher, *The Age of Flight. A History of America's Pioneering Airline*, Greensboro, 2002, p. 146.
9 See: Robert A. M. Stern, Thomas Mellins, David Fishman (eds.), *New York 1960. Architecture and Urbanism between the Second World War and the Bicentennial*, Cologne, 1997, pp. 1007–23.
10 'NYIA 4900 Acres Decentralized Terminals 140 Gate Positions', *Progressive Architecture* (December 1957), p. 76.
11 David Brodherson, '"An Airport in Every City": The History of American Airport Design', *Building for Air Travel. Architecture and Design for Commercial Aviation*, p. 87.

had previously been wooed from among business executives and VIPs, attention now turned to a new market sector. The image that emerges from the advertising campaigns of American airlines is: 'It's "Red Carpet" luxury all the way...'.[8] The flight to happiness was attended by sunny weather, a benign nature, spectacular sunsets, exotic peoples, palm trees, swimming pools and the icons of ancient civilisations: the Pyramids, the Parthenon, and the Colosseum. In 'Red Carpet' luxury, the world was at your feet according to the formula of the appeal of the foreign and the exotic. The target groups were affluent, attractive couples and young families. On board there was impeccable service, ample legroom, entertainment, a separate dining section, and a stewardess to cut up the passengers' meat for them.

On transatlantic flights, the 'tourist class' designation made its appearance in 1951. A year later it was introduced to the European continent. The fare war between scheduled flights and cheap charter flights eventually spread to the regular airlines in the 1960s, where aircraft were now divided into 'economy class' and 'business class'. When the replacement of propeller by jet aircraft made it possible to achieve higher speeds and to reach the farthest corners of the earth within a foreseeable time, air travel for the masses had arrived.

Types of Configuration

Transporter Configuration

The most important post-war airport type was the 'transporter configuration', in which terminal building and aircraft remain physically separate. London's Heathrow (1943–46) was the ideal type of the transporter airport: an overgrown village on an island. Passenger facilities, buildings, and car parks were concentrated on the island. The terminal buildings were connected by a tunnel beneath the runways to the outer road system and by an encircling apron to a star-shaped runway

system correlated with the various wind directions (035, 036, 037).

There was, of course, a major drawback to this set-up: the larger the airport, the longer the distance to the aircraft and the greater the impact of weather conditions. To alleviate such inconvenience, buses were introduced. Switzerland's Zurich airport (1951–53, terminal design by Alfred and Heinrich Oeschger) was a splendid example of the transporter configuration, with the location of the terminal determined by connections with the motorways and the strips for taxiing planes. Shortly before departure time, passengers passed through ticket control into one or two departure lounges to await the buses that would take them to their aircraft. Their baggage, meanwhile, was transported to the plane through the basement. The separation of departure, arrivals and baggage handling over three floors made for a clear and simple organisation of the terminal building (040, 041).

At Idlewild/John F. Kennedy International (opened in 1948, design concept: Wallace K. Harrison),[9] the Heathrow island concept was inflated to an agglomeration of decentralised terminals for the largest American airlines: Terminal City, with parking for 6,000 cars.[10] The central island consisted of a ring road lined by a series of discrete buildings including an International Arrivals Building (design SOM, 1957). 'Each airline planned its own terminal, much like a skyscraper, to be a corporate symbol. And, despite recent complaints, the "delirious airport" is still a great match to the social, architectural, and economic whirl of the 'delirious New York' it serves.'[11] Of the seven 'branded' airline buildings, that of Trans World Airlines (designed by Eero Saarinen, completed 1962) is still the most exciting (042, 043, 044, 045, 046).

Finger and Satellite Configuration

As the number of flights increased and the number of passengers per aircraft grew, the transporter configuration became less and less convenient. Airports

047 Gatwick Airport's round terminal, nicknamed 'Beehive,' designed by Hoar, Marlow & Lovett, 1936. Since 1956, it has been used as an office building.

048 Gatwick's new terminal building, designed by Yorke, Rosenberg & Mardall, 1958. The new building offered a better connection to ground transportation.

047

048

049 Ground plan, Schiphol Amsterdam Airport, M. Duintjer Architects with NACO (Netherlands Airports Consultancy), 1963–67.

050 Amsterdam Airport Schiphol, 1963–67.

051 Schiphol's interior, designed by Kho Liang Ie. The photograph shows the seating developed especially for this airport.

052 The signage at Amsterdam Airport Schiphol, designed by Benno Wissing (Total Design). This communication system set new standards: green signs indicated the location of service elements, and yellow signs provided vital directions for passengers.

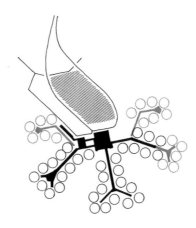

049

050

051

052

designed on the model of Heathrow and Idlewild were extended with 'fingers' (piers) and satellites. In the US, the finger concept had already been discussed in 1939 and ten years later it was implemented in Baltimore Friendship International Airport (design 1948, opened 1950), followed by Philadelphia (1955), Milwaukee (1955), St. Louis (1956), Cleveland (1956) and Chicago O'Hare (Y-shaped finger concept designed by van Naess and Murphy, completed in 1963).[12]

Gatwick Airport (designed by Hoar, Marlow & Lovett, 1936), situated 40 kilometres south of London and linked to the city centre by train, was the first European airport to acquire piers. The visual core of the terminal, the glazed Montebello Tower, consisted of three cylinders of reinforced concrete. A novelty for those years was the narrow, flexible, canvas-covered telescopic walkway that connected the gate and the fuselage of the aircraft (047). A severe drawback of pre-war Gatwick was that its closed shape was not conducive to enlargement. When expansion became necessary at the end of the 1950s to relieve the growing pressure on Heathrow, a new terminal building (designed by Yorke, Rosenberg & Mardall, 1958) was built. The central premise of this rectangular building was the direct link with road and rail transport. In the axis of the rectangle, a 300-metre-long, finger-like covered walkway connected the terminal with the gateways. A terrace on the roof of the finger was open to the general public (048). Two more fingers, projected at the corners of the rectangle, were built in 1964. The larger European airports – Rome-Fiumicino, Milan-Linate, Copenhagen, and Amsterdam-Schiphol – all followed Gatwick's example.

In the late 1960s, early 1970s, the new Schiphol (designed by Duintjer and NACO, completed in 1967), was rated the most passenger-friendly airport in Europe.[13] In those early days, the semi-open, compact mini-city (passenger terminal, control tower, freight depots, offices, parking, infrastructure and four 3300-metre-long concrete runways) was not marred by vast asphalted parking lots or a chaotic landscape of hotels,

multi-storey car parks, and miscellaneous airport services. Typologically, however, it was an old-fashioned airport whose disadvantages had to be overcome by a system of piers served by moving walkways and linked to aviobridges that could be adjusted to the different sizes and door heights of the numerous aircraft types. The beating heart of the airport was designed in such a way that all the facilities were under one roof (049, 050, 051, 052).

Centralised Transfer Machine

Saarinen's innovation for Dulles International Airport (Chantilly, Virginia, opened in 1962) would do away with piers and tentacles of any kind (053, 054). In one fell swoop he shortened the distances passengers had to walk, reduced the high cost of taxiing aircraft, and did away with buses by introducing height-adjustable mobile lounges. The concept, which in fact dated from 1939,[14] had recently been updated by the American architect Victor Gruen, another critic of the rapid and expensive obsolescence of airport designs: 'Ultimately, when dimensional growth has defied reason (as in Idlewild), it renounces its function of a centralised terminal and explodes into a series of satellite junior terminals loosely connected by parking lots'.[15] Gruen's alternative was radically centralist: a large, circular terminal inside which the land-based transport picked up and set down, and on the outside (airside) a 'transfer vehicle' that would take travellers to the waiting aircraft (055). Saarinen designed a single, central building for Dulles and developed the 'people mover', which he had no doubt seen in drawings by Gruen. The air-conditioned mobile lounge (capacity 90 passengers) was built by the Chrysler Corporation and fitted out with red carpet, symbol of Air Age luxury (056).

Forceful architectural inventions though they were, TWA and Dulles did not bring the perfect airport any closer. The advent of jet aircraft had now changed the parameters, and what was required was typological leap, a complete reorganisation of traffic flows in the

12 Wood Alexander Lockhart, *Airport Development and Design: A New Architectural Problem*, Ann Arbor, 1972, pp. 127–46.
13 For example: Corin Hughes-Stanton, 'Schiphol Puts Passengers First', *Design* (December 1968), p. 48.
14 According to Lockhart (p. 151), the idea both of the pier and of the mobile lounge was developed in 1939 by Fellheimer and Wagner. For more on Dulles, see Antonio Román, *Eero Saarinen. An Architecture of Multiplicity*, New York, 2003, pp. 109–23.
15 Victor Gruen, 'Tomorrow's Airport', *Progressive Architecture* (December 1957), p. 108.

053 John Foster Dulles International Airport (Chantilly, near Washington, D.C), Eero Saarinen, 1958–62. The airport is now known as Washington Dulles International Airport.

054 The interior of Washington Dulles with its tandem seating, especially designed by Charles Eames for the airport.

055 'Model for the Airport of the Future' designed by Victor Gruen, Progressive Architecture, December 1957.

056 The 'mobile lounges' at Washington Dulles Airport combined the functions of waiting room and bus.

053

054

057 Ground plan, Berlin Tegel Airport, von Gerkan, Marg & Nickels, 1969–74.

058 For the interior of Berlin Tegel, the architects also used the hexagon form of the terminal building.

059 For Berlin Tegel, parking possibilities close to the gate and the potential for expansion were high priorities in planning the airport.

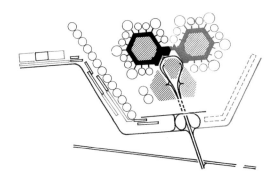

057

058

059

060 Sketch, Terminal 1, Paris Roissy Charles de Gaulle Airport, Paul Andreu, March 1967.

061 Escalators inside the cylindrical Terminal 1 at Paris Roissy Charles de Gaulle Airport.

062 Roissy Charles de Gaulle 1, Paul Andreu, 1967–74. Parking is found on the upper levels of the building. The satellite buildings with the gates are accessed by tunnels.

16 'Plane Talk', *Industrial Design*, (October 1970), pp. 3–57.

terminal was a *sine qua non* of passenger comfort in the jet age.[16] Aeroplanes now carried 500 or more passengers who were disgorged into the terminal in an erratic stream. The model that was developed for new airports in both Europe and the US harked back in part to the central building on an island which doubled as parking space; in fact, a giant transfer machine. The cheapest airport was regarded as an infrastructural turntable that kept walking distances to a minimum and occupied as little space as possible. In terms of layout and facilities, the modern airport was starting to look like a real city. Kansas City International Airport (Kivett & Myers, 1968–72), for example, consists of one gigantic circular island ringed by three slightly smaller islands. The central island contains a tower (offices and air traffic control) and one or two lower buildings, the rest of the space being taking up by parking lots. The island's perimeter is a ring road with exits to the three smaller circles which are in turn ringed by a road whose outer edge is lined by low buildings containing the gates to the apron where the aircraft are parked (069). The striking aspect of this concept is its single-minded focus on the automobile, resulting in vast parking lots: the space inside the three smaller islands is likewise given over to parking as are large parts of the buffer space between the central island and its satellites.

European airport designers aimed at greater concentration, making their buildings considerably taller than those in the US. While airside was reconfigured with piers and satellites, landside was organised so as to incorporate car parking into the (circular or polygonal) terminal building, thereby turning the airport terminal into a traffic roundabout and, with the aid of lifts and escalators, a vertical parking machine. This concept formed the basis for several new European airports, among them Geneva-Cointrin (1968), Cologne-Bonn (1970), Berlin-Tegel (1969–74) (057, 058, 059) and Roissy-Charles de Gaulle 1 (1968–72) (060, 061, 062). These airports were more complex than their American counterparts in that they not only had to handle thousands of cars, but were also required to link up with public transport.

Linear Configuration

One of the first plans based on a linear concept was the proposed master plan for Houston International Airport (Hellmuth, Obata + Kassabaum, 1968, not executed). The plan foresaw a spine with left and right exits from which a series of nine 'paired loops, or demi-modules' extended, bringing aircraft and passengers closer together. Dallas-Fort Worth International Airport (concept: Tippetts-Abbett-McCarthy-Stratton, realized design: Hellmuth, Obata + Kassabaum, 1965–73) is a variation on this theme and arranged as a series of half-circles strung out along a central highway. Dallas-Fort Worth and Tampa International (Reynolds, Smith & Hills, 1970) were the first American airports to be provided with a light rail system to shuttle passengers back and forth between the various terminals and the parking lots (068).

Roissy 2 A–D (1981–94) was modelled on the Dallas-Fort Worth type: an extension or multiplication of an elongated building parallel to the motorway where passengers' cars can be parked underground, level with the gate where their aircraft is parked. The linear system brings all forms of transport together in a single line and then disperses passengers and freight over the various function-specific storeys. The main theme is the oval, with the curves and counter-curves of the terminal façades being a direct reflection of the ground plan (064, 067). The underlying logic was a desire to line the aircraft up in two rows (arriving and departing) which in turn meant projecting the buildings and roads in between; the linearity of the composition is in fact dictated by the motorway. At Roissy 1, choices about where to go are made inside the terminal, at Roissy 2 A-D, outside. At the point where the Roissy 2 A–D modules give way to the modified ovals of Roissy 2 E–F (now with projecting piers) (063) an infrastructural node has been constructed. The linear road system is traversed by the high-speed train line and its glass-roofed station (1994). The traffic node is dramatised vertically by the Sheraton Hotel (1995), itself yet another variation on the oval theme (065, 066).

063 Roissy Charles de Gaulle 2 E–F. Here, the linear concept of terminals 2 A-D were expanded with two narrow annexes. On the left below is the hotel that connects to the TGV station.

064 The ground plan of Terminals 2 A-D forms two ovals. The shape is repeated both in the ceiling construction as well as in the concrete modules in the roadway supports.

065 Sheraton Hotel, Roissy Charles de Gaulle Airport, under which the underground station is located as well and which also marks the transfer to the TGV Station.

066 The system of structural supports at Roissy's TGV Station.

063

064

065

066

067 Aerial view, Paris Roissy Charles de Gaulle Airport.
From left to right: Terminal 1 (1967–74), Terminal 2 A–D
(1972–891), the Sheraton Hotel and the TGV Station (1990–971)
as well as Terminals 2 E and F (1990–2003).

067

068 Ground plan, Dallas-Fort Worth International Airport, planning studies by Tippetts-Abbett-McCarthy-Stratton, execution by Hellmuth, Obata + Kassabaum 1965–73.

069 Kansas City International Airport, Kivett & Myers, 1968–72. Brief routes from automobile to the gate was the starting point in the planning of this airport.

069

068

In the 1970s, changes to the airport type consisted chiefly in the erosion of the existing lucid design principles. The rash of plane hijackings and terrorist attacks during these years necessitated greater terminal security. Terminal space was accordingly divided into secure and insecure areas separated by strictly monitored bottlenecks. The upshot was longer walking distances and much reduced transparency.

Innovation in the 1980s and 1990s related primarily to the architecture of already existing types, which was now required to enhance the airport's image. This meant celebrating the terminal by architectural means and led to both the car park and the shopping mall being incorporated into the terminal building, thereby underlining the economic surplus value for airports of visitors who do not fly at all. Rhein-Main international airport at Frankfurt, for instance, started out as a drive-in system with satellites. Terminal Mitte (designed by Giefer, Mäckler & Kosina, 1965–72) comprised a three-storey underground car park, tram, and railway stations, a double-deck elliptical road system for picking up and dropping off passengers and the halls with check-in counters for piers A, B, and C. The Y-shaped terminal configuration offered a maximum of plane bays on the outside and a maximum concentration of facilities on the inside (070, 071). The seven-storey office block has a concrete frame, aluminium curtain walls and different types of glass.

In 1985, a steep increase in passenger numbers and freight traffic forced the airport authorities to develop a long-term expansion plan for the airport. Two phases were carried out between 1985 and 1994. One element of the expansion was Terminal Ost (designed by Joos, Schulze, Krüger-Heyden, in consultation with O.M. Ungers and Perkins & Will, 1990–94). The building is 550 metres long with a partially transparent roof. The core of the terminal is a large, bright concourse where the roof construction manifests as an extra façade (072). Terminal Mitte and Terminal Ost are connected by a monorail.

Guided (E)Motion

Airports are volatile environments where comfort and a reassuring design are essential to mitigate stress. The terminal creates a stoical environment that transforms individuals into an orderly passenger flow. The time spent in the airport (eating, drinking, shopping) is as important a commercial factor as the disciplined movement towards the boarding area; both require architectural design. The amorphous mass is persuaded and coerced into docility, browbeaten into automatic behaviour and steered by signals and signs. In order to traverse the globe via the universal highway in the air, hundreds of passengers willingly allow themselves to be shut up for hours in a steel tube with tiny windows, to be fastened into cramped seats and subjected to a variety programme presented by uniformed wardens trained to guard the emotional economy of the cargo against excesses.

This logistical regime demands symbolism and emotional streamlining. Clients and designers assume that the traveller subconsciously associates air travel with speed, light, sky, comfort and efficient service. The designer confirms these associations with glass, light colours, comfortable furniture, and a smoothly efficient passenger processing system. His aim is to suffuse all his objects with the lightness of the Air Age.

Universal though the highway in the air may be, pre-war airport architecture was initially required to express two things: the function of the airport and the national character of each country, or in the case of minor airfields the demands of the local commissioners.

Travellers should, after all, be able to distinguish between their place of departure and place of arrival. Simplicity was emphasised because of the likelihood that the buildings would need to be extended. This very "flexibility" should be expressed in the design. If the buildings are constructed of light "flowing" materials rather than of solidly anchored blocks of masonry, the

070 Frankfurt Airport, Terminal 1 (centre), Giefer, Mäckler & Kosina, 1965–72.

071 Ground plan, Frankfurt Airport, Terminal 1

072 Frankfurt Airport, Terminal 2 (East), Joos, Schulze, Krüger-Heyden, with OM Ungers and Perkins & Will, 1990–94.

070

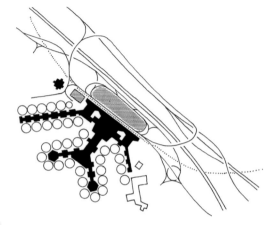

071

072

17 Wallace and Wright, *Airport Buildings*, p. 85.
18 I am grateful to Professor Bohdan Tscherkes for making the relevant historical material available to me.

airport may achieve some of the beauty of design of aeroplanes themselves.'[17] Transparency in every sense of the word, lightness and adoration of light, suggest minimal resistance and consequently a smooth take-off and landing.

None of this applied in the former Eastern Bloc countries, where airports were little troubled by growing pains and developed a rhetorical formula all their own. The long, baroque terminal building at Ukraine's L'viv airport (designed by Russian architect Ivan Zholtovsky, completed 1958), which on the landside looks like a temple, is embellished with a bell tower and two airside pavilions topped by domes. The latter is borne by columns in the shape of overalled male proletarians with rolled-up sleeves. In one of the pavilions, suspended by a cable, there hung a bust of Lenin that fixed arriving passengers with its penetrating gaze. After the travellers had weathered the whole customs and immigration ritual, they emerged into the representative section of the terminal where they were brought up short by a wall-filling mural depicting a rural idyll centred around Little Father Stalin. Welcome to the communist Utopia.[18]

Shell Roofs as Fifth Façade

The 1950s saw the emergence in the United States of numerous designs in which terminal areas were spanned by concrete shell roofs. The dominant architectural motif was no longer egalitarian transparency but a distinctive silhouette. Inside the terminal, moreover, the curved forms of the shell roof gave rise to a dramatic play of light and shadow.

Between 1951 and 1956, the architectural firm of Hellmuth, Yamasaki, and Leinweber designed a terminal with a shell roof inspired by Roman cross vaults for St. Louis. In the waiting area, with its high glass walls, chairs designed by George Nelson were arranged in rows of six.

This building was actually an important influence for the most spectacular example of the genre, in terms of design and symbolism: the TWA Terminal at Idlewild (later John F. Kennedy International Airport), New York. The central concourse, which on the airside is linked by two bridges to the aprons where the planes are parked, is covered by four concrete shell roofs (044). Saarinen wanted to make the TWA terminal a place of movement and transition by dramatising the rites of passage, like the walk through the Y-shaped column to the tube like bridges (045).

His decision to use shell roofs to express the chosen symbolic form ('bird in flight') generated a fascinating interior without a single straight line. In this curved space Saarinen designed not only the check-in counters, signs, seating, concession stands and advertising displays, but the cosmopolitan areas for eating and drinking as well (046). He also designed the luxurious Ambassador Club restaurant; the other four (London Club, Paris Café, Lisbon Lounge, and a lowly snack bar) were designed by the office of Raymond Loewy/William Snaith, Inc. and were more down to earth in both price and ambience. None of the restaurants tried to compete with the decor of the generic space or with the airside view.

At Dulles International Airport in Washington, D.C., Saarinen effected the architectural metamorphosis of the hangar (utilitarian garage for aeroplanes) into terminal (public garage for passengers). The utility is ennobled by the shell roof that is stayed by cables between two rows of reclining concrete columns. In search of a single striking image, Saarinen took his cue from contemporary product design and the demand for 'corporate identity design' (in his case, an allusion to the capital's federal architecture). The image he came up with emphasised the building as a graceful sculpture and took account of the different aspects the building presented to the automobile traveller. The mise-en-scène behind the vertical composition of the terminal building was one of multiple layers experienced at different moments during the approach to the airport. As the traveller turns on to the airport approach road leading to the sunken car park, the building appears to rise up from its foundation and hover between heaven and earth. Nearing the terminal, the huge colonnade becomes visible. In order not to disrupt this image, the control tower was placed at the rear of the terminal building:

Every detail, from the approach road to the graphics, has been designed to create an atmosphere of restraint and decorum – and the structure itself makes the passenger aware of the moment: the formal columns subtly recall Federal architecture of nearby Washington, while the light sloping roof with the enormous panels of open glass between columns remind the passenger of a graceful hangar.[19]

The interior retains the vast size of the hangar but the services have their own scale so that the traveller continues to experience the overarching shell roof above a freely divisible space (053, 054).

In 1958, Charles and Ray Eames produced a film for Saarinen, *The Expanding Airport,* that extolled the advantages of the mobile lounge for both the airlines and the public. It formed part of Saarinen's presentation of his new design for Dulles Airport.[20] The architect also asked the Eames to design comfortable and attractive chairs for the lounges at Dulles Airport. His request happened to coincide with a similar commission from Murphy and Associates, who were busy designing two terminal buildings for Chicago's O'Hare Airport (four semi-autonomous buildings with finger piers, a cylindrical restaurant of reinforced concrete and a cable-stayed roof).[21] The outcome was the durable and comfortable Tandem Sling Seating (1962). This chair type was also used for Tampa International Airport (1972), Phoenix's Sky Harbor Airport (1984), and John Wayne Airport, Orange County, California.

Transparency

The architecture of the 1960s and 1970s was conceived in terms of elegance, speed, light, and air, and realised with masses of glass, light colours and comfortable furniture. At Zurich Airport the different functional elements of the terminal – main hall and two side aisles – were expressed on the outside: the office block with traffic tower in one aisle was rather closed, the main hall appeared very narrow at the landside entrance and became wider and brighter as it approached airside, while the restaurant area – parallel to the gates – was one and all glass. The architecture choreographed the ritual passage from darkness to light.

In 1950, Frederick Gibberd and Partners (project architect: George Dunton) designed the Central Terminal Area of London Airport (Heathrow): a control tower some 40 metres high with a T-shaped base and a visual control room on its roof, a passenger terminal, and the Eastern Apex Building containing operational rooms, crews' quarters, and viewing terraces for the public. All three buildings have a steel frame based on a 3.6 by 3.6 metre module and filled with bricks or glass blocks. The ceilings and roofs consist for the most part of pre-cast concrete elements. In the terminal, a spacious passenger concourse was guaranteed architecturally by placing a glass wall along the entire length of the building (037). This glazed gallery connected all the side passages providing amenities for the public. One fork of the concourse led to the restaurant, which in turn gave access to the roof gardens, laid out with lawns and beds containing shrubs and flowers and paved with walkways made of a variety of materials. The brown brick of the walls formed a fine contrast with the green grass of the roof gardens and the silvery aluminium of the aeroplanes.

The Conran Design Group designed the vandal-proof interior and furniture for the Terminal One building (1969). Their designs for kiosks, currency exchange booths, and furniture was to set the standard for later airport interiors. The designers succeeded in developing a different and exciting concept that is now immediately recognisable as typical of the 1960s: free-standing, circular display cases with a very delicate construction, enhancing their transparency. The accompanying retail spaces were also circular but larger and more introverted. A genuine innovation was the circular baggage foreman's booth, constructed entirely of reinforced

19 Maude Dorr, 'Portraits in Architecture: A Review of the Most Recent Buildings of the Late Eero Saarinen', *Industrial Design,* (May 1963), p. 63.
20 Eero Saarinen's friendship with Charles Eames dated from before the war, when they worked together on experiments in standardised furniture design. They also collaborated on the celebrated Case Study Houses 8 and 9. Between 1945 and 1978, Charles and Ray Eames produced at least forty chair concepts for the retail market. The Eames Office had first experimented with mass produced chairs for schools and stadiums. Pat Kirkham, *Charles and Ray Eames. Designers of the Twentieth Century,* Cambridge (Mass.), 1995.
21 Brodherson, '"An Airport in Every City"', pp. 83–84.

073 Ground plan, Paris Orly Airport, Aéroports de Paris architectes, directed by Henry Vicariot, 1961.

074 The motorway Route Nationale 7 runs beneath Orly's terminal and runways.

075 View of the main building and the west fingers of Paris Orly. The roof of the upper terrace was designed by Jean Prouvé.

076 Main hall, Terminal Building, Paris Orly. On the right are the airline counters.

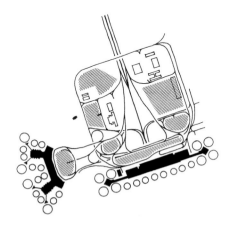

073

074

075

076

glass fibre on a chromed steel base. The rubbish bins, telephone booths, and customs and immigration furniture all belonged to the same design family: rounded form, white fibreglass and chromed steel streamlining. Even the modular furniture for passengers was specially designed for this airport (038, 039).[22]

The five-storey Gatwick passenger terminal (1958) is a concrete skeleton based on a module of 6.1 metres. The skeleton is clad in panels of steel and glass with wooden window frames. The U-shaped operations block, one storey high, and the finger pier were pure steel constructions with a curtain wall (048). The same sustained transparency characterises Orly-South (Paris), a new terminal inaugurated with great fanfare in 1961 (Aéroports de Paris architects, Henry Vicariot chief architect). The building, a steel skeleton construction 200 metres long and 70 metres deep and hung with glazed curtain walls, stands in the middle of the airport. At the east and west ends it is extended with a two-storey 'finger', giving it an airside frontage of 700 metres (073, 074). The main building consists of eight levels, two of which are below ground and contain the technical services and storage areas. The above ground floors contain a shopping mall of 1500 square metres and – on the airside – restaurants and terraces. In the central hall are steel columns faced with dark green natural stone, the walls and above all ceilings are finished with reflective anodised aluminium ('Orly-blond') and the floor is laid with white quarry stone from the Bourgogne (076). Monolithic architecture in grey, white and black, Orly never gives the impression of weight. The terminal building is one big show window.

The original Schiphol terminal (1967) consisted of a single, horizontally articulated building laid out as a horseshoe around an island. The various functions were kept organisationally and spatially separate. In order to provide sufficient docking spaces for aircraft, three piers were constructed on the airside (050). The building was zoned vertically as well horizontally, with parking in the 'basement' and the arrival and departure halls stacked above this. The top floor contained cafés for visitors, bars and a restaurant with seating for 1200 and a panoramic view of the airport. The simply but expressively designed interior contributed greatly to the spatial experience. The designer (Kho Liang Ie) had identified certain 'panic points' and used his design to foster a sense of calm and confidence, not least through the proportions and the colour scheme which were geared to clarity and good organisation. For example, the colour green denoted services, yellow was used to indicate the routes to be followed by passengers (052). The waiting areas were a breath of fresh air: instead of the customary small, isolated departure lounges with tiny shops, incessant loudspeaker announcements, snow-filled television screens, and a chronic shortage of seats, he designed islands with rows of exceptionally comfortable chairs (051). Heavily trafficked floors were laid with ceramic stone, those in the waiting areas with black textured rubber. The main departure hall was free of kiosks and pavilions selling consumer goods so that there was no clash between advertising and the airport signage system. On the top floor there were kiosks aimed at transit passengers and here the advertising was abundant but still strictly controlled.

Kho Liang Ie designed all the individual elements inside the building including the telephone booths and the furnishings in the main control centre and the air crew quarters. His design concept for kiosks and telephone booths was elegant in its simplicity: curved glazed walls mounted in angle sections.

The standard of finish, both in design and material, is immaculate – particularly in details like the staircase rails, the balconies, and the three kinds of showcase. Other examples are the south cafeteria in the lounge – whose service is wooden framed on a concrete base, covered in tiles, with thick PVC foot rests and charming decorative lights – and also the construction system used for the shops.[23]

22 'Conran Design at Heathrow', *Architectural Design* (February 1969), p. 394.
23 Hughes-Stanton, 'Schiphol Puts Passengers First', pp. 52–53.

24 Serge Salat and Françoise Labbé, *Paul Andreu. Metamorphosis of the Circle*, Milan and Paris, 1990, p. 30. See also Paul Andreu, *J'ai fait beaucoup d'aérogares…Les dessin et les mots*, Paris, 1998.

Monoliths

The new central terminals built in the 1960s and 1970s required an architectural concept of their own. The departure point was the architectural expression of the concept of the transport machine. Roissy 1 is the prime prototype of this kind of terminal. The curved line in the form of a series of semi-circles was expressed in three different ways at Roissy – as rotunda (Roissy 1), ellipse (Roissy 2 A–D), and ellipse with peninsulas (Roissy 2 E–F) – and clad in a palette of restful colours: white, grey, and black (067).

The entire megastructure of Roissy was designed by Aéroports de Paris, with Paul Andreu as chief architect. The roads, bridges, water tower, traffic control tower, the terminal exterior and interior have a more or less uniform design. The concrete main building of terminal 1 is linked by two-storey, 250-metre-long tunnels to seven satellites around which the aircraft are parked (062). Andreu invested all his energy in guaranteeing the functionality of the cylindrical organisation of the space and in the strictly modular construction of the building.[24] The circle is not simply the formal motif of the design, but also the basic organisational principle. The terminal is an organism without façade, a condenser that swallows up masses of people and spews them out. The forms follow one another as an assemblage without breaking points. The cylinder has a hollow centre that conjures up the effect of a moment of reflection. The void is criss-crossed by diagonal escalators, which transport departing passengers from the dark, up through the void towards the light (061). Above they see the open sky, and beneath them is a gushing fountain.

High-Tech Design

Given the numerous calls to make terminal buildings elemental (skeletal or exposed construction), light, transparent, and flexible, it was only to be expected that the so-called high-tech architects would apply themselves intensively to airport design. In the 1980s and 1990s, the celebration of the tectonic composition of terminals was allied to two familiar building types: the arcade and the station concourse, both hybrids of street and interior. The passengers move through elongated, uncluttered spaces that look like a transparent arcade or a station concourse. The spaces, lined with shops, bars, and cafés, are bathed in light.

In the new Hamburg International Airport (designed by von Gerkan, Marg und Partner, 1993–94), the passenger facilities are arranged in three parallel, elongated strips: the landside transport facilities, the passenger terminal, and the 500-metre-long boarding pier with footbridges to the aeroplanes branching off at right angles. Two rows of six massive, reinforced concrete pillars, each sprouting four slender, diagonal steel tubes, support the roof. The new terminal is open and brightly lit and looks like a simple space frame construction (077, 078). The curved form deprives it of conventional front and rear façades while the side elevations are flanked by rectangular office buildings.

The ultimate high-tech airport is Stansted (design: Norman Foster, 1986–91) which marries the glorified hangar with the nineteenth-century railway station. Stansted, too, aspires to be a single terminal building capable, thanks to its modular structure, of being endlessly extended with new modules without any sense of alienation from the mother building (079). This white structure, which can be viewed as one gigantic roof, accommodates all the public amenities on a single level with one unambiguous concourse catering to both arrival and departure (080, 082). Technical services and car parking are accommodated in the building's plinth (081). The projecting trussed roof and branching, tree-like groups of pillars follow a set pattern and modulate the daylight penetration. Stansted looks on the one hand like a minimalist square glass box, on the other hand like a daring celebration of tectonics. Both aspects find one another in the metaphor of light:

The arrival is in a huge cave from which the passenger gradually ascends to a huge luminous tent. After passing through clearly organised stages of preparation, and

077 Terminal 4, Hamburg Airport, von Gerkan, Marg und Partner, 1993–94.

078 Interior view, Terminal 4, Hamburg Airport.

079 Perspective drawing of Stansted Airport, Norman Foster, 1986–91. The two already build satellite buildings are connected with an underground train to the modularly constructed main building. In case there is a need for expansion, two further sketched satellite buildings can be constructed.

080 Clarity and transparency guarantee easy passenger orientation at Stansted.

081 A cross sectional drawing shows the structural supports for the ceiling.

082 In the 'trunks' of the 'structural trees' that with four steel columns support the ceiling contain service elements.

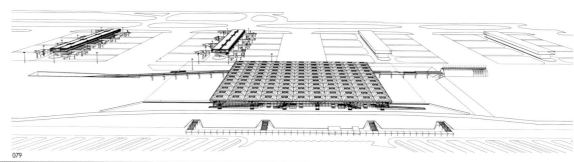

079

080

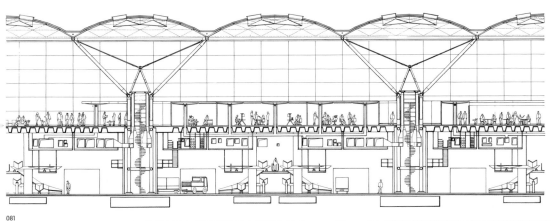

081

082

25 Peter Davey, 'Stansted', *The Architectural Review* (May 1991), p. 45.

arriving at a point where the initiate can contemplate the heavens, he is plunged underground again to arrive at a jetty, whence he boards his aerial vessel.[25]

Although the airport as transfer machine and as social space can never satisfy everybody's demands and wishes, designers persist in their frantic efforts to create a relaxed environment capable of assuaging the physical and psychological perturbation that is part and parcel of air travel (the fear of flying, a nervousness about terrorist attacks or disasters, and the discomforts of jet lag, unpleasant smells, and loud noise). If anything has become clear in the Air Age, it is that an entirely adequate planning of airports is an impossibility, not only because technical and logistical aspects are the prime determinants, but also because unpredictable geopolitical complications (war, terrorism, and epidemics) and commercial trends all exact changes in airport design. Typological and architectural purity are inevitably compromised as a result. Parking facilities, obvious entrances, short walking distances, a linear organisation of traffic flows, avoidance of intersecting flows, first-rate signage and security, all vie for preferential treatment and will never be perfectly balanced. An airport is a place for commercial exchange, a complex system of structures around which is woven an endless cycle of production, construction, demolition, maintenance, and different types of work. Perfection, itself historically and culturally contingent, has a limited shelf life.

HAMBURG
LINZ
BRUESSEL
LOURDES
PRAG
AMSTERDAM
ODESSA

tra

vel

A TRIP THROUGH TIME
IN THE AIRCRAFT CABIN

BARBARA FITTON HAUß

Almost a century ago, the first aeroplane passenger took a seat next to Wilbur Wright between the kite-like wings of the Wright Brothers' modified Flyer 3 biplane, which hopped 200 metres before touching down again.[1] Since then, air travel has become a commonplace means of world-wide mass transport. While today's average airline passenger typically associates enclosed spaces, cramped seats, lacklustre food service on tiny trays, and inhibited productivity or uninspired entertainment with the fastest mode of long distance travel, the adventure and romance of commercial flight in previous decades is unknown to most.

The evolution of the aircraft cabin has been largely neglected as a subject of aviation or design history, as the former has focused on the technical developments of aircraft and the latter on other tasks of industrial design. With thousands of different aeroplanes flown by hundreds of commercially operating airlines during the past century, it would be impossible to present a comprehensive history of the passenger cabin. However, each decade produced distinctive interior features and types, partially dictated by technological advancements, but also by the increasing influence of professional designers on the cabin environment.[2] In the process, the aircraft cabin eventually emancipated itself from spatial solutions presented by land and water-bound modes of passenger transportation and engendered interior designs reflective of and specific to travel by air.

The first regular passenger air service did not rely on aeroplanes at all, but was established in Baden-Baden on 23 August 1910, with sightseeing tours flown by the German airship LZ-6. In the same year, the Zeppelin LZ-7 initiated inter-city service on routes between Frankfurt, Baden-Baden, and Düsseldorf. The first scheduled airline service on the American continents employed a flying boat, transporting a single passenger between St. Petersburg and Tampa, Florida, beginning in December 1913. However, the first viable passenger transports did not appear until after World War I, when domestic and international airlines were founded in Europe and North America.[3]

By the early 1920s, the passenger's outdoor perch had improved somewhat over Wright's precarious tandem seat. In a pre-flight advisory to its pioneer passengers, KLM (Royal Dutch Airlines) advised: '[K]eep away from the propeller [...] don't hang over the side of the aircraft or bother your pilot [...] – you could lose your hat. Don't throw things overboard; refrain from alcohol several hours before a flight, and don't eat split peas, beans, brown bread or any food which could cause excessive gas in the intestines. Visit the toilet before leaving.'[4] In-flight amenities included leather overcoats, helmets, goggles, hot water bottles, cotton earplugs, and (perhaps more realistic than today's floatation device) a parachute.

Parallel to the post-war conversion of World War I bombers for commercial transport, the open cockpits of smaller planes were gradually supplanted by enclosed passenger cabins.[5] Their interiors were as varied as the planes themselves, ranging from the spartan, boxy cabin of the 12-passenger Farman F-60 Goliath (1919) (083, 085), to the carriage-like interior of a 1919 Hawa F 10 triplane with all-over button-upholstery and facing sofa seating, to the living room ambience of a KLM Fokker F.III (1921) with traditional leather armchairs chained to the floor.[6]

The Junkers F 13, built in Dessau beginning in 1919, was revolutionary inside and out (✈002, 084).[7] The world's first all-metal transport aircraft, it was a single-engine low-winged monoplane designed to carry four passengers. Instead of climbing up a stepladder to reach an open cockpit, passengers ascended footsteps mounted on the down-sloping cantilevered wing to enter the cabin through a side door. Around large windows and a small electric ceiling light, the surfaces of the entire cabin were covered with the same upholstery fabric as the seats, giving it the elegant appearance of a contemporary motorcar and augmenting the comfort of the primitive heating system.

1 Charles Furnas, who worked with the Wright brothers at Kitty Hawk, went up alternately with Wilbur and Orville Wright on 14 May 1908. A less often cited claim is that Henry Farman and Ferdinand Léon Delagrange made the first passenger flight in France on 29 March 1908, although there is disagreement about who piloted the plane.
2 In his introductory essay to the exhibition catalogue Building for Air Travel, Zukowsky outlines the contributions of industrial designers to aircraft interiors in the first scholarly review of this subject. His bibliographical references were an invaluable resource. See John Zukowsky, Building for Air Travel, New York and Munich, 1996. I am equally indebted to Jochen Eisenbrand for sharing research material. I would also like to thank Melissa Keiser at the National Air and Space Museum in Washington, D.C. and Rick Watson at the Harry Ransom Humanities Research Center in Austin, Texas for their friendly support.
3 After several failed start-ups, airline consolidation and government subsidies helped European airlines to become established in the mid-1920s. US legislation allowed its airmail to be put to private tender in 1925, effectively creating a subsidy for air passenger service. By 1930, the Hoover administration had grouped 23 regional airlines into three national carriers.
4 Mary Edwards and Elwyn Edwards, The Aircraft Cabin: Managing the Human Factors, Aldershot, 1990, p. 12.
5 One of the earliest enclosed cabins was constructed in 1913 by Igor Sikorsky for perhaps the largest plane of its time, the Bolshoi Bal'tiskii, also known as the Grand. The cabin was fully glazed around the front half and accommodated six passengers on four armchairs and a sofa, with an additional recreation table.
6 L'aérien francais inaugurated the first international public air transport with the Farman F-60 Goliath from Paris to London on 8 February 1919.The Hawa (Hannoversche Waggonfabrik) F 10 and KLM Fokker F.III are illustrated, respectively, in: Wolfgang Wagner, Der deutsche Luftverkehr: Die Pionierjahre 1919-1925, Koblenz, 1987, p. 208; Gerald Nason, 'Inside-Up: Interior Design and the Airline', The Architectural Review (December 1966), fig. 6.
7 The F 13 series of 322 planes built between 1919–32, a time when many planes were constructed individually, speaks for the modernity of both the F 13 and Junkers' production facilities in Dessau.

083 The civilian version of the Farman F-60 Goliath, developed in 1918 as a bomber, offered seating for 12 passengers.

084 The Junkers F 13, the first airliner with an all metal body and cantilever wings, offered space for four passengers and could fly a distance of 1000 km.

085 The cabin of the F-60 Goliath was fitted with wicker chairs.

083

084

085

The two seats and aft bench were equipped with safety belts,[8] and a sliding front window separated the cabin space from the partially open cockpit.

From a design perspective, perhaps the most significant feature of the F 13 was its passenger seat. Constructed out of thin corrugated sheet metal and Duralumin tubing, it not only preceded, but also directly inspired the tubular steel furniture produced by Marcel Breuer, Walter Gropius, and others at the Dessau Bauhaus beginning in 1925.[9] Junkers developed corrugated metal seats as early as 1915 for the Ju 1 (nine years before Jean Prouvé's earliest sheet metal furniture), and perfected the F 13 seat in four versions during flight tests beginning in 1919. The final version joined a U-shaped tubular frame tipped on its side to an angular metal seat structure in a form that predicts the development of the cantilevered chair as it evolved between 1926 and 1927.[10] However, passenger comfort obviously demanded the envelopment of the bare metal frame in thick padding and leather or fabric upholstery, obscuring its structural form not only to occupants, but also to later generations of design historians.

In the mid-1920s, the aircraft interior began to acquire a few standard features, and nascent airlines introduced early forms of in-flight service and even entertainment. Dutch aircraft manufacturer Anthony Fokker's popular trimotor F.VII/3m had wicker seats for eight to ten passengers, as well as sliding windows to alleviate airsickness (a common phenomenon in the turbulence encountered at low altitudes), and what is reported to be the first onboard toilet.[11] To distract passengers from noxious engine fumes, high noise levels, uncomfortable temperatures, and vibration, Britain's Imperial Airways employed wind-up gramophones and hand-cranked movie projectors as early as 1925.[12]

The successful American debut of Fokker's F.VII/3m at the Ford Reliability Tour in 1925 inspired the design of the all-metal Ford Tri-Motor, which went into series production just a year later (➜165). The first important commercial aeroplane developed in the US, the Ford Tri-Motor dominated American air service into the early 1930s. Despite the moniker 'Tin Goose' and complaints about excessive noise, extreme temperatures, heavy vibration, and a toilet described as 'a hole punched through the fuselage', the Tri-Motor had an attractive interior that is representative of 1920s aircraft. The structure of the aircraft cabin as we know it today is reflected in six rows of single seats separated by a central aisle, each positioned at a window. Wicker seats (chosen for their light weight, and sometimes substituted with upholstered metal-frame chairs) had leather or fabric-covered cushions. In some planes, curtains around the large windows softened the hard lines of the interior and, together with individual electric sconces at every seat, created something of a homey atmosphere. Polished or painted plywood panelling concealed most structural parts and added Art Deco touches to the unified cabin space. The suspended net hatracks found in some Tri-Motors were common cabin features well into the 1930s, when they were eventually replaced by open overhead apparel racks.

Night flying and meal service soon placed new demands on the aircraft interior.[13] Luft Hansa established its first night route in 1926 with the Junkers G 24 between Berlin and Königsberg (now Kaliningrad), marking the way with revolving spotlights at 25 to 30 kilometre intervals and neon or gas signals mounted on masts and rooftops in between. The two Albatross L 73's (subsequently dubbed 'Flying Sleepers') on routes between Berlin-Vienna and Berlin-Malmö were equipped with eight deeply reclining seats and four day chairs that could be converted into two night berths (086).[14] KLM followed in 1931 with a long-distance interior arrangement on the Fokker F.XII for the Amsterdam–Batavia (now Jakarta) route. In a room-like cabin shared with the radio operator and navigator, made spacious by its sparse furnishings and modern décor, four passengers sat in leather-upholstered tubular steel lounge chairs (087).

8 The safety belt was introduced as early as 1910, following accidents in which the pilot and/or passenger were thrown from the plane. Its invention has been attributed to several different people, including Glenn Curtiss, Benjamin Foulois, and Albert J. Engel.
9 Helmut Erfurth, Der Stahlrohrstuhl und sein Entwicklungsweg durch das Industriedesign, Dessau, 1986. The author documents the collaboration between Junkers and the Bauhaus, which moved from Weimar to Dessau in 1925 and sought out the technological capabilities and experience of local industries. Junkers also produced a garden chair derivative of the F 13 seat in 1920–21 (p. 13).
10 Ibid., pp. 6 and 8.
11 Edwards and Edwards, The Aircraft Cabin, p. 12.
12 As part of an Imperial Airways media event in 1925, the black-and-white silent film The Lost World gained distinction as the very first in-flight motion picture: 'Inflight Entertainment: Historical Firsts', World Airline Entertainment Association: www.waea.org/ife.htm; see also: Keith Lovegrove, Airline: Identity, Design and Culture, New York and Kempten, 2000, pp. 92 and 98.
13 The first commercial night route was introduced from Paris to London in 1922.
14 Erich H. Heimann, Die Flugzeuge der Deutschen Lufthansa, 3rd ed., Stuttgart, 1987, p. 56 and Addendum 2. This was apparently a high-density configuration, as an arrangement with eight seats converting into four beds is also documented. See also Karl-Dieter Seifert, Der deutsche Luftverkehr 1926–1945, Bonn, 1999, p. 27.

15 Mart Stam described this airplane seat in the article 'Neue Stühle', *De 8 en opbouw* (July 23, 1938). At the time, he was working with Anton Lorenz and Hans Luckhardt on an aircraft seat design that was never produced. Fridtjof F. Schliephacke, 'Der Bewegungsstuhl 1700–1984: Entwicklungsgeschichte des mechanisierten Sitzens' (1984), typescript, Archiv der Akademie der Bildenden Künste Berlin, p. 290.

16 The first airborne meal is reported to have been served on the Russian Sikorsky *Ilya Muromez* in 1914, a four-engine biplane with an imposing wingspan of 34.5 metres that was originally designed as a 10-passenger transport, but then modified and produced in series as a WWI spy plane and bomber. See Edwards and Edwards, *The Aircraft Cabin*, p. 10; J. Roeder, *Giganten am Himmel: Großflugzeuge 1910 – heute*, Munich, 1982, pp. 24–26.

17 Construction of the Junkers G 31 beginning in 1926 made a deep impression on leading figures at the Bauhaus. Under the leadership of László Moholy-Nagy, the metal workshop newly opened in September 1926, utilising some machinery that was had been generously provided by Junkers. Marcel Breuer even designed seats for the G 31 in early 1926; however, they were not produced. In a 1973 interview, Marianne Brandt recalled regular excursions to the Junkers plant, where the 'Bauhäusler' and their guests were 'especially impressed by the aircraft assembly '. See Helmut Erfurth, 'Symbiose von Kunst und Technik: Das Bauhaus und die Junkerswerke in Dessau', *Die Metallwerkstatt am Bauhaus*, ed. Klaus Weber, Berlin, 1992, especially pp. 93–94.

18 Just one month before the G 31 went into service in May 1928, Luft Hansa signed a 15-year contract with Mitropa (Mitteleuropäische Schlafwagen- und Speisewagengesellschaft AG) in an effort to match the well-established food service on Central Europe's passenger trains (Seifert, Der deutsche Luftverkehr 1926–1945, pp. 55–57).

19 National Air and Space Museum (NASM) Archives, Wash. D.C., file AB-581872-01: 'Performance of Boeing Model 80-A: Eighteen-Passenger Tri-Motored Transport', p. 2 (typescript).

20 NASM Archives, file AB-581872-01: 'Boeing System's Transcontinental Air Liners Typify Peak of Aircraft Construction' (typescript).

The backrest could be manually adjusted to three different positions, while a horizontal footrest slid out from beneath the seat to create a full-length recliner.[15] Large luggage trunks – presumably one did not fly to Batavia for a short visit when the trip itself took almost a week – could accompany passengers behind or underneath their seats.

At some point passengers' desire to eat en route must have outweighed their propensity toward airsickness, and airlines began to introduce in-flight food service.[16] Prior to this, passengers on long-haul routes had taken their meals at restaurants during fuelling and maintenance stops, just as they had slept in hotels during overnight pauses. But as the range and size of aircraft increased, so did the sophistication of onboard meals. While prepared box lunches and drinks could be stored and served from a simple pantry closet, the need for a galley to provide more substantial service was soon recognised. One of the earliest planes to incorporate food preparation facilities into its design was the 15-passenger Junkers G 31 (1926), which gained fame as the 'Flying Dining Car' (088).[17] Junkers' design engineer Ernst Zindel obviously had a modern train interior in mind when he divided the cabin space of the G 31 into three compartments with varied groups of facing seating on either side of a central aisle. Each compartment had crank-down glass windows, two electric ceiling lights for night flying, ventilation and heating, and a convertible berth arrangement. The small galley provided cooking equipment and storage for tableware, thermos jugs, and fresh food that was prepared and served onboard by a Mitropa steward (089).[18] Passengers enjoyed their meals on linen tablecloths with china, silver, glassware, and even fresh flowers.

On the other side of the Atlantic, the influence of passenger train interiors on the aircraft cabin was equally evident. Boeing's first true passenger airliner, Model 80, entered service on the Chicago–San Francisco route in 1928. The aim of Boeing's chief engineer, Claire Egtvedt, to rival the luxury of transcontinental trains is evident in a Boeing press release that points out the cabin's 'noticeable resemblance to the interior of a modern railway coach'.[19] This desired impression was validated by passengers, who came to refer to the Model 80A (a more powerful 18-passenger version) as the 'Flying Pullman' (090, 091). The entire cabin was finished in polished dark mahogany as the exterior veneer of three-ply sheathing with a core of balsa wood for sound insulation. The rich brown wood was complemented by polished black walnut seats upholstered with curled hair and sedan cloth. An interesting feature of the reclining seats was a locking device on the legs enabling them to be removed from the cabin in less than 15 minutes. In this way, cabin space could be easily reallocated for mail or express freight service. Since the designated route was often flown at night, special attention was given to the illumination of the cabin with 27 electric lights, including dome lights as well as shaded wall lamps with individual switches next to each outboard seat (the slightly wider fuselage allowed three seats per row, moving the narrow aisle off-centre). Overhead aluminium water tanks provided electrically generated hot and cold water in the lavatory, and a lead to the cold water tank even serviced a drinking fountain mounted on the rear wall of the cabin.[20]

In comparison to the aeroplanes actually flown at the time, several 'jumbo' projects designed by pioneering aviation engineers in the 1920s deserve to be remembered for their visionary audacity. The earliest dates back to a patent awarded to Prof. Hugo Junkers in 1910 for a flying wing that would carry 100 to 1000 passengers across the Atlantic in one-and-a-half days. This idea informed Ernst Zindel's design in 1920 for a long-range landplane (Junkerissime) with seating for 56 in its monowing. Windows in the ceiling, floor, and forward edge of the thick wing would have provided spectacular aerial views of the landscape as one passed over it at 160 km/h. Junkers again took up the idea in 1923 with the J 1000 project, a flying wing for 80 to 100

086 Lufthansa's Albatross L 73, also called 'Flying Sleeping Car.'

087 The cabin of the Fokker F-XII on the KLM route Amsterdam–Batavia (today Jakarta). Equipped with seats made of tubular steel.

088 Cabin, Junkers G-31, with 15 seats, 1928. In the same year, Luft Hansa served food on board for the first time.

089 Galley, Junkers G-31.

090 Boeing, Model 80 A, 1929.

091 Cabin, Boeing Model 80 A, Boeing Air Transport. This posed photo was taken in early 1930, before in May of that year the first stewardesses began service. Their uniforms, unlike the one depicted here, had no similarity to a nurse's uniform.

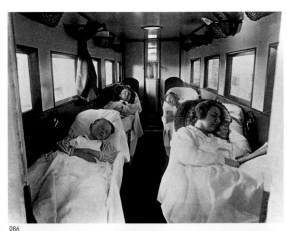

086

088

090

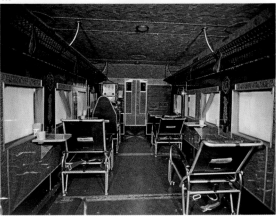

087

089

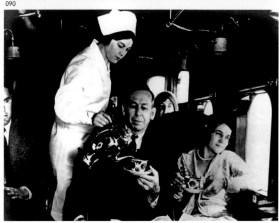

091

092 Aerial Express, William Whitney Christmas and Vincent
Burnelli, drawing, 1928.

093 Junkers J 1000, a flying wing with space for 80 to 100
passengers, drawing, 1923.

094 Junkers J 1000, model, 1924.

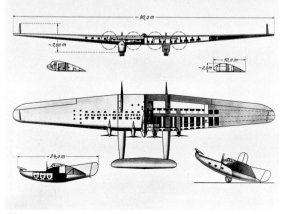

092

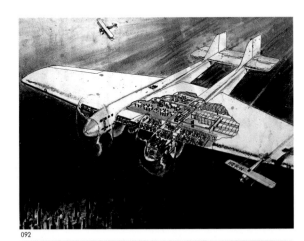

093

094

095 Airliner Number 4, cut-away drawing of deck 7, Norman Bel Geddes, 1929.

096 Airliner Number 4, back view, Norman Bel Geddes, 1929.

097 Airliner Number 4, model, Norman Bel Geddes, 1929.

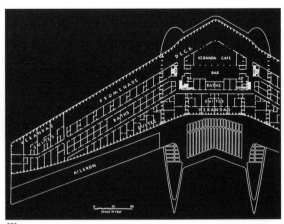

095

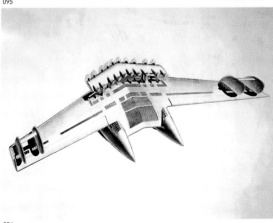

096

097

098 Junkers G-38, 1929. Thanks to a height of 1.8 m on its front side, this plane held room for four to six passengers.

099 Cabin design of a Luft Hansa Junkers G-38. The compartments are placed on different levels.

100 The Handley-Page HP 42, 1930. The travel velocity of this 'hotel of the skies' was only 150 km/h.

101 The cabin design of the Handley Page HP 42.

098

100

099

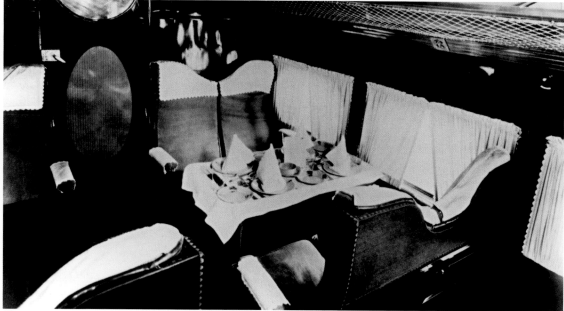
101

passengers (plus 10 crew members) to be powered by four turbine engines (an anticipated improvement over contemporary diesel engines). With a span of 80 metres – compared to the 65 metres of today's Boeing 747 – the wing provided space for 26 two-person or six-person compartments, while the twin fuselage of the canard design accommodated a dining room and an observation deck (**093, 094**).[21] A comparable ten-engine transatlantic transport was designed in 1928 by another German, Edmund Rumpler, in the form of a flying double boat with a monowing spanning 88 metres and accommodating 135 passengers.[22]

Similar projects surfaced in the US at roughly the same time. William Whitney Christmas, in collaboration with Vincent Burnelli, devised the 1928 Aerial Express, an intercontinental monowing aircraft for approximately 100 passengers (**092**). Intimate forward seating compartments, a large central dining room and adjacent kitchen, a variety of lounges, fuel tanks, and cargo holds were planned in the space of the 80-metre wing span. The double fuselage housed crew quarters, lavatories, and a long 'saloon'.[23] Certainly the most extravagant of the early 'jumbo' projects was Norman Bel Geddes' Air Liner Number 4, designed in 1929 in association with aeronautical engineer Dr. Otto Koller (**095, 096, 097**). The huge V-shaped wing (160 metre span) resting on five-story twin pontoons was to be powered by 20 motors with six back-up engines onboard. Comfortable sleeping accommodations were to be provided for 451 passengers, whose needs on their journey across the ocean would be satisfied by 155 crew members. The lazy cruising speed of 160 km/h might explain Bel Geddes' provision of four tennis courts, six shuffle-board courts, a gymnasium with showers and private dressing rooms, a solarium, a playroom for children, a doctor, hairdresser, library, promenade deck, and a dining room for 204 patrons with an orchestra platform. Air Liner Number 4 aspired to nothing less than 'the same view and conditions as on the finest ocean liner'.[24] Although none of these planes ever got

past the drawing board, aviation experts acknowledge them as theoretically realistic aeronautical designs, though far ahead of their time with respect to powerplants and passenger capacity.

The largest landplanes introduced around 1930 were, in fact, Junkers' G 38 (1929) and the British Handley-Page HP 42 (1930) – yet they could hardly have been more different. Despite the stifling restrictions on German engine and aircraft construction imposed by the Treaty of Versailles, Junkers maintained its vanguard role in aviation design with the 30 to 34 passenger G 38 (**098, 099**).[25] As the plane that came closest to realising Junkers' 1910 patent, its imposing all-metal monowing had a span of 44 metres and was 10 metres deep on the centreline with a 1.8 metre thick profile. This made it possible to place four to six passenger seats in the forward space of the wing, with an unmatched view through windows in its leading edge. Two more passengers were seated in the glazed nose, since the cockpit was mounted above it, and the remaining 26 occupied three cabins in the fuselage. The staggered cabin compartments in the G 38b each had distinct colour schemes (green, blue, and red). A completely equipped galley and bar facilitated steward service from the fore. Toilets and a lavatory were also provided, and the small aft compartment was reserved for smoking.

While chief engineer Ernst Zindel wanted Junkers' aircraft cabins to reflect the functional comfort of a continental train interior, Imperial Airways' Handley-Page HP 42 emulated the plush trappings of an English drawing room (**100, 101**). In spite of its anachronisms (including fabric-covered wings and a fuselage of mixed materials), the slow, ungainly biplane became the flagship of Imperial Airways in the early 1930s. It was also popular with passengers, who enjoyed its fanciful interior and, on some routes, five-course dinners. Fore and aft cabins accommodating a total of 24 to 38 passengers were separated by the central fuselage, where baggage space, lavatories and the

21 See Wagner, *Der deutsche Luftverkehr*, pp. 108–113; Heinz J. Novarra, *Junkers Grossflugzeuge*, Stuttgart, 1988, pp. 8–9, 104.
22 See Wagner, *Der deutsche Luftverkehr*, pp. 112–115.
23 Rudolf Braunburg, *Als Fliegen noch ein Abenteuer war: Der Passagierflug von den Anfängen bis in die Nachkriegszeit*, Dortmund, 1988, pp. 88–89; 'Christmas', *Aerofiles: A Century of American Aviation*: www.aerofiles.com/_ca.html; Joe Yoon, 'Aerospace History Questions' (5 August 2011), Aerospaceweb.org: www.aerospaceweb.org/question/history/q0038.shtml.
24 Norman Bel Geddes, *Horizons*, 2nd ed., New York, 1977 [1935], pp. 109–21.
25 Only two models were built, the prototype G 38a (1929, designation D-2000) and the slightly larger G 38b (1931, D-2500). Both flew with Lufthansa between 1931 and 1940. The airline began using the conjoined name in 1934.

26 Eric Niderost, 'Handley Page's Slow and Stately H.P.42', *Aviation History* (July 2000), *The History Net*, Online, 30 May 2003. A cutaway drawing of the HP 42 is published in: Braunburg, *Als Fliegen noch ein Abenteuer war*, pp. 76–77. An excellent photographic print of the biplane's cabin in Lovegrove's *Airline* (p. 85) is incorrectly identified as an Armstrong-Whitworth Argosy, a smaller plane also flown by Imperial Airways at the time.

27 Daniel C. Sayre, 'Gentility in the Air', *The Technology Review* (January 1934), pp. 127–128.

28 *Pioniere des industriellen Designs am Bodensee*, ed. Zeppelin Museum Friedrichshafen, Friedrichshafen, 2003, p. 119

galley were located due to the proximity of the four engines mounted on the wings' bracing struts. The cabins had elaborate wood panelling with inlaid scrollwork, sofa-style seats with floral-patterned upholstery, chintz curtains, and a ceiling with profiled panels. No flying train this – the HP 42 established a reputation as 'a virtual hotel of the air'.[26]

The most important cabin innovations in the new American passenger planes of the early 1930s were not visible interior elements, but perceptible improvements in cabin environment and infrastructure. The breakthrough of the monocoque, twin-engine, streamlined airliner with a smooth metal skin and retractable landing gear, as represented by the Boeing 247, Douglas DC-1/DC-2, and Lockheed Model 10 Electra, brought not only a significant increase in cruising speed (115 to 160 km/h faster than the Ford Tri-Motor's 160 to 196 km/h), but also improvements in sound insulation and more sophisticated heating and ventilation systems. A multi-layered shell consisting of a thick layer of insulating material such as kapok, airspace, and a layer of felt between the exterior metal skin and the cabin lining reduced the noise level within the cabin from an almost deafening 120 decibels measured in some early tri-motors to 70 decibels, a level at which one could comfortably converse. Vibration was reduced by replacing plywood or bakelite wall panels with fabric cabin lining and inserting rubber connections between the frame and floor, under chair supports, and around fixed windows and doors. Instead of producing heated air by passing fresh air directly past the hot exhaust pipe of the engine in an enclosed cylinder – with the possibility that exhaust fumes might enter the system – fresh air was taken in through a scoop near the nose and heated over a steam radiator connected to a small exhaust-heated boiler.[27] Thermostats regulated the temperature automatically.

A distinct advantage of the DC-2 (104, 105) cabin (production model of the prototype DC-1) over the Boeing 247 and the Lockheed 10 Electra was the fact that the entire length of the floor was free from structural obstacles. Double wing spars penetrated the cabin of the Boeing 247, making it necessary to cushion the spars and install U-shaped footsteps in the aisle so that passengers and crew could step over them (102, 103). The Lockheed plane also had a heavy truss passing through and over the cabin floor behind the first row of seats. In general, however, all three interiors were similarly rudimentary: 10 to 14 upholstered metal-frame armchairs at a generous 40-inch (101.6 cm) pitch in single-seat rows facing forward, curtained windows, overhead apparel racks with netting, a utilitarian aft lavatory, and a simple service cabinet.

A factor that hindered the development of larger landplanes prior to World War II was the lack of adequate airport facilities, especially at more remote destinations in the Southern Hemisphere. Seaplanes, on the other hand, could land on lakes or in sheltered harbours. Another advantage of the seaplane over the landplane was that it did not need the heavy undercarriage required for landing on hard ground, thus permitting an increase in the overall size of the plane. Although the seaplane has almost disappeared from the public consciousness as a mode of commercial air travel, the largest and most luxurious passenger transports in the 1930s were flying boats.

The Dornier Do X, built in 1929 in Friedrichshafen, was the largest and most luxurious of them all, but also the least successful from a commercial standpoint (106, 107, 108, ✈ 340). For the interior, Dornier contracted with Swiss architect Emil Rau and the Zurich-based company J. Keller & Co.; furnishings were manufactured by the Knoll company in Stuttgart.[28] The middle of three decks was reserved for passengers and included a bar, a smoking salon, a series of spacious lounges, a sleeping compartment, lavatories, and a fully-equipped electric kitchen. Except for the big portholes, it is hard to believe that the cabin compartments of the Do X were not spaces in a fine hotel. Turkish carpets, elegant armchairs, elaborate curtains, and printed wall coverings provided

102 Die Boeing 247 (1933) was the first low wing American airliner to feature retractable wheels.

103 In the cabin of the Boeing 247, two ribs of the wing cut through the cabin.

104 Douglas DC-2, 1934.

105 Cabin design, Lufthansa Douglas DC-2. The backrest of the seats could be adjusted by means of a crank-driven cog wheel mechanism.

102

103

104

105

106 The Dornier Do X, section drawing.

107 The Dornier Do X on its presentation flight in New York, 1931.

108 Passenger accommodations on the Dornier Do X.

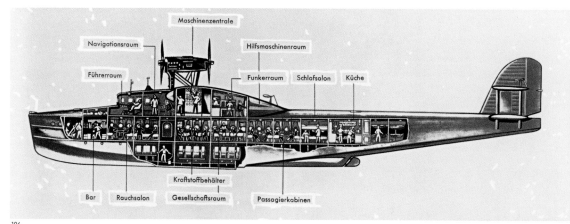

106

108

107

an appropriate setting for sumptuous meals served on linen tablecloths with specially designed porcelain. Although the Do X received a lot of publicity after a 1929 test flight on Lake Constance with 169 people on board (normal capacity 72) and a transatlantic tour to Rio de Janeiro and New York City in 1931, its twelve engines did not provide enough power to make it suitable for regular route service.

While flying boats by Dornier (Germany), Latécoère (France), and Short (➔388) (Britain) dominated the skies and waters of Europe and its foreign ports, Pan American Airways inaugurated passenger service to Pacific and Caribbean destinations with US-built flying boats. Pan Am wanted to shorten the travel time on its Pacific routes by eliminating overnight hotel stops. Rather than relying on aviation engineers, the airline sought out the services of Norman Bel Geddes – who had established one of the first industrial design offices in the US in 1927 – to equip its new flying boat with sleeping facilities. Geddes' work on the Martin M-130 China Clipper beginning in 1933–34 was not only one of the earliest collaborations between an aircraft manufacturer, an airline, and a consultant industrial designer, but also set lasting standards for pre-war passenger transports (109, 110, 111, 112).[29]

Pan Am's original plan called for separate night and day interiors that could be exchanged during stops at company airbases en route.[30] Geddes' office did an independent analysis of long-range passenger comfort requirements and proposed a single flexible day-night interior that met the airline's stringent weight restrictions. Few structural changes could be made, so Geddes utilised extant bulkheads to divide the fuselage into room-size compartments and also relocated bulkhead doors off-centre to create enough space for six berths per compartment (rather than four). Clever dimensions, removable armrests, and hinged frame elements made it possible to use the same equipment for sitting and sleeping. Contrary to Pan Am's practice of preparing meals ashore, Geddes devised a complete, compact

galley with hanging shelves for glassware, cooling and cooking facilities, and a roll-away cabinet so that semi-prepared meals could be finished onboard. Gender-specific toilets were provided, and the lounge functioned as a dressing room at the beginning and end of the day (with a magazine table that unfolded into two wash basins with running water!). The problems of ventilation, vibration, heating, and cleaning were also addressed by installing cup-shaped vents and lights, cork flooring, and removable slip covers for furnishings and walls. Great attention was paid in selecting materials that were both lightweight and durable for bedding, curtains, and upholstery. Notable details were leather hassocks that doubled as life preservers, non-skid tabletops of sponge rubber and felt, and the 5 degree tilt of galley surfaces to counteract the plane's position in flight. Geddes was not exaggerating when he wrote, in 1945: '[W]e went into the problem in a very thorough manner and produced items of passenger comfort that were so basically sound that they are still in general use'.[31]

Rather late in the game, US airlines began to seek better ways to transport their passengers across the vast North American continent. While the Boeing 247, DC-2, and L-10 Electra made transcontinental travel faster, their small capacities and rudimentary interiors were serious limitations. In 1935, American Airlines approached Douglas with a request for a stretched and widened DC-2 that could include convertible berths. This resulted in the legendary DC-3 (➔008), first built and delivered in June 1936 as the Douglas Sleeper Transport (DST) (118, 119, 120), with the standard 21-passenger dayplane following two months later (121).

American Airlines' Flagship Skysleeper and United Air Lines' DST Mainliner had almost identical interiors that match drawings for United by industrial designer Henry Dreyfuss in the collection of Cooper-Hewitt National Design Museum.[32] Although these drawings are dated shortly after the first deliveries of the DST, they include detailed notes on materials and colours, as well

29 Geddes' work on the Martin M-130 proved that he was not just an ingenious visionary designer, but also capable of producing workable and innovative solutions for extant aircraft. Subsequent Pan Am Clippers, particularly the Boeing 314 (113, 114, 115, 116), have striking similarities with the Martin M-130 and were obviously based on Geddes' China Clipper interior. The claim that Pan Am actually contracted with Geddes in 1936 to design the Boeing 314 interior (M.D. Klaás, *Last of the Flying Clippers: The Boeing B-314 Story*, Atglen, PA, 1997, pp. 31–34) could not be substantiated in primary sources and was modified by the book's author in a personal letter dated 30 July 2003 to refer only to the evident influence of Geddes' M-130 design on the B-314 Pan Am interior.

30 Harry Ransom Humanities Research Center, The University of Texas at Austin, Norman Bel Geddes Papers, JF #291.1: Pan American Clipper Aircraft: Case History, 15 October 1946.

31 Harry Ransom Humanities Research Center, The University of Texas at Austin, Norman Bel Geddes Papers, JF #291.1: NBG memorandum to Miss Maxon, 16 October 1945.

32 Cooper-Hewitt National Design Museum, Henry Dreyfuss Papers, TMS Box #V-898, Archive Box 6: United Airlines Transport Co. 1936.

109 Martin M-130 China Clipper, Pan American Airways, 1934.

110 Martin M-130 China Clipper, cabin. The interior décor was designed by Norman Bel Geddes.

111 Martin M-130 China Clipper, cabin in night configuration. Using curtains, the sleeping compartments are separated.

112 Martin M-130 China Clipper, cabin in daytime configuration. At night, two wash basins could be pulled out from the middle table.

109

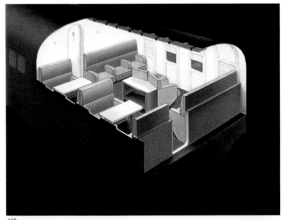

110

111

112

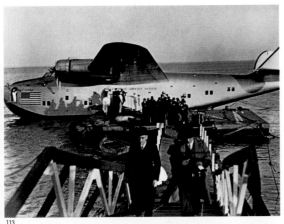

113

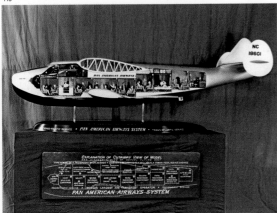

114

115

116

117

113 In 1939, a year after its first flight, Pan American Airways' Boeing 314 Yankee Clipper was the first airliner to fly non-stop across the Atlantic.

114 Boeing 314, section model.

115 The cabin interior of the Boeing 314, here in the day configuration, was similar to Bel Geddes' design for the Martin M-130.

116 Cabin of the Boeing 314 in the night configuration.

117 The Boeing 307 Stratoliner was the first airliner with a pressurised cabin. The two rear compartments show the day configuration, the two front compartments the night configuration.

118 Drawing of a cabin design of the Douglas Sleeper Transport for United Airlines, Henry Dreyfuss. The drawing is dated 14 December 1936.

119 Cabin, Douglas Sleeper Transport (Douglas DC-3) in the day configuration. The edition of Vogue on the seat of the passenger on the left dates from 11 March 1936.

120 Cabin of the Douglas Sleeper Transport at night. Every two double seats could be folded out to form a bed, while a further could be pulled down from the ceiling.

121 Standard design, cabin, Douglas DC-3.

122 Douglas DC-3 in the United Airlines Skylounge-Version with swivel chairs.

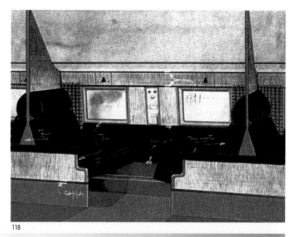

118

120

121

119

122

as actual fabric samples. Furthermore, they show striking similarities to Dreyfuss' cabin designs from the 1950s and clearly reflect the philosophy outlined in a 1956 interview: 'Dreyfuss believes that people are acclimatized to rooms, not long tubes [...] So he likes to divide the tube-like cabins into compartments. This, he believes, makes passengers feel at home and relax, reducing trip fatigue'.[33] Ceiling-high partitions divided the DST cabin into three main compartments with facing double-width seats. The room-like quality of the space was enhanced by low balustrades running down either side of the aisle with an interruption at each compartment and a double function as inboard armrests. The colour designations on the drawings – copper, buckskin tan, brown, rich walnut veneer, and alumilite metal mouldings – reflect Dreyfuss' conviction that 'earthy, muted colours' inspired emotions of comfort and security.[34] Sleeping and dining facilities on the DST rivalled those of contemporary flying boats, albeit in a smaller space. Overnight passengers were accommodated in seven seat-to-berth conversions and seven fold-down upper berths. With a length of 196 cm and enclosing curtains, they were an air traveller's dream. The private two-person Skyroom next to the forward galley and separate toilets and washrooms for men and women were additional features that echoed the amenities of flying boats.

However, it was the standard 21-passenger DC-3 dayplane that made air travel popular and airline profits possible; by 1939, it was carrying an overwhelming percentage of the world's commercial passengers. The DC-3 shows an early appearance of open rigid overhead storage racks and – in United Air Lines' luxurious 14-passenger Skylounge configuration – large swivel lounge chairs that could be turned towards centre to make a foursome around a card table, make an intimate twosome for dining, or be comfortably reclined with a hassock for the feet (122).[35]

The Focke-Wulf Fw 200 Condor was quite similar to the standard configuration DC-3, with rows of single and double seats on either side of an off-centre aisle

(➜016, 123). Semi-rigid overhead racks and individual reading lights integrated into the ears of passenger seats were just two innovative features on the 26-passenger Condor, which set world speed and distance records in 1938 on a non-stop flight from Berlin to New York and a four-hop trip from Berlin to Tokyo. Typical for commercial German planes, however, the passenger cabin was still divided into distinct compartments. The continued influence of the train interior was even stronger in the case of Junkers' last great commercial aircraft, the Ju 90 ('Der Große Dessauer') (➜015, 124). The cabin, designed by chief engineer Ernst Zindel in collaboration with Lufthansa representatives, looked like a virtual transplant of a luxury train interior with five identical compartments of facing seating for 40.[36] Even the luggage racks of metal tubing were placed perpendicular to the fuselage directly above the high-back bench seats, instead of running along the cabin walls.[37] According to one of the first stewardesses on the Ju 90, the non-food items in her pantry included a daily newspaper, bandages, games, and – as an early example of business-class service – a portable typewriter in case a passenger wanted to dictate a letter.[38]

World War II paradoxically brought both an interruption and a dramatic advance in commercial aviation design. Commercial planes introduced just before the war were converted to military use for the duration of the conflict (e.g. Fw 200, Ju 90, Boeing 307 Stratoliner). Some planes designed as pre-war commercial transports went into production in military versions (DC-4, Lockheed C-69 Constellation). Conversion plans for specifically military aircraft were put forth by designers in anticipation of post-war civilian applications (Convair Models 37 and 39, Avro York). The war then left behind a highly superior airport network, and post-war aircraft benefited from new materials such as aluminium alloys, Polaroid glass, plastics, and synthetic textiles.

33 George Christian, 'Comfort in Airline Cabin Design Makes Dollar Sense', Aviation Week (May 14, 1956), pp. 92–93.
34 Ibid.
35 Musée de l'Air et de l'Espace (Paris Le Bourget), Documentation, DC-3 file: 'United Air Lines presents the Mainliner' (brochure).
36 Recalling the design process for the Junkers Ju 90, Zindel elaborated the reasons for dividing the cabin space into train-like compartments. Quoted in: Novarra, Junkers Grossflugzeuge, p. 28.
37 The British De Havilland D.H. Albatross flown at the same time by Imperial Airways had a very similar arrangement (Nason, 'Inside-Up', p. 415, fig. 16).
38 Braunburg, Als Fliegen noch ein Abenteuer war, p. 128. An interior photo of the Do X also shows a seating arrangement around a small table with a typewriter (p. 72).

39 See Zukowsky, *Building for Air Travel*, p. 17 and note 5.

40 A contemporary colour rendering of the TWA Stratoliner was printed in *Collier's: The National Weekly* (June 6, 1940; reproduced in Angela Schönberger, ed., *Raymond Loewy: Pioneer of American Industrial Design*, Munich, 1990, plate 5. Another source naming Loewy as designer of the Stratoliner together with furniture supplier Marshall Field's (Chicago) is: 'Boeing 307 Stratoliner: The World's First High-Altitude Airliner', Seattle, 1989, p. 10. A black-and-white photo of the TWA interior is shown on p. 11 (NASM file AB-582070 Boeing 307 DOCS).

41 Christian, 'Comfort in Airline Cabin Design', p. 95.

42 See Novarra, *Junkers Grossflugzeuge*, pp. 126–29.

43 Cooper-Hewitt National Design Museum, Henry Dreyfuss Papers, TMS Box #V-894, Archive Box 2, 1972.88.232.320. Some of the 85 photos in this folder appear to be from a different Dreyfuss project (Lockheed Electra L-188?), since the fuselage section and window shape differ from the XC-99. For Loewy's more realistic conversion plan for the Convair Liberator bomber, see: J. Gordon Lippincott, 'Industrial Design: Using the New Materials', *Interiors* (May 1944), pp. 57–61, 85–88. Only two Model 37 conversions were built, one of which was flown for a short time by American Airlines.

44 The Stratocruisers delivered to United Air Lines and Northwest Airlines had square windows, while the planes for Pan Am, SAS (Scandinavian Airlines System), AOA (American Overseas Airlines) and BOAC (British Overseas Airways Corp.) were fitted with round windows. Colours and fabrics also varied widely. See: Peter M. Bowers, *Boeing Aircraft Since 1916*, London, 1989, pp. 365f.

45 Egtvedt's original design is documented in 'Tests Being Given Altered B-29 for Use as Transport', *The Buffalo Evening News* (15 November 1944). An artist's rendering shows the lounge, staircase and upper deck in a section drawing of the fuselage. Highly detailed technical drawings by WDTA for the Stratocruiser (dated 1946) are preserved on microfilm at Syracuse University, Bird Library, Dept. of Special Collections, Teague Papers: Boeing Stratocruiser, Microfilm 35,17. Noteworthy contemporary reports include: Society of Industrial Designers, ed., *U.S. Industrial Design 1949-1950*, New York, 1949, pp. 104–05; 'Stratocruisers With the Teague Touch', *Interiors*, July 1947, p. 20.

The Boeing 307 Stratoliner (➜ 005, 117), which went into service in 1940 as the first commercial airliner with a pressurised cabin and a cruising altitude of 7000 metres, evolved as a transport version of the military B-17 Flying Fortress. Its great civilian potential was hindered when the eight 307s delivered to Pan Am and TWA were mobilised under the military designation C-75. The 'exceptionally impressive' interior of the Stratoliner (as mentioned in a contemporary press report) closely resembled the layout devised by Norman Bel Geddes for Pan Am's flying boats: compartments of facing three-person seating with removable armrests and hinged backrests for conversion into two-tiered berths. However, the row of single port-side seats remained uninterrupted, creating a more spacious feeling in the aisle. Attribution of the 307 interior has been disputed, but it appears that Howard Ketcham was responsible for Pan Am's planes, while Raymond Loewy took credit for TWA's interiors.[39] Their contributions were probably restricted to surface finishes, colour schemes, and fabric selection, resulting in a more restrained PAA interior and a very colourful TWA cabin with contrasting patterns: stars on the seats, leaves on the carpet, wood-grained bulkheads, and striped curtains.[40] This reflected Loewy's philosophy that a 'soft look' with 'charm and gaiety' would instil confidence in the inexperienced traveller.[41]

Although first introduced in 1938, the 46-passenger DC-4 did not enter commercial service until 1946, with an interior that was twice the size of the DC-3 but shared many common characteristics. Junkers' ambitious EF 100 project (1940–41) for a four-engine 75-passenger airliner never got off the drawing board, although models and a mockup of the bar area (once again with fascinating metal seat shells that look like forebears of plastic designs from the 1960s) are documented in photographs.[42] One of the most interesting wartime projects was Henry Dreyfuss' conversion plan for the Consolidated Vultee XC-99 or Convair Model 37 (125, 126). This huge six-engine aircraft – like a 1940s premonition of the Airbus A380 scheduled to enter service in 2006 – could transport 400 fully-equipped soldiers on two decks extending the complete length of the fuselage. Dreyfuss' design for 204 commercial passengers included five and six-abreast rows in main cabins on both decks, spiral staircases fore and aft, private two-person staterooms below, two central lounges, a large galley, and spacious restrooms. A photographic series in the Dreyfuss Papers (Cooper-Hewitt) shows mockup sections of the aircraft, which drew an order from Pan Am for fifteen; nevertheless, this plane was only built as a single prototype and never entered commercial service.[43] Without tourist class tickets for the mass public and a more economical powerplant, a bird of this size was not quite ready to fly.

Another fascinating post-war hybrid was the Boeing 377 Stratocruiser, a civilian version of the C-97 military transport (127, 128, 129, 130, 131). The guppy-like shape of the Stratocruiser resulted from its Siamese-twin fuselage, which offered extra cargo and passenger space on the lower deck. While Boeing engineer Claire Egtvedt was responsible for much of the basic interior, the aircraft manufacturer turned to the industrial design office of Walter Dorwin Teague Associates to refine and vary the cabin space for six different airline customers.[44] In what became one of the most fruitful collaborations in aviation history, Frank Del Guidice established a Seattle branch of WDTA in March of 1946 in order to work directly with Boeing engineers. The Stratocruiser continued the tradition of luxury service offered on large long-range planes with a spacious sleeper configuration in the main cabin and a popular lower-deck lounge. WDTA modified the lounge concept put forward by Egtvedt in 1944, turning the spiral staircase so that the bar could be positioned behind the steps, where it would not interfere with passenger traffic.[45] A wall-size mirror behind the curved lounge seating created the illusion of greater space. Teague also streamlined the interior with sweeping lines and uninterrupted surfaces, and integrated light and call buttons and ash trays into

123 Cabin, Lufthansa Focke-Wulf FW 200 Condor. The chair airs feature individual reading lights.

124 From the arrangement of the seats to the design of the luggage rack, the cabin of the Junkers Ju 90 is reminiscent of the interior design of a train.

124

123

125 Convair Model 37, section drawing, 1945. This plane, with an interior designed by Henry Dreyfuss, was a converted World War II military aircraft.

126 Lounge in a mock up of the Convair Model 37. Only a prototype was built of this plane.

125

126

127 The long-term collaboration between Boeing and Walter Dorwin Teague Associates began with the Boeing 377 Stratocruiser, first used in 1949.

128 Section drawing of a Boeing 377 Stratocruiser.

129 Lounge of the Boeing 377 Stratocruiser, lower deck.

130 Cabin of the Boeing 377 Stratocruiser, upper deck.

131 While in the Douglas Sleeper Transport two opposing chairs could be made into a bed, in the Boeing 377 Stratocruiser two seats behind one another combined to form a bed. An additional bed could be clapped down from the ceiling, as in the DC-3.

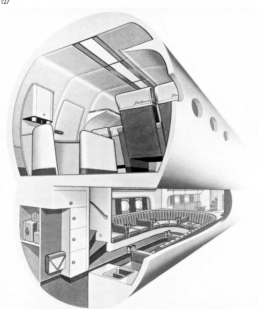

128

129

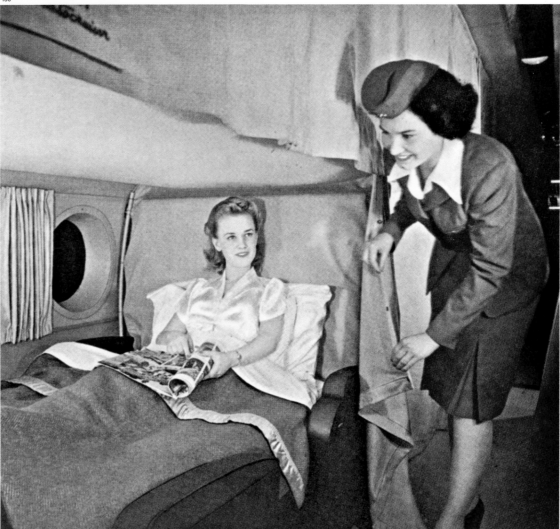

131

132 Section drawing and floor plan of the DC-6.
E. Gilbert Mason designed the cabin interior.

133 Douglas DC-6, 1947.

134 DC-6, drawing of the cabin in night configuration,
1945. The upper berth had its own window, reading
lights, and mirror.

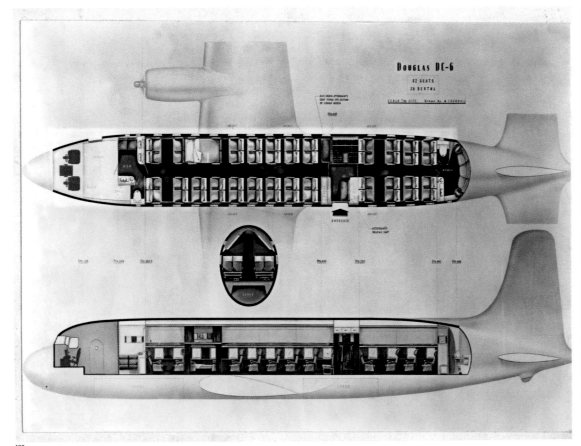

132

133

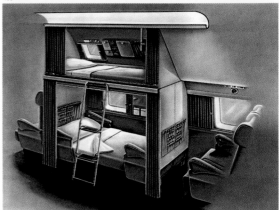

134

135

46 The Sherman Fairchild Collection of Aeronautical Photographs at NASM Archives contains photographic documentation of an extensive series of (unattributed) drawings for the DC-6, including images 1A-39329, 1A-39334, 1A-39257-39262. The attribution of these drawings to E. Gilbert Mason and Associates is established in: Society of Industrial Designers, ed., *U.S. Industrial Design*, p. 109.
47 For technical details on the history of Douglas seats, see Schliephacke, *Der Bewegungsstuhl*, pp. 293 and 300 (figs. 334/335, 347–49, 367–71); 'High Chairs', *Industrial Design* (February 1961), pp. 54–55 (figs. 1–3 and photos 6–9).
48 In a paper presented at the SAE National Aeronautic Meeting in April of 1946, Eastern Airlines architect/engineer Walther Prokosch addressed the problem of lap-held food trays and stated: 'It should be possible to design a tray support which will be collapsible into the arm rest, simple in operation, and sturdy. [...] [T]he tray could be designed to double as a work surface between meals' (p. 101). Prokosch also proposed a flat airsick container for seat pockets to replace the rigid bucket-style containers that were stored under seats at that time. NASM FO-09-4030-25, file heading: Aircraft Design. Passenger Cabin 1940–49: Walther Prokosch, 'The Planning of Cabin Interiors for Transport Aircraft' (typescript).
49 Cooper-Hewitt National Design Museum, Henry Dreyfuss Papers, Industrial Design, Box 4, 1972.88.151. Dreyfuss discusses this interior in: Society of Industrial Designers, ed., *U.S. Industrial Design*, pp. 46–47.
50 Documented, respectively, in: Schliephacke, *Der Bewegungsstuhl*, pp. 478 and 480, figs. 564, 587, 588; 'Air France, Lockheed "Super Constellation"' (April 1955, brochure).
51 'Enter the Viscount', *Industrial Design* (August 1955), pp. 27–33.
52 'Living room aloft for new turboprop planes', *Interiors* (June 1957), pp. 122–23.

the seats' armrests. Although Boeing offered a 100-passenger high-density configuration utilising the lower deck for ticketed seats, airlines preferred to use the extra space to pamper a smaller number of high-paying customers when the Stratocruiser entered service in 1949–50.

Douglas Aircraft entered the post-war commercial airline business with the DC-6, which began service in 1947 with accommodations for 52 to 86 passengers (132, 133, 134). A complete cabin concept for the DC-6 was produced by the industrial design office of E. Gilbert Mason in 1945.[46] The sophisticated sleeper arrangement included special personal amenities for the upper berth, with an individual reading light, personal storage, a fold-out vanity mirror, and a relatively large window (in comparison to tiny upper-berth window slats on previous sleepers). Continuing a Douglas tradition of innovative seating reaching back to the DC-1, the reclining DC-6 seat was operated by, a newly patented hydraulic system.[47] Mason's seat design had distinctive sweeping armrests, contoured cushions, and a sculptural headrest moulded out of latex foam rubber, the successor to heavy coil-spring and hairpad upholstery. The problem of balancing food trays on a lap pillow (common for standard row seating well into the 1940s) was solved with a detachable tray table that could be inserted into the front of the armrest.[48] Strong and lightweight, the table was also capable of supporting a portable typewriter.

Lockheed engaged Henry Dreyfuss to design the interior of the C-121 Super Constellation – arguably one of the most elegant aircraft ever built (✈022, 135). For this purpose, Dreyfuss established a resident design staff in Burbank headed by William Purcell (similar to the Teague team in Seattle). Photos of a KLM Super Constellation mockup (c. 1949) in the Dreyfuss Papers reflect the designer's conviction that the space of the fuselage should be broken up by inserting bulkheads, concealing longitudinal lines and mixing natural materials such as textured fabrics, leather, and wood.

The elegant lounge is furnished with low-backed perpendicular seating and varied tables. Pleated silk curtains, wall panels with a decorative world map, and a space reserved for natural flowers enhance the lounge's domestic character.[49] Super G Constellations flown by other airlines offered similar luxury, such as Lufthansa's Senator class with fully reclining seats and full-length footrests, or Air France's *Parisien Spécial* service with private sleeping compartments and two lounges. Regardless of the airline, the main cabin remained largely unchanged, with double-seat rows along a middle aisle, open storage racks, and large square ceiling lights.[50]

The dominance of US aircraft in the world market at the end of the war motivated the British to perfect two revolutionary powerplants and adapt them to commercial applications: the propeller-turbine and jet (turbofan) engines. As the first turboprop passenger plane, the Vickers Viscount made its first flight in 1948 and entered commercial passenger service on British European Airways (BEA) in 1953. Noteworthy design features of the Viscount were the large oval windows by Vickers engineer George R. Edwards, and a fold-down seat tray introduced by BEA that has since become ubiquitous on commercial aircraft. Charles Butler's redesign of the Viscount interior in 1953–54 for Trans Canada Airlines and the Washington-based carrier Capital Airlines is a specific example of cultural styling that increased the appeal of the plane to North American customers.[51] Butler made liberal use of vinyl-covered Fiberglas and Duracote (PVC) aluminium for the ceiling and hatrack, as well as other plastic surfaces.

The US answer to the Viscount was the Lockheed L-188 Electra, which entered service in 1959. Again, Lockheed turned to Henry Dreyfuss for a distinctive interior design. Dreyfuss' solution was a veritable 'living room aloft' with an unusual seating concept.[52] Between widely spaced rows of facing triple seats, Dreyfuss inserted a pair of seats with a small table between them. A table lamp that could have been lifted directly from a home interior served as a screen between the passengers sitting in the middle triple seats. The twin seats were set at a slight inward angle to increase legroom. Low seat backs added to the 'club' atmosphere intended for commuter flights on the short to medium range Electra.[53]

Parallel to the development of the Vickers Viscount, De Havilland introduced the first commercial jet airliner – the D.H. 106 Comet – to the world in 1949, with route service starting on British Overseas Aircraft Corp. (BOAC) in 1952 (→028, 136). The advent of the jet age in commercial aviation ushered in a new design approach to the aircraft cabin. This went hand in hand with the decision by the International Air Transport Association (IATA) to introduce Tourist Class fares in 1952. As an airline engineer had pointed out in 1946, 'The faster we can get from one place to another the less we have to worry about [...] comfort requirements'.[54] It was only a matter of time before the rational use of cabin space would become paramount, and passenger comfort sacrificed to passenger capacity, engendering the seat-packed tube so familiar to today's average airline customer. However, this did not occur overnight, and there were many examples of luxurious accommodations on passenger transports of the 1950s that could still be considered airborne rivals of the ocean liner.[55]

The interior of the Comet 1A, as documented in an Air France brochure from the period, retained one lounge area with facing seating for eight, but placed the remaining passengers in a unified main cabin with nine rows of forward-facing four-abreast seating. The galley was just behind the cockpit, and gender-specific washrooms and toilets were aft. A BOAC plan and section show an almost identical layout with only seven rows of seats due to the generous 45-inch (114-cm) pitch of BOAC's luxurious Slumberette recliners.[56] In this very first jetliner, first-class luxury was mainly a product of a comfortable reclining seat combined with fine food service and, above all, the prestige of travelling at an amazing 740 km/h, approximately 225 km/h faster than any other commercial aircraft flying in 1952.

When the Comet streaked onto the scene, US manufacturers were caught flat-footed, but a series of catastrophic accidents in 1954 due to metal fatigue caused by cabin pressurisation at high altitudes – one must remember that the Comet was travelling in uncharted territory at 10670 metres – grounded the British jet. By the time the Comet 4 series was deemed airworthy in 1958 (only after an unprecedented wreckage retrieval operation and pressure tests on an existing fuselage in a huge water tank), the Boeing 707, Douglas DC-8, and Convair 880 were poised to enter the competition.

With a cruising speed of 925 km/h and room for 126 to 152 passengers, the Boeing 707 set lasting standards for the commercial jetliner when it entered service in 1958 (→027, 137, →344). This was equally true of its interior, again designed by Teague Associates. The prime principles of flexibility and easy maintenance were realised with recessed floor tracks for variable seat configuration, easily removable prefabricated wall and ceiling panels, and partially cantilevered seat rows with fold-up armrests. The wall panels of vinyl-laminated aluminium could be customised with embossed textures or colour-printed graphics. Portable track-mounted partitions made it possible to divide the cabin into different class sections (until then single-class cabins were common practice, with airlines using newer planes with roomier configurations for first-class travellers and older models for tourist flights). Over 100 small windows offered views independent of row alignment, and two integrated plastic blinds – a tinted sun filter and an opaque cover – replaced window curtains.[57] Indirect fluorescent cove lighting augmented dome lights in the ceiling. The passenger service units were a hallmark feature of the 707, rectangular pods hanging under the open baggage rack that contained call buttons, air inlets, reading lights, no smoking/seat belt signs, loudspeakers, and emergency oxygen equipment.[58] The location of PSUs was adaptable to seat configuration.

As a whole, WDTA's 707 cabin design represented a radical departure from the philosophy behind many

53 Designers have always agreed that the seat is the most important element in the aeroplane interior, which is why Dreyfuss, E. Gilbert Mason and especially Warren McArthur devoted considerable resources to aircraft seat design. Typically, aircraft manufacturers and airlines turn to specialised companies for their seat selections. See Jochen Eisenbrand, 'More Legroom Please', in this publication.
54 NASM file FO-09-4030-25: Aircraft Design. Passenger Cabin 1940–49: Albert P. Elebash, 'Passenger Aircraft Facilities – Design and Operation', paper presented at the SAE National Air Transport Engineering Meeting (Chicago, December 1946, typescript).
55 It is noteworthy that the US$ 675 price tag (today approximately US$ 8650) of a round-trip transatlantic ticket on the Boeing 314 Clipper in 1940 more than rivalled the price of a high-sea cruise.
56 See Helmut Gerresheim, De Havilland Comet, Stuttgart, n.d. [1980s], pp. 47–49.
57 Double-pane windows with interior air circulation eliminated the need for a water trough at the bottom of each window to collect heavy condensation, as was typical on unpressurised aircraft. See NASM file FO-094030-20: H. O. West (United Air Lines Transport Corp.), 'Interior Finish and Arrangement of Transport Airplanes', paper presented to the Natl. Aircraft Production Meeting of the Society of Automotive Engineers, Washington, DC (March 1937, typescript).
58 Individual emergency oxygen masks were first introduced on the Comet 4 in 1958. As a back-up system for the pressurised cabin, they had come a long way from the tubes through which passengers could 'sip' bottled oxygen on flights over high mountain ranges in the 1930s. See NASM file FO-904030-20: Arthur E. Raymond (Douglas Aircraft Co.), 'Designing to Please the Air Traveller', paper presented at the Natl. Aircraft Production Meeting of the Society of Automotive Engineers, Los Angeles (15–17 October 1936, typescript).

136 Cabin, De Havilland 106 Comet, British Overseas
Airways Corporation, c. 1952.

137 With the cabin of the Boeing 707 (here a view of the
1956 mock up), Teague Associates set the standard for the
interior design of airliners. This was particularly true of the
modular wall panels and the passenger service units, with
integrated signal buttons, fresh air jets, and reading lights.

136

137

aircraft interiors of the 1950s, whose designers integrated domestic elements in order to make the cabin environment feel 'familiar' (and therefore reassuring) to a broadening spectrum of airline passengers. Teague believed that one could also inspire confidence and security in the passenger by eliminating wooden surfaces and 'the textile look', replacing them with metals and synthetic materials in harmony with a jet's sleek exterior. This approach established an interior specific to air travel and no longer imitative of other modes of transportation or residential styling.

Pre-production mockup sections of cabin interiors were standard by this time: Lockheed had even built a full-scale mockup of Dreyfuss' L-188 Electra interior that incorporated lighting and air conditioning systems.[59] But Boeing went to unprecedented lengths to sell its new jetliner by authorising Teague to build a full-scale mockup of the 30.5-metre-long 707 cabin in an eighth-floor Manhattan loft for a half million dollars (one-tenth of the purchase price). When it was finished in 1956, journalists and airline executives were invited to take simulated flights on the 707 mockup. Working galleys and lavatories with running water, sound effects mimicking the roar and drone of jet engines, pilot's announcements, variations in dome lighting ranging from white daylight to red dusk to midnight star-scattered blue, and a team of stewardesses ensured that the experience was as close to flight as one could get without leaving the ground. Boeing evaluated over 15 different airlines' responses to the mockup by encouraging representatives to leave written comments, which were then sorted and analysed.[60] BOAC, for example, indicated that 'colours & pattern do not reflect quality & good taste according to British', while an unidentified airline didn't like the pink ceiling. The 57 different comments on the PSU included one request to 'provide Muzak to each seat', TWA wanted floatable seat cushions, and numerous airlines felt that the hatrack was too high. Airlines traditionally had a major say in the design of cabin interiors, but Boeing's attention to specific preferences

and criticisms – combined with Teague's spectacular mockup – helped the company to sell a billion dollars worth of 707 jets even before the first delivery.

The Boeing 707's two direct jet competitors, the Convair 880 and the Douglas DC-8, offered interesting alternative solutions for individual passenger controls. In the Convair 880, consultant industrial designer Harley Earl also placed the service panels overhead, but set them flush with the bottom of the rigid hatrack, so that their upward protrusion into the rack provided regular divisions (138). He also dropped canopy-like sections of the ceiling at every fifth seat to interrupt 'the tunnel-effect that plagues all planes'.[61] For the DC-8, staff designer J.A. Graves integrated all of the passenger controls and fixtures into the seat (139, ✈224, ✈225). Passengers had access to cold air, a stewardess call button, and a fold-up tray table in the seat back directly in front of them. An individual reading light was located just to the right of the headrest (a solution seen on the Focke-Wulf Condor in 1938!), and an ashtray was integrated into the armrest. This arrangement won praise from contemporary critics, including some visitors of the 707 mockup who found the seat controls to be superior to Boeing's PSU.

The need for short-range jetliners was first answered by Sud-Aviation's S.E. 210 Caravelle, which entered service with Air France, SAS, and Finn Air in 1959 (✈030, 140, 141). The most distinctive interior design feature of the Caravelle, developed under the direction of chief engineer Pierre Satre, was its droplet-shaped window, still surrounded by conventional curtains. The strong longitudinal lines of wall panels, hatracks, and ceiling elements ran uninterrupted from fore to aft, creating a sweeping, elegant perspective. Regular four or five-abreast seating added to the unified effect of the cabin, which held 64 to 80 passengers. Following the example of the Caravelle, Boeing also used an aft-mounted engine configuration on its first short-range jet, the 727. The passenger service controls on Boeing's second jet were directly integrated into the flat hatrack.

59 The design process for the L-188 Electra is described in detail in: 'Dreyfuss Designs Electra', *Industrial Design* (October 1957), pp. 88–92.
60 Syracuse University, Bird Library, Dept. of Special Collections, Teague Papers, Box 25: 'Analysis of Comments New York Mockup, from May 1, 1956 to July 1, 1957' (WDTA, New York, typescript).
61 *Interiors* (September 1958), pp. 100–03. Both jets are introduced in this transportation issue.

138 Cabin, Convair 880, designed by Harley Earl, 1958. The pattern of the plastic wall coverings was designed by Dorothy Draper.

139 In the Douglas DC-8, the designer J. A. Graves integrated all passenger service elements into the chair. Scandinavian Airlines had their DC-8s individually designed by Finn Juhl.

140 Drawing, lounge of the SE 210 Caravelle, Eastern Air Lines.

141 The SE 210 Caravelle, designer and chief engineer, Pierre Satre. Starting service in 1959 for Air France and SAS, this plane was set apart by its drop-shaped windows.

140

138

139

141

142 For the Boeing 747 – here tourism class in a 1:1 Model – that finally established the aeroplane as a means of transportation for the masses, Teague Associates set new standards of cabin design, such as enclosed overhead bins.

143 The Tiger Lounge in a mock-up of the Boeing 747. Special elements like such lounges were offered to the airlines by the manufacturers, but for reasons of space and costs, seldom realised.

62 'We Design Only for People ...', *Industrial Design* (October 1970), pp. 40–43; 'Design for Air Travel', *Industrial Design* (October 1970), pp. 34–38.
63 The wide-body concept proved so popular that Boeing developed a retrofit kit for its single-aisle jets (also offered as a production option beginning in 1972). By lowering the ceiling and inserting sculpted recesses on a lateral axis with indirect fluorescent lighting, adding wash-lit reveals to the window panels, and installing enclosed overhead bins with flush-mounted passenger service controls, Boeing aimed to enhance the longevity of the 707, 727, and 737 models with the 'Superjet' look. See: 'Flight in Space', *Industrial Design* (January/February 1972), pp. 50–53.
64 Sayre, 'Gentility in the Air', p. 129.

All in all, the many jet interiors that followed the first trailblazers could be described as variations on a theme, more or less limited to different colour schemes, graphic wall panel designs, seat textiles, and minor details in lighting and passenger controls.

The most dramatic change in cabin architecture to date was catalysed when Boeing announced the 747 'jumbo' jet in 1966 (→ 032, 142). Reductions in air fares, an explosion in air-passenger traffic, and increasingly crowded skies provided market conditions that would finally support an airliner that could carry up to 490 passengers – double the capacity of any transport in service when the 747 was certified in 1969. With a cabin 2.44 metres high, 6.1 metres wide, and 56.4 metres long, the size of the 747 permitted the Teague office (still under the direction of Frank Del Guidice) to usher in a 'new era in jet environment'.[62] The auditorium-like space and wide-body twin-aisle configuration presented a new challenge to designers, but also offered completely new possibilities.

One of the most resourceful decisions of Boeing/Teague was to place interchangeable service modules (galleys, lavatories, and storage units) transversely between aisles rather than against outboard walls. This flexible arrangement not only created more window seats, which were at a premium with nine- or ten-across seating, but also broke the cavernous interior into room-like spaces containing 60 to 100 passengers. The service islands could be centrally accessed from both aisles, which was advantageous for passenger traffic and food service, and also provided forward walls for movies or artwork. Relatively flat sidewalls added room to window seats, and architectural reveals around the windows made them seem larger while dispersing more light into the interior. Enclosed overhead bins above the centre section and along both sides of the fuselage provided secure space for carry-on luggage, since passengers had acquired the habit of putting much more than their hats onto overhead storage racks.[63]

A telltale exterior feature of the 747, the bump on the forward fuselage, resulted from the requirement of a hinged nose through which bulk freight could be front-loaded. The fairing of the raised flight deck provided upper-deck space that was originally used as a crew rest area or as a lounge accessed by a spiral staircase from the first-class cabin in the nose. This 'extra' space was subject to the greatest variation in styling and design, as extravagant lounge examples from different airlines show. When the spiral staircase proved to be hard to navigate, it was replaced by a right-angled, and then a straight staircase. In the stretched fairing of the 300-series, the upper-deck cabin could accommodate up to 99 economy passengers. A spacious lounge concept for a reserved area in the baggage hold was also developed in a 1972 Boeing mockup, the most spectacular feature of which was a vertical viewing port designed like a glass-topped cocktail table. Orange shag carpeting, jungle prints, and brown leather gave the Tiger Lounge an unmistakable 1970s look (143). But growing competition and the 1978 US Airline Deregulation Act put increasing pressure on airlines to squeeze as many ticketed seats into their planes as possible, and concepts like the Tiger Lounge were soon threatened with extinction on commercial carriers.

As an increasing number of passengers found themselves relegated to a decreasing amount of personal space with no view to distract them, airlines had to come up with a way to keep them entertained. This situation had been anticipated by a prescient commentator on the novelty of radio navigation aids in 1934, who imagined 'the super-speed, super-blind, super-dull all-fog airplane flight' and noted that 'already individual radio head sets and even movies thrown against a screen at the end of the cabin have been experimented with as counter-irritants'.[64] By the mid-1940s, Pan Am had installed movie equipment on its DC-4s and Lockheed Constellations, but there was some criticism that the generalised loudspeakers forced everyone to watch a film

144

144 A Lufthansa DC-10-30. The 1974 DC-10 was Douglas' first widebody aeroplane.

145 Cabin design, American Airlines DC-10.

146 In the L-1011 Tri Star, a galley developed by Lockheed-Designer R. J. Robillard and Sundberg-Ferar was installed in the lower deck to offer more space for passenger seats.

147 The cabin of the Lockheed L-1011 Tri Star, designed by the office of Sundberg-Ferar, featured in the central axis small closets that also served as dividers.

145

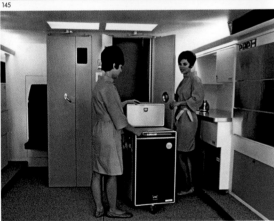
146

147

65 Elebash, 'Passenger Aircraft Facilities', pp. 4–5.
66 Musée de l'Air et de l'Espace (Paris Le Bourget), Documentation, Boeing 747 file: 'Boeing 747' (brochure); www.waea.org/ife.htm (n. 5).
67 Scott Kelly, 'MoTown's Transit Paradox', *Industrial Design* (May 1968), pp. 22–27.
68 Barbara Allen, 'Mess Halls in the Air', *Industrial Design* (May 1968), pp. 28–33. The author names Lockheed design engineer R. L. Vernon as the initiator of the idea in 1967 and mentions that Lockheed had applied for a patent.
69 'Mass Transportation: In the Air', *Industrial Design* (November 1966), pp. 42–43. This enthusiasm was shared by international airlines: Boeing received orders for 122 SSTs from 26 different airlines before the program was cancelled; 15 airlines had submitted options for 69 Concordes by January 1967. Only 16 production Concordes were built and sold exclusively to Air France and British Air.

whether they wanted to or not.[65] In 1961, a movie-theatre owner from Tennessee perfected an automatic back-projection system with 16mm film reels and individual earphones. His company, Inflight Motion Pictures, custom-designed movie and audio systems for 747 customers, and by 1971 (aided by Trans Com's new 8mm film cassette) in-flight movies and short subject programming were an expected amenity on long-distance flights.[66]

Douglas and Lockheed were also developing wide-body jets in the late 1960s, with the DC-10 entering service one year after the Boeing 747 in 1971, and the L-1011 Tri-Star following in 1972. Not as large as the 747 (capacity 255 to 380), the DC-10 was introduced with an attractive 2-2|2-2 seat configuration in tourist class and 2-2-2 in first class (**144, 145**). This eliminated the unpopular middle seats created by the original 2-4-3 configuration in the main cabin of the 747. Douglas enhanced the central bank of quadruple seats by placing a 20-cm-wide divider between the two centre seats, thereby providing seat-side stowage and an extra table surface. However, the wider seats and aisles praised in both manufacturers' publicity material were soon forfeited to an extra seat in each row on many airlines, resulting in a 2-4-3 configuration (without the central divider) on the DC-10 and a 3-4-3 plan on the 747.

Lockheed's L-1011 Tri-Star went to great lengths to offer its passengers a roomier and more comfortable environment (**146, 147**). The on-site consultant industrial design office of Sundberg-Ferar (who, like Harley Earl, hailed from the Detroit automotive industry) convinced Lockheed to furnish the first class of the L-1011 with executive seats and to equip the coach cabin with first-class seats at a 36-inch (91.5 cm) pitch.[67] Sundberg-Ferar's centreline divider separating the quadruple section into paired seats was high and wide enough to accommodate a man's jacket on an interior hook, likewise serving as an effective screen between the middle seats. A new food-service concept featured a below-deck galley system,

which was also considered for the Boeing 747 and offered as an option on the DC-10. The idea originated with Lockheed, however, and the L-1011 seems to have been the only aircraft in which the underfloor galley was actually implemented.[68] Lockheed designer R.J. Robillard collaborated with Sundberg-Ferar on the functional and appearance aspects of the food system. Dual elevators transported both food and personnel up to a minimal service centre in the main cabin. Wide-body capacity also made the introduction of service carts with standardised meal trays necessary in order to feed several hundred people during the shorter service window at high cruising altitudes. An unanticipated problem posed by the service carts was that passengers had difficulty getting past them to reach the toilets, all of which were located aft in the main cabin of the L-1011.

Conceived before the wide-body jets, but considerably longer in development, the Concorde represented the epitome of air travel into the twenty-first century (➤**264**). In the early 1960s, four contenders entered the race to produce the first commercial supersonic transport: Sud-Aviation (later Aerospatiale France) and British Aircraft Corporation in a cooperative effort on the Concorde, the Soviet Union's Tupolev, Boeing, and Lockheed. Expectations at the time were euphoric: in 1966, aviation experts predicted that 'by 1980 a total of 800 SST's [...] will have taken over up to 45 per cent of the air travel market. Close to 2000 SST's may be in service by 1990'.[69] The Tupolev Tu-144 was the first to become airborne, taking flight two months before the Concorde at the end of 1968 and breaking the sound barrier in June 1969 (➤**034**). However, the Concorde beat the Tu-144 into regular commercial service in 1976, and remained there until 2003, whereas the supersonic Tupolev flew only seven months before being withdrawn from commercial service in June 1978. Lockheed (**148, 149, 150**) and Boeing (**151, 152**) presented their plans for supersonic prototypes with full-scale interior mockups in 1966. Boeing won the US government

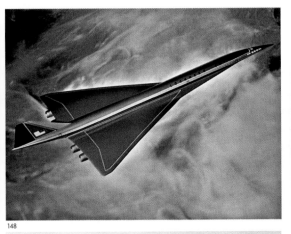

148

151

148 Lockheed participated in the competition for the construction of an American supersonic jet with the design L-2000 SST. Drawing from 1966.

149, 150 Part of the proposed design of the L-2000 SST were new serving carts and maintenance modules designed by Henry Dreyfuss in 1965. The plane was never built.

151 Boeing's planned supersonic jet, the SST 2707, in a 1966 drawing. This plane also never was built.

152 Planned interior of a Boeing SST 2707, Teague Associates.

153 The cabin in Air France's Concorde, designed by Raymond Loewy.

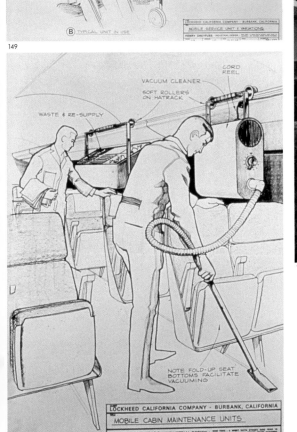

149

150

152

153

70 Frank Spadaro, 'A Transatlantic Perspective', *Design Quarterly* (Winter 1992), pp. 20–26.

71 Kenneth Dowd and Alan Anderson, 'Time Share', *Aircraft Interiors International* (April 2002, offprint), no page numbers.

72 Robert Welsh, 'High Stakes in the Air', *Innovation: Journal of the Industrial Designers Society of America* (Summer 1998), pp. 10–13; Aaron Betsky, 'Changing Flight Patterns', *Metropolis* (September 1994), pp. 33–37.

contract to build a prototype, but government funding was rescinded in 1971 and the project was abandoned.

Ironically, the most expensive and prestigious means of air transport in recent time – the Concorde – offered very little room for cabin variation. Although the airlines hired prominent figures for successive redesigns of the Concorde interior – including Raymond Loewy (153), Pierre Gautier-Delaye, and Andrée Putman for Air France and Charles Butler, Landor Associates, and Product Design Factory for British Airways – their refurbishments were largely limited to colour schemes, surface treatments, and new seats in a straightforward cabin with four-abreast rows and shallow overhead storage bins. It is no coincidence that the most intriguing supersonic cabin design was also the largest: Boeing's SST 2707 was planned for 277 to 300 passengers (as compared to the Concorde's standard 100 to 108). Teague Associates' interior had three main cabin sections divided by bulkheads and a cantilevered string of groovy overhead storage containers with retractable video monitors that would have looked quite at home on Star Trek's USS Enterprise.

The 1970s witnessed the take-off of a new international player, the European Airbus consortium. Airbus has lived up to its name with a no-nonsense approach to air travel, focusing on standardisation, efficiency, economy, and utility both from engineering and design perspectives. The basic model of the Airbus family, the A-300, filled a gap in the market as the first short-to-medium range wide-body commercial transport when it entered service in 1974 (➤ 033, 154). A number of design offices worked on the twin-engine, two-aisle plane, but the original 'Atlas' interior was largely attributable to the design team of Deutsche Airbus under Uwe Schneider with Horst Sommerlatte and others. From the beginning, it was the aim of Airbus 'to utilise as many of the same parts and systems as possible among the different aircraft types'.[70] It is in keeping with this philosophy of 'commonality' that Airbus developed the A340 and A330 models, which entered service in 1993–94, with the same constant fuselage section as the original A300. Not only performance specifications (engines, range, capacity), but also interior arrangements can be mixed and matched in the A330/340 'family'. Besides different cabin configurations, a range of optional modular cabin units are offered, including lower deck passenger lavatories, three types of crew rest areas, and beverage bars.

Boeing responded to the new competitor in the early 1980s with the 767 and 757 models. Yet it was not until the introduction of the wide-body twinjet 777 in 1995 that Boeing came out with a truly distinctive new cabin concept (155). The boxy, angular contours of the company's previous jets were replaced by a curvilinear architecture 'that drew its inspiration from the soaring flight of birds'.[71] The flowing interior profile integrated sidewall panels, light strips, stowage bins, and ceiling panels in an undulating wave across the upper cabin. Large retractable bins (initially introduced on the 767) increased overhead centreline clearance and improved physical access to window seats. Combined with warmer lighting, this design also incorporated the psychological theory that 'people need less proximate personal space if they perceive an environment as spacious' (or, as a more sceptical commentator put it, 'perceptual reality is considered at least as important as whether your knees hit the seat in front of you or not').[72] One of the foremost design goals of the WDTA team led by Robert Welsh was to provide a flexible interior arrangement that would allow airlines to respond to changing market conditions over the plane's 25 to 30-year life span. Previously, galleys and lavatories had been removable, but assigned to fixed positions. Boeing and WDTA created flexibility zones on the 777, making it possible to position such units in different areas on the plane. Boeing plans to adapt this 'new signature look' to its other jets (much as the 747 widebody cabin was retroactively adapted to its single-aisle predecessors), meaning that it may very well shape future travellers' image of the aircraft cabin.

154

154 Cabin, Airbus A 300. The goal of Airbus' designers to design the individual cabin elements in such a way that they could also be used in other Airbus models.

155 The cabin of the Boeing 777, developed by Boeing and Teague Associates, is characterised by flowing lines.

155

156 The Airbus A380, scheduled to begin service in 2006, will have two decks and fly approximately 555 passengers.

157 First class upper deck of a 1:1 model of the Airbus A380.

158 Conceptual study of a first-class lounge on the lower deck in Airbus widebody aeroplanes (A340/A380). Concept/Design: EADS LG-AS Advanced Design and Marc S. Velten for AIRBUS ECDT as part of TIBS (Technology and Integration of On-Board Systems).

159 The Boeing 7E7 Dreamliner, currently in planning, is to go into service in 2008.

160 The cabin of the Boeing 7E7 will have larger windows and luggage racks than current plane models.

156

157

158

159

160

Airbus is presently developing the first twin-aisle, twin-deck airliner for a market that continues to demand greater capacity coupled with reduced operating costs. The A380, with a standard layout for 555 passengers, is scheduled to enter service in 2006 (156, 157, 158). The staggering complexity of such a project is reflected in the fact that Airbus has 16 different development and production sites scattered across Europe, with multiple teams contributing to cabin design.[73] The A380's two full-length passenger decks can be operated independently as distinct cabins with separate galleys and toilet facilities. Again, Airbus is developing a wide variety of interior options that can be individually selected by airline customers. However, it remains to be seen if the luxurious first class mockups, spacious lounge areas, duty free shop, bars, and crew rest facilities designed for the A380 will take precedence over a potential seating capacity of at least 650 passengers. Judging from present commercial aircraft configurations, 84 economy passengers will occupy roughly the same amount of cabin space as 22 first class travellers.

A noteworthy trend that continues in the A380 interior is the 'cocooning' effect engendered by new seats and information technology. In contrast to the social interaction that characterised prestigious modes of transport prior to the jet age, privacy and personal entertainment/communication are the measure of twenty-first century luxury. First class options offered by Airbus on the A380 include recliners embedded in shells with lateral wings, or forward/rearward couplings with moveable privacy screens echoing the seating developed by the design firm Tangerine for British Airways in the year 2000.[74] New multi-media systems already introduced on the A340-600 (Airbus In-Flight Information Services) and Boeing jets (Connexion) offer not only on-demand video and audio and games, but also laptop connections and satellite Internet access. Lufthansa is testing new wireless LAN-technology on its 747s and plans to introduce the FlyNet system on other long-range aircraft

in 2004. Even the cramped budget passenger can 'cocoon' on newer planes like the Boeing 777, which provides a personal media centre with flat interactive seat-back screens throughout its economy cabin.

What does the future hold? In a volatile airline market that has been shaken by terrorism, war, and a sluggish world economy since the turn of the millennium, it is hard to tell. Boeing recently shelved its plans for a Sonic Cruiser (designed to fly at barely subsonic Mach 0.98) after investing several years and substantial funds in development, and is now pursuing a new concept for a mid-size long-range jet with extensive use of advanced composite materials in the airframe. The stronger, corrosion-resistant composites would permit a level of cabin pressure equivalent to 1830 metres above sea level (as opposed to the current 2440 metres) and a ten-percent increase in humidity, lessening the dehydration and fatigue of passengers. According to chief interior designer Klaus Brauer, initial ideas for the 7E7 ('E' for 'efficiency') Dreamliner include soft flowing lines, individual seats, and even fluorescent surface foils that could imitate the Northern Lights (159, 160).[75] Boeing recently solicited the input of young design students to conceptually retool some of the company's present jets. The results of this project – scenic overlooks through picture windows, stadium seating, vending machines, a transparent dome, standing-style seats for short flights – may not be seen on any aircraft soon, but they have elicited enthusiasm from Boeing engineers for their creative potential.[76]

The most futuristic project presently under consideration is a monowing aircraft that could hold up to 900 passengers. The still elusive Blended Wing Body concept amazingly harks back to Hugo Junker's 1910 patent in the infant years of aviation (161, 162, 163). Both Boeing and the European research teams ONERA (Office National d'Etudes et de Recherches Aerospatiales) and DLR (Deutsches Zentrum für Luft- und Raumfahrt) are exploring the commercial possibilities of all-wing structures that have thus far been restricted to military

73 Design teams in France and Germany (Toulouse, Laupheim, and Munich), supported by a wide range of consultants and suppliers, are developing the cabin design and interior components of the A380. The A380 interior will be installed at assembly facilities in Hamburg. Robert Gotschy (Head of Industrial Design, Airbus Aircabin, Laupheim) and Marc Velten (Manager Advanced Design, EADS Deutschland, Munich) generously provided information on newer Airbus projects.
74 Ottagono (December 2000/January 2001),
pp. 52–53.
75 Andreas Spaeth, 'Heiße Luft am Himmel über Paris', Süddeutsche Zeitung (21–22 June 2003), p. V1/1.
76 This 13-week project was initiated by The Boeing Corporation and WDTA and supervised by design instructor Steve Montgomery at the Art Center College of Design in Pasadena. See Jeffrey Goldfarb, 'Expo – Taking to the Skies', Industrial Design (January 2001), p. 11.

77 In a cooperative project (Hamburg University of Applied Sciences, Technical University of Munich, EADS Airbus, DaimlerChrysler Research, iDS Hamburg, COMTAS Aerospace), design engineers and students have been exploring the problems and possibilities presented by unconventional aircraft configurations. Academic supervisors of the A20.30 BWB project are Prof. Werner Granzeier (Hamburg), Prof. Dr.-Ing. Dieter Schmitt and Dipl.-Ing. Stephan Eelman (Munich). I am indebted to Prof. W. Granzeier for the provision of material and information on the BWB project.

78 Henry Dreyfuss, *Designing for People*, 2nd ed., New York, 1967 [1955], p. 120.

79 'We Design Only for People...', *Industrial Design* (October 1970), p. 40.

80 Charles Butler, 'What's Wrong With Aircraft Interiors', *Airlift* (April 1959), pp. 28–29.

81 Larry Stapleton, Teague's director for client services. See Betsky, 'Changing Flight Patterns', p. 33.

82 Hulme Chadwick, 'Modern Air Transport Interior Design', *Art & Industry* (January 1946), pp. 73–79.

83 Betsky, 'Changing Flight Patterns', p. 35.

applications. The technical advantages of a BWB – load capacity and fuel efficiency that cannot be achieved with conventional aircraft – stand in contrast to the immense challenge of making its interior space emotionally acceptable to passengers. Its huge size has inspired concepts for onboard movie theatres, bars, lounges, promenades, fitness rooms, compartmental seating, and private first-class cabins, once again reviving the dream of a flying ocean liner. Planners are considering layouts that would address the divergent needs of various groups, such as senior citizens, families with small children, or passengers with specific ethnic or religious affiliations. But the scarcity of windows, the problem of emergency evacuation, and the unsettling spectre of an air disaster with such a large number of people aboard a single aircraft present untested psychological barriers.[77]

The design of the aircraft cabin has always been subject to highly restrictive parameters, not only regarding size and shape (memorably compared to 'a huge, inelastic pickle' by Henry Dreyfuss),[78] but also with respect to 'producibility, maintenance, durability, safety, accessibility, weight and flexibility', as WDTA president Milton Immermann summarised in 1970.[79] Within these parameters, the role of the industrial designer has ranged from decorator/stylist to architect/engineer. In 1956, Charles Butler complained that the designer was typically brought into the planning of an aircraft too late to influence engineering decisions and then 'expected to do the impossible with vinyl, colors and fabrics'. He called for 'the engineering group, the passenger service and marketing people, and the interior designer [to] work together from the very beginning in creating the ultimate for the passengers'.[80] Almost fifty years later, the realisation of this vision is apparent in a Teague executive's observation that the Boeing 777 'was the first airplane in which the needs of the interior set the design of the exterior'.[81] The present design process for the A380 confirms this integrative approach.

Ironically, the design elements most readily noticed by the average air traveller – colours, fabrics and surface treatments – are largely dictated by transient fashions. Although designers themselves have sworn by colour psychology since the 1940s, a comparison of their conclusions merely reveals an adherence to prevalent tastes. For example, British designer Hulme Chadwick declared in 1946 that 'blue is [...] probably the worst colour that could be used' in an aircraft interior.[82] He advocated neutral backgrounds with bright accents. Fast forward to the 1990s, and a USAir spokeswoman elaborates the airline's new colour scheme: 'Bright colors get people agitated, but blue is so soothing'.[83] The earthy colours of the 1940s, the gold and silver-accented synthetics of the 1950s, the psychedelic patterns of the 1970s, the corporate blues and greys of the 1990s: the air cabin has always kept pace with contemporary styles.

Yet less outwardly perceptible aspects of cabin design have a much greater influence on the passenger's overall flight experience. These elements have transformed the enclosed space of flying machines over the past century. Early aircraft cabins were modelled on automobile and train interiors in direct competition with these modes of ground transportation. Flying boats and larger landplanes attempted to imitate the luxurious social spaces of hotels or even ocean liners. New post-war materials encouraged designers to develop specific solutions for the aircraft cabin while creating a reassuring environment for a broadening spectrum of passengers. The jet engine not only brought enough speed and capacity to the aircraft to make it a viable means of mass transportation, but also inspired a non-derivative cabin interior that set new standards. Temperature and humidity, ventilation and pressurisation, sound insulation, lighting, individual seat controls, food service, seating comfort, lavatory facilities, and in-flight entertainment largely determine passenger satisfaction and continue to form the focus of designers' efforts. As commercial aircraft steadily increase in size, their interior architecture has

161 Study for the Blended Wing Body A20.30., Hochschule für Angewandte Künste, Hamburg and Technische Universität, Munich.

162 Study, entry area, Blended Wing Body A20.30, Industrial Design Studio.

163 Study, lower deck, Blended Wing Body A20.30, Industrial Design Studio.

161

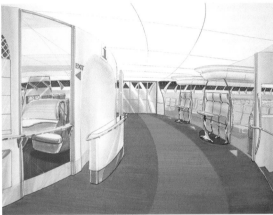

162

163

84 My final and most heartfelt acknowledgement goes to June Fitton, who spent 23 hours on a DC9-30, a DC10-30, a Boeing 737, and a Bombardier CRJ so that she could entertain her grandchildren while this article was being written.

more potential variability, but remains ultimately accountable to the air transport market. The seat-packed tube will be with us as long as most people make ticket price their top priority when booking a flight. So if you happen to be reading this on a plane, you might find that a trip through time offers more diversion than a trip through space.[84]

'MORE LEGROOM PLEASE': A HISTORICAL SURVEY OF THE AIRCRAFT SEAT

JOCHEN EISENBRAND

Translation by Barbara Fitton Hauß

Chair design thus becomes a major problem. [...] All in all, it is nearly true to say that the airplane is built around the seat. – Arthur E. Raymond, 1936[1]

The seat is easily the most important ingredient in the airplane interior. Make a man comfortable, and everything looks rosy to him. He can relax, his food tastes better, the trip will seem hours shorter. – Henry Dreyfuss, 1955[2]

Travellers on a train can get up and walk to the dining car, and bus and automobile passengers can make regular stops to stretch their legs. The air passenger, in contrast, must spend almost the entire duration of a trip in his or her seat. From this perspective, seat quality and seat spacing are the most important elements of air cabin design. The passenger's desire for adequate legroom, however, stands in opposition to the financial necessity of the airlines to fit as many customers as possible into a cabin. The less space between seat rows, the greater the capacity, resulting in higher revenues per flight. This conflict of interest between the comfort requirements of air passengers and the spatial constraints of commercial airlines is a fundamental condition of aircraft seat design and production.

To compensate for the limited amount of space in an aeroplane, aircraft seats are constructed with mobile elements: adjustable backrests and foot supports must allow different seating positions without encroaching on the personal space of neighbouring passengers. Standard features of today's seats include an integrated folding tray table, a seat pocket for safety information, an in-flight entertainment system in the armrest, and a life vest under the seat cushion. The designer's task is made even more difficult by a number of additional requirements: aircraft seats must be especially lightweight, since every gram translates into increased operating costs; safety specifications require a construction that will withstand stress of up to 16G in crash tests; furthermore, all materials must adhere to stringent flammability regulations. Finally, the seat must offer the highest possible degree of comfort on flights as long as ten

hours not only to the average-sized passenger, but to people who are big and small, fat and thin. All in all, no easy task: it is not surprising that the construction of aircraft seats quickly evolved into a highly specialised industry that supplies both aircraft manufacturers and individual airlines.

Wicker and Aluminium: Seats in the Ford Tri-Motor

The quest for ideal materials and a perfect form in passenger seat design is almost as old as air travel itself. Even in the 1920s, some aeroplanes were developed, manufactured and flown over a relatively long time-span. Consequently, a single aeroplane model was often equipped with different seat versions during the course of its commercial service. Various interior arrangements of the Ford Tri-Motor (1926–28), for example, offer insights into the earliest developments in the production of aircraft seats.

Into the 1930s, the Ford Tri-Motor was one of the most important passenger aeroplanes in commercial service on the North American continent. Approximately 200 models were built. The cabin accommodated twelve passengers in six rows with a central aisle. The earliest Tri-Motors had woven wicker seats with leather-covered cushions (**164, 165**). Since wickerwork is lightweight and flexible, woven chairs were common in the early years of passenger aviation. As early as 1919, wicker seats made by the English company Dryad were used in the Vickers Vimy, a military aeroplane that had been converted for civilian transport service.[3] Claude Dornier also installed wicker furniture in the Superwal and other flying boats, and in landplanes such as the Merkur (**166**). At the beginning of the 1930s, Norman Bel Geddes complemented the built-in seating in Pan American Airways' China Clipper with individual wicker pieces.

Another seat model used in the Ford Tri-Motor was a hybrid construction made of rattan and metal. The two front legs of the three-legged wicker chair were reinforced with thin steel tubing. The back leg, a rectangular

1 Arthur E. Raymond, 'Designing to Please the Air Traveller', Transcript of a paper presented to the National Aircraft Production Meeting of the Society of Automotive Engineers, Los Angeles, 15–17 October 1936, p. 3, National Air and Space Museum Archives, file FO-094030-20.
2 Henry Dreyfuss, *Designing for People*, New York, 1967 (1st ed. 1955), p. 121.
3 Eva B. Ottillinger, *Korbmöbel*, Salzburg and Vienna, 1990, pp. 168 f.

164 Aeroplane chair, wicker, c. 1925. Vitra Design Museum.

165 Cabin, 4 AT or 5AT Ford Tri-Motor, Transcontinental Air Transport.

166 Cabin of a Dornier Superwal with wicker seating, c. 1926.

167 Aeroplane chair, wicker with aluminium support, also used in the Ford Tri-Motor. Vitra Design Museum.

164

166

165

167

168 Cabin, Ford 4-AT Tri-Motor, Transcontinental Air Transport.

169 Aeroplane chair, aluminium, c. 1930 (covering and cushions: replicas, 2003).

170 This pneumatic cushion was placed in the leather upholstery of the aluminium chair. The makers applied for a patent in 1930. Vitra Design Museum.

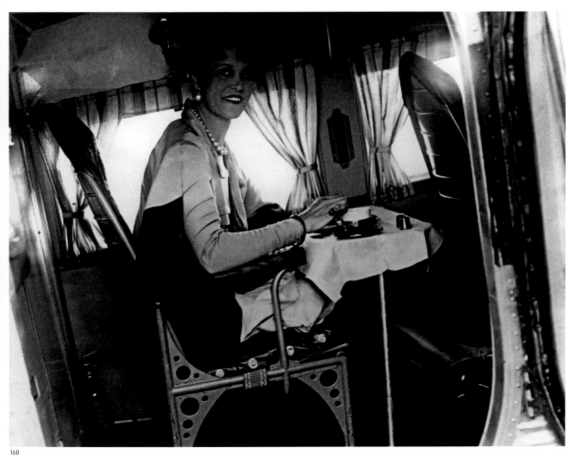

168

169

170

171 Aeroplane seating with aluminium frame, c. 1940.
Vitra Design Museum.

172 Aeroplane seat, Model 154 2D, 1943. Designed
by Warren McArthur, these seats were installed in the
Douglas C-54.

173 Aeroplane Seating No. 158, Warren McArthur, 1944.

174 Aeroplane Seating Model No. 358A-2,
Warren McArthur, c. 1945.

175 Warren McArthur Corporation advertising brochure, 1946.

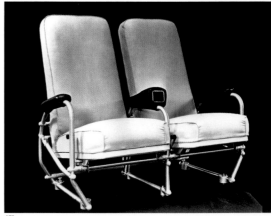
173

174

171

172

WARREN McARTHUR ROLL CALL

ALASKAN AIRLINES	HUGHES AIRCRAFT
AMERICAN AIRLINES	LOCKHEED AIRCRAFT
BEECH AIRCRAFT	GLENN L. MARTIN
BELL AIRCRAFT	MID-CONTINENT
BOEING AIRCRAFT	NATIONAL AIRLINES
CANADAIR LTD.	NORTH AMERICAN
CHANCE-VOUGHT	NORTHROP AIRCRAFT
COLONIAL AIRLINES	NORTHEAST AIRLINES
CONSOLIDATED VULTEE	NORTHWEST AIRLINES
CONTINENTAL AIRLINES	PAN-AMERICAN
CURTISS-WRIGHT	PENN-CENTRAL AIRLINES
DELTA AIRLINES	REPUBLIC AVIATION
DOUGLAS AIRCRAFT	RYAN AERONAUTICAL
EASTERN AIRLINES	SIKORSKY AIRCRAFT
FAIRCHILD AIRCRAFT	TATA INC. INDIA
GOODYEAR AIRCRAFT	UNITED AIRLINES
GRUMMAN AIRCRAFT	WESTERN AIRLINES

TRANSCONTINENTAL & WESTERN AIR
K.L.M. ROYAL DUTCH AIRLINES
LINEAS TRANSCONTINENTALES DE-AERO
TRANSPORTES, S.A.

WARREN McARTHUR CORPORATION
ONE PARK AVENUE   NEW YORK CITY
T R A N S P O R T A T I O N   S E A T I N G

175

wooden strut, ran from the top of the backrest to the floor and was sheathed in sheet aluminium below the seat (167). Leather upholstery also augmented the spartan comfort of this chair. A pocket for reading material was sewn into the back cover of the chair, much like the ones common today. Leather was a preferred upholstery material not only because of its durability, but also because 'the dust of the airports' could be easily removed by 'quickly washing it off with water and mild soap', as noted in a contemporary report.[4]

In spite of their popularity, wicker chairs had two major disadvantages: they were flammable, which made them a potential source of danger, particularly in the technically unsophisticated era of early aviation. Furthermore, the technique of wickerwork precluded the construction of an adjustable backrest.

These problems were solved by chairs made out of aluminium tubing, which gradually replaced the wicker seats in the Ford Tri-Motor (168, 169).[5] The seat surface and backrest of one metal model were connected by a joint that could be manoeuvred with a lever positioned underneath the seat. This made it possible to slide the seat surface forward, while the backrest reclined backward in a proportional movement. Thanks to the use of aluminium and the minimal amount of material, these seats were both robust and amazingly lightweight. The seat surface consisted of a leather cushion snapped to the metal frame and supported by tensile belts. Perforated metal was used for bracing between the legs, and corrugated sheet metal gave added strength to the backrest. This type of seat was also used on other aeroplanes, such as the Boeing 247, indicating that the first specialised aircraft seat manufacturers were already active at the beginning of the 1930s.

The seat cushions in the aeroplanes of the 1920s and 1930s were usually filled with kapok, animal hair, or feathers. New, lighter foam rubbers eventually supplanted these traditional padding materials. As early as 1934, seats with moulded foam cushions were installed in the Sikorsky S-42 flying boat.[6] Passengers in the Douglas DC-3 made themselves comfortable on latex foam

cushions around 1944.[7] Underneath the leather cover of the Ford Tri-Motor's aluminium seat, there was an inflatable rubber cushion with a valve:[8] the lightness of this type of padding could hardly be surpassed. Although this system was patented in 1930, it seems to have been in use only for a short time (170).[9] Years before the development of the pressurised cabin, pneumatic cushions must have been somewhat problematic under conditions of changing air pressure. Interestingly, today's aircraft designers are once again exploring the idea of using air as a means of cushioning.

Aluminium Aircraft Seats by Warren McArthur

The triumph of aluminium as a favoured material in aircraft construction began in the USA around 1930.[10] At about the same time, furniture designers started to experiment with aluminium, which had an aura of 'newness' to it, despite the fact that it had been known since the nineteenth century.[11] In 1930, the designer Warren McArthur (1885–1961) founded a furniture company in Los Angeles specifically for the purpose of developing furniture made out of aluminium tubing.[12] Parallel to this, he began his first design studies for aircraft seating. Following the relocation of his company to Bantam, Connecticut, McArthur began with the production of aircraft seats on a large scale in 1935. His preferred materials were aluminium and magnesium, for which he and his engineers developed new processing methods and applications.[13] During the 13 years of its existence, the Warren McArthur Corporation produced more than 250 seat models for different aircraft. The majority of these were destined for military use – over 85 percent of the aircraft used by the US military during World War II were equipped with seats from McArthur.[14] But the company also produced over 40 different models for passenger seating (172, 173, 174). Early versions of McArthur's aircraft seats can be identified by the reinforcement rings around the connections between tube sections, which are also a typical feature of his furniture designs.

4 'Übersetzung aus Aviation vom Februar 1931 über Innen-Ausstattung von Flugzeugen. Von John F. Hardecker', Deutsches Museum Munich, Junkers Archive, file 0305 T11 Junkers Flugzeugbau 1919–33 – Flugzeugteile und Zubehör.
5 See Douglas J. Ingells, The Fabulous Ford Tri-Motor, Fallbrook, 1968, p. 38.
6 Albert P. Elebash, 'Passenger Aircraft Facilities – Design and Operation', typescript of a paper presented to the Society of Automotive Engineers, National Air Transport Engineering Meeting, Chicago, 2–4 December 1946, p. 5. National Air and Space Museum, file FO-904030-25. In comparison, see: 'Igor I. Sikorsky Presents the S42. The Development and Characteristics of a Long-Range Flying Boat.' Paper presented to the Royal Aeronautical Society, London, 15 November 1934. http://www.sikorskyarchives.com/s42.html.
7 R.(ichard) M.(oss), 'High Chairs', Industrial Design, February 1961, p. 54.
8 See Elebash, 'Passenger Aircraft Facilities', p. 5.
9 The Vitra Design Museum Collection contains one of these seats. The rubber cushion bears the label: 'Patented October 7, 1930'.
10 While the Ford Tri-Motor had a steel frame covered with aluminium sheeting, the Boeing 247 was the first aeroplane in the USA with a frame made out of an aluminium alloy, followed by the highly successful DC-3. See Sarah Nichols, 'Aluminum by Design: Jewelry to Jets', Sarah Nichols (ed.), Aluminum by Design: Jewelry to Jets, New York, 2000, pp. 34 ff. Also Sarah Nichols, 'Highlights: Aviation', Aluminum by Design, p. 236. In Germany, Junkers pioneered the development and application of aluminium alloys and introduced the Junkers F 13 with great success in 1919: the first aeroplane with a fuselage and wings made of Duralumin, an aluminium-magnesium alloy with high tensile qualities. Junkers also used the same material in the construction of aircraft seats. See the essay by Barbara Hauß in this publication.
11 Nichols, Aluminum by Design, p. 31.
12 McArthur had begun with the construction of furniture in the mid-1920s by using steel tubing for gas lines and automobile gaskets. Sarah Nichols, 'Highlights. Warren McArthur', Aluminum by Design, p. 216.
13 'Light Metal Seating', Modern Metals. The News Journal for Light Metals, 1.6 (July 1945), p. 15. I am greatly indebted to Nicholas Brown, Camden/Maine, for valuable references, numerous illustrations and extensive information on the Warren McArthur Aircraft Corporation.
14 Ibid., p. 14.

15 When the remainder of the 'Warren McArthur Corporation for the production of passenger, pilot and co-pilot aircraft seats' was put up for sale, it included an offer of 14 US patents for the construction of metal furniture, as well as raw materials (steel, magnesium and aluminium) at a price of US $ 350,000. Unpaginated, undated typescript in the Lorenz Archive, Vitra Design Museum.

16 Fridtjof F. Schliephacke, Der Bewegungsstuhl, typescript, Akademie der Bildenden Künste, Berlin, p. 291.

17 R.(ichard) M.(oss), 'High Chairs', p. 54.

18 Fridtjof F. Schliephacke, 'Erinnerungen an Hans Luckhardt – Erfinder, Konstrukteur, Architekt', Brüder Luckhardt und Alfons Anker, ed. Achim Wendschuh, Berlin, 1990, p. 99.

19 Schliephacke, 'Erinnerungen an Hans Luckhardt', p. 105. In the correspondence held between Anton Lorenz and the Mücke-Melder-Werken beginning in January 1936 on producing an aircraft seat prototype, a Thonet seat is mentioned that was being built 'at the time' for Air France. Lorenz Archive, Vitra Design Museum.

20 Correspondence between Anton Lorenz and NKF Hodermann, Lorenz Archive, Vitra Design Museum. See also: Fridtjof F. Schliephacke, 'Hans Luckhardt – Verzeichnis der Modelle und Entwürfe. Stahlrohrmöbel und Bewegungsstühle', Wendschuh (ed.) 1990, pp. 305–10.

In a print advertisement published in November 1946, Warren McArthur listed over 40 customers of his aircraft seats, including practically every important airline and aircraft manufacturer in America (175). In spite of this evident success, the company was forced to close in 1948, perhaps due to the loss of a large percentage of military contracts after the war ended.[15] In the meantime, however, aluminium had established itself as a lightweight and robust material for the production of aircraft seating.

Patented Comfort for Sitting and Reclining

Next to the goal of reducing weight with the use of lighter materials, the second great challenge in aircraft development was to increase passenger comfort. Apart from the aspect of upholstery, this could be best achieved with dynamic and adjustable seat elements. The first technical advancements focussed on an adjustment mechanism for the backrest: ranging from a simple locking lever underneath the seat of the Ford Tri-Motor, to a crank-driven cog wheel mechanism in the DC-2 (1933) (176),[16] to a complex spring system that was built into the armrest of an early seat on the DC-3 (1936). From the mid-1940s onward, such systems were replaced by compact hydraulic cylinders, which were also easier to maintain.[17] What all of these seats had in common, though, was a backrest that required manual adjustment, while the angle of the seat surface remained fixed. In comparison, the designs developed by German architect Hans Luckhardt (1890–1954) went much further.

Luckhardt had been designing tubular steel furniture since the end of the 1920s. At almost the same time, he had started to explore 'the problems of comfortable seating by means of adjusting the seat and back surfaces of armchairs'.[18] He shared his interest in ergonomics with Anton Lorenz, a patent attorney who managed the rights to Mart Stam's cantilevered chair and several Breuer pieces, while also serving as director of the legal division for copyright protection at Thonet, the furniture

manufacturer, between 1933 and 1935. Lorenz and Luckhardt began to collaborate on the development of automatically adjustable and collapsible reclining armchairs in 1933. Thonet constructed the first prototypes of their designs around 1935, including an aircraft seat made of tubular steel (178).[19]

Both this chair and the following models were based on the idea that the redistribution of body weight alone should allow the user to achieve different sitting and reclining positions. Thanks to a so-called driving gear, the backrest, seat surface, and leg support were synchronised in a coordinated movement and remained in balance regardless of the chosen position.

In 1937, Lorenz and Luckhardt contracted with the Neue Kühler- und Flugzeugteile Fabrik Kurt Hodermann for the manufacture of a second, improved aircraft seat prototype (177). This time, they used tubular magnesium, which is lighter than steel. Lorenz presented the seat to airlines in France and England, but he was also anticipating an order from Lufthansa.[20] In the meantime, the patented system went into series production at Thonet: The furniture manufacturer produced reclining armchairs bearing the name Siesta Medizinal beginning in 1938–39 for both therapeutic and domestic use.

With the aim of establishing scientifically based parameters for optimal sitting and reclining positions, Anton Lorenz initiated an experimental study at the Kaiser Wilhelm Institute for Industrial Physiology in Dortmund in 1938. In a trial series, test persons were submerged in a water tank that was enclosed on one side with clear glass plates. In order to keep the face just above water, a rope was strung underneath the buttocks as the body's presumed centre of gravity. The test subjects were then photographed in the position of total relaxation that their bodies assumed underwater. The various results of the separate photographs, showing physical outlines and anatomical positions, were traced and superimposed upon one another. The resultant averages reaffirmed the advantages of Luckhardt's construction: in a relaxed state, which ensures the greatest degree of comfort and recuperation, the

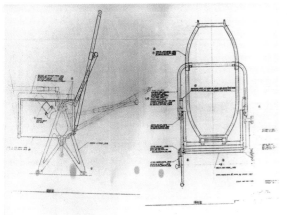

176 Design plan, aeroplane seat, KLM DC-2, 1934.

177 Aeroplane seat with a frame of tubular magnesium, designed by Hans Luckhardt, prototype c. 1937, produced by Neue Flugzeugteile und Kühler Fabrik Hodermann.

178 Aeroplane seat, frame of tubular steel, prototype c. 1935, designed by Hans Luckhardt, produced by Thonet Paris.

179 'The Anatomy of Sitting and Reclining', Thonet advertising brochure, c. 1938–39. Vitra Design Museum.

176

THONET
PARIS

178

Die Anatomie des Sitzens und Liegens

und ihre Auswirkungen auf Diagnostik, Behandlung und Liegekur

Thonet „Siesta Medizinal" System Luckhardt D. R. P.

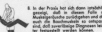

Die Entwicklung der vollkommenen Entspannung

1. Steckt nicht eine Art instinkthaften Triebes dahinter, wenn viele Menschen so „überzwerch" in einem Sessel sitzen und dazu behaupten, dieses „gesellschaftsunfähige" Sitzen sei für sie das bequemste?

2. Diese Knicklage, die ja die meisten Menschen während des Schlafes einnehmen, ist ohne Zweifel nicht anerzogen und demnach als Hinweis darauf anzusehen, daß sa ähnlich wohl die vollkommene Entspannungslage sein müßte.

3. Der Versuch, sich durch Überschlagen der Beine Bequemlichkeit, also Entspannung zu verschaffen, ist fast allen Menschen eigentümlich. Daß der Körper dabei jedoch n a c h v o r n e r u t s c h t, weist darauf hin, daß diese Art des Sitzens der Entspannungslage noch nicht sehr nahe ist.

4. Diese doppelte rechtwinklige Knickung des Körpers bei „korrektem" Sitzen wirkt so ermüdend, daß diese Stellung als Ausgangspunkt für die Erforschung der optimalen Entspannungslage überhaupt nicht in Frage kommen kann.

5. Nachdem festgestellt ist, daß der Mensch seine Lage im Schlafe etwa vierzigmal wechselt, dabei aber selten Oberkörper, Oberschenkel und Unterschenkel in einer Lage hat, kann als erwiesen gelten, daß die dargestellte Lage keine Entspannung herbeiführt.

Gerade die besonders negativen Ergebnisse zeitigenden Lagen (z. B. Nr. 4 und 5) haben ergeben, daß hiebei stets zwei Muskelgruppen gegeneinander wirken. Beide sind sie in Wechselwirkung gespannt und entspannt, und diese Spannung hält auch an, wenn der Körper scheinbar vollkommen ruhig gebettet ist. Scheinbar! Denn auch in diesem Falle erweist die Untersuchung mit dem Stethoskop oder mit dem Elektrokardiographen das Vorhandensein von Muskelströmen als Zeichen dafür, daß eine tatsächliche Entspannung nicht

vorhanden ist. Es muß aber irgendwie eine Lage geben, die eine vollkommene Entspannung auslöst und die irgendwie in der Nähe der dargestellten Lage Nr. 1 bis 3 liegt. Den Weg dazu weist uns die Unterwasser-Forschung. Das spezifische Gewicht des Körpers ist ja bei fast vollständigem Eintauchen gleich dem des Wassers. Bewegungen der Gliedmaßen geschehen also im Wasser praktisch ohne jede Belastung durch das Gewicht der Gliedmaßen selbst.

6. Versuche in dieser Richtung haben nun ergeben, daß der Körper unter Wasser immer wieder und unwillkürlich eine ganz bestimmte Knicklage einnimmt, also die Entspannungslage sein muß, da sie ja durch die Aufhebung des Gewichtes ohne Spannung zustande kam.

7. Auf die Gegebenheiten außerhalb des Wassers übertragen, müßte also der Körper so, wie hier skizziert, gebettet werden, um vollkommen entspannt zu sein.

8. In der Praxis hat sich dann tatsächlich gezeigt, daß in diesem Falle die Muskelgeräusche zurückgehen und daß auch die Bauchmuskeln so entspannt sind, daß zuverlässige Diagnosen leichter festgestellt werden können.

9. Ein genaues Studium dieser Knicklage führte zu der Erkenntnis, daß fünf Stützungs-Elemente notwendig sind, um dem Körper die vollkommene Entspannung zu geben: a) Unterstützung der Muskulatur des Schultergürtels, b) der Arme, c) der Rumpf-Muskulatur einschließlich der Gegend der unteren Lendenwirbelsäule, d) der Oberschenkel- und e) der Unterschenkel-Muskulatur.

10. Aus diesen fünf Elementen heraus (siehe auch oberes Titelbild) entstand der Thonet-Medizinal-Stuhl sowohl für die ärztliche Praxis, als auch für Liegekuren, dessen praktische Anwendung die folgenden Seiten zeigen.

179

180 Aeroplane seat with a magnesium tube frame, designed by Hans Luckhardt, produced by Thonet Paris for Air France, c. 1938. Vitra Design Museum.

181 Promotional photograph, Thonet Paris, c. 1938.

180

181

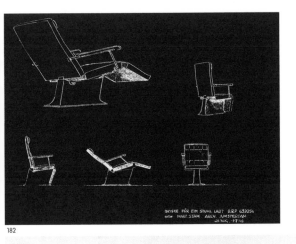

182 Design for an aeroplane chair by Mart Stam, patented by Hans Luckhardt and Anton Lorenz, 1938.

183 Designer Hans Luckhardt on a prototype of his aeroplane seat using rectangular aluminium tubing, Junkers, c. 1939–40.

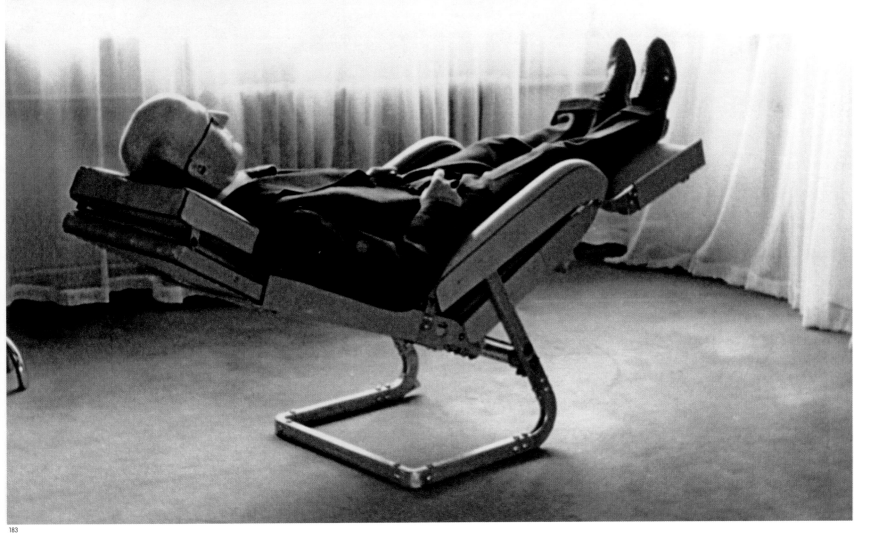

184 When the last beds in aeroplanes disappeared in the mid-1950s, the airline began to advertise their new 'sleeper seats'.

185 Lufthansa's Comforette seats were introduced in 1957 in First and Deluxe-Class on the Super Constellation.

184

185

human body takes a position of angular recumbence, with the arms slightly bent at the elbows and the legs raised and slightly angled.[21] An ergonomically shaped reclining armchair must, then, support the body at five points: across the shoulder girdle, underneath the arms, in the lumbar zone, and under the thighs and calves (179).[22]

Finally, the third aeroplane seat Luckhardt developed according to these principles made it into series production and, subsequently, into the air. The 'world's first automatically adjustable aeroplane seat' was produced in a small series by the Thonet company in Paris with a frame made of magnesium tubing. In 1938, Air France installed the seat for trial purposes on planes flying the night route between Paris and Algiers (180, 181).[23]

At the same time, Anton Lorenz commissioned Mart Stam to develop an alternative design after the latter had discussed the Air France seat in a published article.[24] The major difference between Luckhardt's design and his own was in the frame: Stam's base took the shape of an upside-down T that ran under the middle of the seat on a longitudinal axis. However, this chair was never produced (182).[25]

Lorenz and Luckhardt were also negotiating with the aircraft manufacturer Junkers. In early 1939, the Siesta sleeper seats were installed in a Junkers Ju-90 mockup, where they were competing directly with an 'English aircraft seat' (183). The Siesta seat apparently did not enter into series production for Junkers because it required too much space: passengers at the window seats would have to climb over the extended footrest of their neighbours to reach the aisle.[26] This remains a problem even today: The comfort of an individual passenger cannot be increased at the expense of the person in the next seat, in spite of – or precisely because of – the limited amount of space.

In the same year, Anton Lorenz emigrated to the United States. He contacted American Airlines in 1945 in hopes of finding a new customer for the 'Adjustable Reclining Aircraft Chair' that he had developed together with Luckhardt. His aim was to convince the airline of the chair's suitability for transcontinental DST (Douglas Sleeper Transport) flights between New York and Los Angeles. These planes were equipped with two passenger seats that could be joined at night to make a single bed, with another berth folding down from the cabin ceiling. Lorenz argued that his patented construction would replace the function of two seats with just one, thereby saving the airline space, weight and money without forfeiting passenger comfort.[27] With this proposal, however, Lorenz proved to be ahead of his time.

New Reclining Comfort in the 1950s

Eight years later, at the end of 1953, American Airlines announced that it was discontinuing Sleeper Service on the DC-6 (successor of the DST). The shorter duration of flights due to faster planes such as the DC-7 eliminated the need for airborne beds.[28] In order to maintain resting options for their passengers onboard, however, the airlines began to introduce more comfortable seats, with backrests that could be deeply reclined, and retractable footrests, similar to the earlier solution put forth unsuccessfully by Anton Lorenz. The introduction of tourist class travel in the early 1950s also forced the airlines to establish distinguishing characteristics for their first class service – which they did with an emphasis on seating amenities. In the mid-1950s, TWA ran large-format advertisements in American daily newspapers praising the comfort of the Siesta (!) Sleeper Seats installed in the first class of the airline's Lockheed Super Constellations (184).[29] At roughly the same time, Lufthansa introduced the 'Comforette' seat in its first and deluxe classes (185).

A Pan American World Airways advertisement in a German periodical bears witness to the transformation in the interior design of commercial aeroplanes that was taking place: In the Stratocruiser, passengers could choose (for the last time) between sleeping compartments with 'feathery softness' and PAA's newly

21 Schliephacke, 'Erinnerungen an Hans Luckhardt', pp. 105 f.
22 Brochure of the Thonet company, 'Die Anatomie des Sitzens und Liegens', 1938–39, Vitra Design Museum Archive. Illustration printed in Schliephacke, 'Erinnerungen an Hans Luckhardt', p. 109.
23 Ibid., p. 100. According to Schliephacke, 47 seats were installed in one plane. Lorenz records that the first contact and the first delivery were both one year later, respectively, in 1938–39, and that six planes were equipped with a total of 48 seats. Letter from Anton Lorenz to N.M. Graves, 23 March 1945. Lorenz Archive, Vitra Design Museum. The new aircraft seat did not achieve a wider distribution, probably due to the beginning of the war.
24 Mart Stam, 'Nieuwe Stoelen', 8 Opbouw, 9.15 (23 July 1938), n.p.
25 Schliephacke, Der Bewegungsstuhl, p. 294.
26 Carbon copy of a letter from Gebrüder Thonet to Junkers, 27 August 1938, Lorenz Archive, Vitra Design Museum.
27 Letter from J. A. Ferguson, Vice President of the Barcalo Manufacturing Company, and John T. Fisher, American Airlines, 13 June 1945. Carbon copy in the Lorenz Archive, Vitra Design Museum. No documented evidence of a later collaboration was found.
28 'Airline is Ending Sleeper Flights', The New York Times, 20 December 1953, p. 78.
29 New York Journal American, 9 October 1957; New York Herald Tribune, 8 October 1957.

186 Chair frame used in X-ray tests during development of Lockheed's L-188 Electra

187 Prototype of airline seating for the Lockheed Electra, Henry Dreyfuss, 1955.

188 Plastic shell seating for TWA, designed by E. Gilbert Mason, 1961.

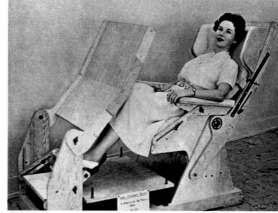

186

187

188

installed 'Sleeperette' reclining seats. It is notable that this new, more comfortable aircraft seat still did not offer the synchronised adjustment of its supporting surfaces, in contrast to the seat developed much earlier by Luckhardt and Lorenz.

Ergonomic Seating Studies in the US

The first scientific studies on aircraft seating were published in the United States in the early 1940s. The furniture manufacturer Heywood-Wakefield, for example, took the physical measurements of almost 4000 people in order to determine ideal seat proportions on the basis of statistical averages. This resulted in a recommended seat pitch (distance between the same point on seats in successive rows) of 100 cm for standard seating and 120 cm on long-haul flights.[30]

In conjunction with the launch of the L-188 Electra, industrial designer Henry Drreyfuss was commissioned by the Lockheed Aircraft Corporation in 1955 to conduct a scientific study on the ergonomic requirements of seat cushioning. The purpose was to establish a seat form that would provide the highest degree of comfort to a majority of passengers on a flight lasting four to five hours.[31] A physician from Cornell University Medical College advised the designer on medical issues.[32] In the previous studies initiated by Anton Lorenz at the Kaiser Wilhelm Institute, the medium of photography had been used; Henry Dreyfuss now utilised X-ray technology. Using available statistics from public surveys, he deducted the physical measurements of the average American man and woman – whom he named Joe and Josephine – and used these as a reference not only in the development of the L-188 Electra seat, but for many other subsequent designs.[33] The first step was to build a mobile wooden mock-up seat based on his models' measurements. Next, several test persons were seated in the mock-up, either in an upright or reclined position, and rolled past an X-ray screen (186). The X-ray images of the pelvis and spine were evaluated with the following conclusions: the seat surface should be neither concave nor convex, but flat; in addition, it should be short and low enough so that the sitter's feet rest on the floor; finally, the backrest should support the lumbar area (187).[34] This last requirement, as previously mentioned, had already been established in the earlier German studies.

Dreyfuss achieved the ergonomic shape of his seat back with polyether foams of varying densities.[35] The conclusions reached in his experiments for the Lockheed L-188 Electra were useful for subsequent contracts, including the design of seats for American Airlines' Boeing 747s.[36] For first class seating, Dreyfuss revived the forty-year-old idea of pneumatic cushioning in order to make the padding adaptable to the individual size and weight of passengers.[37]

Early seat studies did not focus exclusively on the issue of comfort, but also investigated safety requirements. One example is the aircraft seat manufacturer Aerotherm, which produced the L-188 Electra seats according to Dreyfuss's specifications. During the early 1940s, Aerotherm conducted crash trials on aircraft seats. One of the company's primary concerns was the ability of various materials used in the construction of seat frames to absorb shock.[38] Such tests are still indispensable in new seat development and also provide basic standards for certification.

The Ascent of Plastics

In the 1950s, plastics were not only on the rise in the area of consumer products, but also in the field of aeronautics. Initially, there was an increasing use of plastics on commercially flown aeroplanes as upholstery material on the arm supports and backrests of seats.[39] Aerotherm, for example, covered the seats of the Electra with Fiberglas-reinforced vinyl.[40] The seats of the Convair 880 were covered with Mylar, a polyester foil developed in 1952. This washable and printable foil was also used as an exterior finish on cabin surfaces. The seat of the Boeing 707, developed by the manufacturer in collaboration with Walter Dorwin Teague Associates at the end of the 1950s, had a backrest made out of a

30 Elebash, 'Passenger Aircraft Facilities', pp. 5 f.

31 Henry Dreyfuss, 'Lockheed Aircraft Corporation. Chair Design Requirements for Electra 188', 16 December 1955, p. 3. Typescript, Henry Dreyfuss Papers, Cooper-Hewitt National Design Museum.

32 Dr Janet Travell also advised Henry Dreyfuss in other cases, including the development of tractor seats. See Russell Flinchum, The Man in the Brown Suit, New York, 1997, p. 154. As early as 1944, Henry Dreyfuss developed seats with adjustable backrests for the Consolidated Vultee Model 39. The headrest had a small reading light integrated into the left side and an individual speaker in the right side. See J. Gordon Lippincott, 'Industrial Design. Using the New Materials', Interiors, May 1944, p. 86.

33 Flinchum, The Man in the Brown Suit, pp. 175 ff.

34 Dreyfuss 1955, pp. 7 ff. See also R.(ichard) M.(oss), 'Dreyfuss Office Human Engineers a Chair for Airborne Executive Suite', Industrial Design, November 1959, pp. 92 f.

35 R.(ichard) M.(oss), 'Dreyfuss Office Human Engineers a Chair for Airborne Executive Suite', pp. 92 f.

36 Niels Diffrient, 'Design with Backbone', Industrial Design, 17.8, October 1970, pp. 44–47.

37 Ibid., p. 46.

38 'Thermix Engineers Help Make Military, Commercial Planes Safer and Better', Greenwich Time, 14 Sep. 1956, p. 6. Also B.(etsy) D.(arrach), 'Pan American Expresses a New Personality for a New Kind of Travel', Industrial Design, March 1959, p. 37.

39 See illustration of a DC-6 seat in: R.(ichard) M.(oss), 'High Chairs', p. 55.

40 Ibid., p. 56. Also Interiors, June 1955, p. 123.

189 Aida Group's foldable seating for economy class is intended to shorten boarding times.

190 The design group Tangerine developed the first fully flat extendable seating in Business Class for British Airways, 2000. To save space, the seating was installed facing in opposite directions.

191 Qantas' cocoon-like Skybed was created by the Australian designer Marc Newson in 2003.

189

190

191

192

193

192 Aeroplane seating developed by Lantal Textiles and Prospective Concepts, completely cushioned by air.

193 Pneumatic cushion in the airline seating designed by Lantal Textiles and Prospective Concepts.

194 For Japan Airlines, the London designer Ross Lovegrove developed the Skysleeper Solo in 2002.

195 The new Virgin Upper Class Suite, designed by Softroom and Pearson Lloyd, 2003.

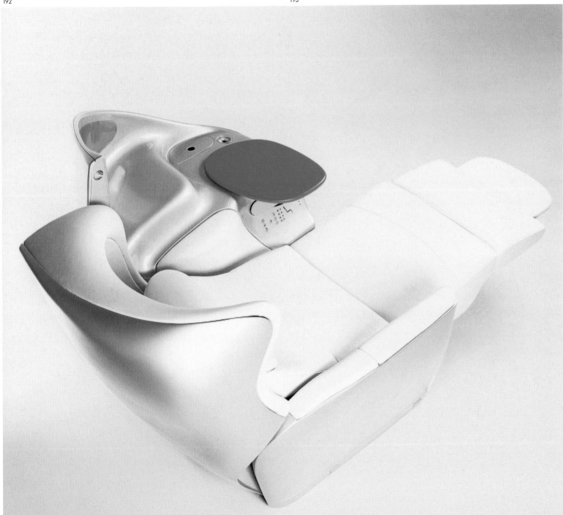

194

195

41 B.(etsy) D.(arrach), 'Pan American Expresses a New Personality', p. 27. Before the introduction of the folding tray table, passengers either had to balance their food trays on their laps, or they used removable trays that could be inserted into slots in the seats' armrests. The integrated tray table became common after its introduction in the mid-1950s and also appeared on the seats of the Douglas DC-8 and the Vickers Viscount. See 'Enter the Viscount', *Industrial Design*, August 1955, p. 33.

42 R.(ichard) M.(oss), 'High Chairs', pp. 52 and 57 ff.

43 Jörg Heuser, 'Service Lift', *Aircraft Interiors International*, May 2003, pp. 40–44.

hard plastic shell enveloped in foam padding. Integrated into the back side was a folding tray table, which has since become a ubiquitous feature on aircraft seats.[41] The first passenger seat made entirely out of plastic was created by the industrial designer E. Gilbert Mason (**188**). In 1961, TWA commissioned him to develop a new seat for its passenger planes. The prototype consisted of top and bottom seat shells made of vacuum-moulded Royalite plastic. The shells were mounted together and the space between them filled with urethane foam and aluminium mesh for reinforcement. The finished double shell was bolted to an aluminium and steel base that was flexibly attached to a horizontal crossbeam with A-shaped leg supports. In this way, it was possible to tilt the static seat shell backwards into a reclining position. Seat and head cushions made of fabric-covered foam were simply attached to the shell with strips of Velcro.

Thanks to the simplicity of this construction, Mason's plastic chairs were one-third lighter than conventional seats. Instead of the approximately 500 parts in other seats, they had just 70. Airlines could also recognise potential savings in the fact that the seats could be installed at a pitch of 87.5 cm, rather than the 97.5 cm standard at the time.[42] Yet in spite of these advantages, this new method of construction did not take hold. However, both hard and soft plastics remained essential materials in aircraft seat construction from then on, whether in the form of shell elements or upholstery. It also appears that the aim of developing seating systems with closer rows – compare the above mentioned numbers with the conclusions of studies conducted in the 1940s – established itself as one of the main goals of the airlines with regard to seat design. Today's economy class seating typically has a seat pitch of approximately 80 cm.

Recent Developments

A comparison of the external appearance of today's economy class seats with those from the 1960s and 1970s reveals but few differences. Most significant developments since then have had little to do with seat construction, but instead focus on the expansion and improvement of in-flight entertainment systems. The controls for these systems, such as volume and channel functions, a headphone socket, and other electronic features, are integrated into the armrests. During the past few years, LCD-screens in seat backs have been introduced for the purpose of offering passengers more diversion from the discomfort of sitting for extended periods on long flights.

Present considerations for economy class seating are primarily devoted to the aspect of efficiency. Together with Airbus, the Aida Group is now developing the first fold-up aircraft seat with the aim of reducing aisle blockage, which commonly occurs when passengers board and disembark the plane (**189**). When the chair is not in use, the seat surface automatically folds up – like seating in theatres – making it easier for passengers to reach their assigned seats or to exit into the aisle. The logic behind this development is that the airlines could shorten the amount of time their planes spend on the ground. This seat differs not only in its construction from conventional models, but also in its aesthetic appearance, for which designers drew inspiration from the seats of contemporary sports cars. In spite of its required stability, the seat is as light as it looks: both the shell and the crossbeam upon which it is mounted are made of carbon-fibre composites.[43]

Aside from such interesting modifications, major improvements in seating and reclining comfort are limited almost exclusively to options for first and business class travellers. Four basic trends can be identified: seats that can be extended into a fully horizontal bed surface, greater privacy, new seat configurations, and the utilisation of pneumatic cushioning systems.

So that their deep-pocketed business travellers feel as comfortable in the air as they do at home, in 2000 British Airways became the first airline to install seats that can be fully extended into a flat sleeping surface. However, since the seat-bed unit requires up to fifty

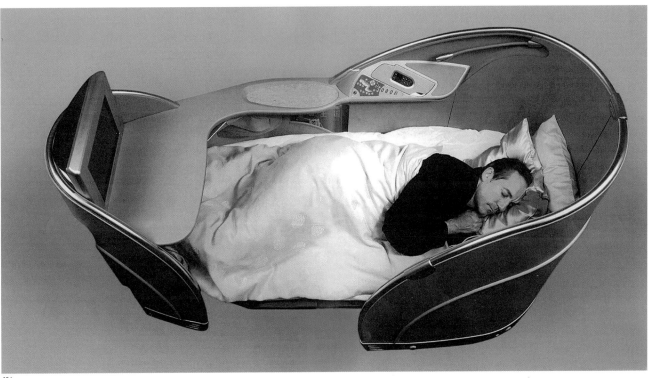

196

44 'Prima Classe/First Class', *Ottagono*, No. 141, December 2000/January 2001, pp. 52 f.

45 See Marion Hume, 'Sitting Pretty', in, *Qantas – The Australian Way*, Sept. 2003, pp. 67 ff; also Anthony James, 'Aussie Rules', *Aircraft Interiors International*, December 2003, pp. 18–24.

46 Using the same concept, BE Aerospace has also developed similar seat models for other airlines. See 'New Direction for Northwest', *Aircraft Interiors International*, Sep. 2003, p. 8.

47 'Air Support', *Aircraft Interiors International*, Sep. 2003, p. 81.

48 Anthony James, 'Double Take', *Aircraft Interiors International*, September 2003, pp. 29–34. Also see Deyan Sudjic, 'The Bed in the Sky', *Domus*, September 2003, pp. 100–09; Henrietta Thompson, 'The Best Seat in the Skies?', *Blueprint*, December 2003, pp. 50 f.

49 Andreas Spaeth, 'Wie man sich bettet, so fliegt man', *Süddeutsche Zeitung*, 28 October 2003, p. V2/2. Brigitte Scherer, 'Zwei Arten zu fliegen', *Frankfurter Allgemeine Zeitung*, 16 October 2003, p. R2.

50 Wallace A. Peltola, 'Eyes Wide Shut', *Aircraft Interiors International*, May 2003, pp. 34–38.

percent more space than their previous seats (at a pitch of 183 cm, as compared to 121 cm), the airline would have lost several seats in a traditional cabin layout. To avoid this, British Airways developed a new seating configuration for its Boeing 747s and 777s in collaboration with the design firm Tangerine: seats are installed in pairs with one facing forward and the other backward (190). In this way, more seats fit into the forward cabin than a typical row plan would allow. By folding their tray tables up sideways, neighbouring passengers create an additional screen between themselves as they repose in opposite directions.[44]

Even more privacy is afforded by Qantas' Business Class Skybed. The airline was able to obtain the services of Australian-born designer Marc Newson for the development of this new seat, who collaborated with aircraft seat manufacturer BE Aerospace.[45] The upright back shell of this model gives it the appearance of a partial cocoon, which opens into a bed that is 200 cm long and 60 cm wide.[46] The shell shelters the head of the resting passenger, while also muffling cabin noises (191).

Japan Airlines also commissioned a well-known designer for its new first class seats. Ross Lovegrove's organically shaped, futuristic looking Skysleeper Solo was distinguished with the Japanese Good Design Award in 2002. The shimmering white surface of the seat shell is accented by a red retractable table, an integrated yellow telephone, and a glowing green light panel (194). Like Newson's design, this seat has inflatable cushioning in the lumbar zone. Since the ergonomic shape of the backrest, necessary while sitting, becomes irritating in a supine position, the advantage of pneumatic padding lies in the fact that the lumbar cushion can be deflated to create a completely flat bed surface. An additional feature of the pneumatic backrest is a pulsating mechanism that 'breathes' air into and out of the cushion, thereby massaging the spine of the sitter.

Moreover, pneumatics save weight. Lantal Textiles, a Swiss producer of fabrics for transport industries, and the Prospective Concepts company developed a seat that relies solely on air chambers for padding (192, 193). The pressure of the air pockets can be adjusted to meet the needs of individual passengers. They also replaced conventional electric motors for the operation of the footrests with a pneumatic system. Depending on the type of aeroplane, these innovations can save up to 1500 kg, according to the manufacturer.[47]

Another novel solution for comfortable airborne repose was recently introduced by Virgin. In the airline's new Upper Class Suite, passengers sit on upholstered leather, but sleep on mattresses. To achieve this combination, Virgin's in-house design team worked together with the design group Softroom and the furniture designers Pearson Lloyd to develop the first aircraft seat with a backrest that folds forward to become part of a bed (195). The surface of the backrest is joined to the top of an ottoman mounted in front of the seat. The unified surface offers enough space for a sleeping passenger to stretch out. The system does have one disadvantage: in order to make the bed, a passenger must first get up. Perhaps as compensation for this, travellers are no longer required to sit in an upright position during take-off and landing, thanks to integrated airbags.[48] Virgin also gained space by placing the seats with their backs to the windows. Since the lower part of the seat faces the aisle, the aisle can be made narrower while still conforming to strict safety regulations.

Many airlines have slightly inclined rest surfaces to save space. The new lounge seats in Lufthansa's business class, for example, recline to an angle of 9 percent, as compared to 13 percent recline.[49] Seat lengths vary between 185 and 200 cm. When it comes to seat width, All Nippon Airways leads the way at the moment with a seat-bed by Tola Design measuring 84 cm across (196).[50] These figures suggest a degree of comfort about which passengers in economy class seating can only dream – until they are awakened by leg cramps and a stiff neck.

AIRLINES AND CORPORATE DESIGN

JOCHEN EISENBRAND

Translation by Julia Thorson

The advent of jet planes in the late 1950s marked the dawn of a new age in the field of commercial aviation, not only in terms of technology but also with regard to design. Airlines were then among the first companies worldwide that developed corporate design programmes to standardise their external presentation and thus set themselves apart from the competition.[1] All internal and external expressions of the company were henceforth to be recognisable through a set of continually recurring characteristics. These deliberately planned corporate symbols replaced the elements of visual communication that had accumulated over the company's history in a mostly ad-hoc fashion. New corporate logos, fonts, and colours now became clearly defined distinguishing features of the airlines. Their uniform application was set out in corporate design handbooks. The guidelines affected printed material such as flight schedules, passenger tickets, and luggage tags as well as the marking of the aeroplanes and the service vehicles on the runways. In handling all these aspects, graphic design was thus accorded a significant role in the image of the airlines. But the parameters of corporate design extended even further, covering things like personnel uniforms as well as industrial design and interiors. Individually designed passenger cabins, the interior furnishings of the ticket offices and the profile the airlines put forth at airports now emerged as an important component of how the companies presented themselves.[2]

In face of the expansive commissions that accompanied the development of corporate design programmes in commercial aviation, this type of design-based identity formation offered a new attractive field for graphic and industrial designers. The extensive nature of the commissions and the specifications down to the smallest detail furthermore gave designers more influence on the uniform implementation of their designs. As a consequence, international air travel began in the 1960s to develop its own aesthetic, about which Andy Warhol enthused: 'Airplanes and airports have [...] my favorite graphics and colors [...].'[3] With the numerous collaborations between airlines and designers, it is likely not surprising that the first comprehensive publication on corporate design was published in 1967 by a graphic designer who had himself helped shape the images of a number of airlines – FHK Henrion.[4]

As the examples of BOAC, Swissair, Pan Am, Lufthansa, KLM, SAS, Braniff, and others below will show, the reasons for the growing importance of the airlines' corporate image lay in technological advances as well as in the resulting new economic and sociocultural contexts. The transformation of corporate design thus seems to be a reflection of general developments in civil aviation. Though the golden age of airline design did not get underway until around 1960, there were already some initial efforts by airlines to create corporate identities both in Europe and in the United States back in the early days of commercial aviation.

The Beginnings

Regular scheduled service in commercial aviation commenced in 1919, when planes, pilots, and airfields were in ample supply following World War I. In France alone, eight airlines were founded, in Switzerland three.[5] The Deutsche Luft Reederei began the first continuous daily national passenger service between Berlin and Weimar, while the aircraft manufacturer Farman offered the first daily international connections between Paris and Brussels. A number of private airlines joined together to form the International Air Traffic Association (IATA) to better coordinate scheduled air service. In the early days of the aviation industry, the expansion of route networks and technological advances were so predominant that matters of design initially played only a minor role.

Beginnings in Europe

At the outset, the airlines in Europe covered different route networks. Overlaps in service were rare. Since the preference was to fly aircraft types manufactured domestically, the fleets themselves differed from one another as well. Hence there was initially little need to

1 Other companies that developed their own corporate design programmes early on were Olivetti, IBM, and Braun.
2 The uniforms of the flight attendants also came under the auspices of corporate design. See Joanne Entwistle's contribution to this volume, 'Fashion Takes Flight'.
3 Andy Warhol, The Philosophy of Andy Warhol (From A to B and Back Again), San Diego, 1977, p. 160.
4 F.H.K. Henrion and Allan Parkin, Design Coordination and Corporate Image, London and New York, 1967.
5 R.E.G. Davies, A History of the World's Airlines, New York and Toronto, 1964, pp. 10 ff.

6 Roosenburg's association with KLM continued on future projects. In 1928/29, he built the first reception building with control tower at Amsterdam's Schiphol Airport and an administration building for the airline in The Hague (1940–1947). See Colin Wells, 'KLM – A History of the Future', *The Image of Company – Manual for Corporate Identity*, ed. F.H.K. Henrion, The Hague, 1990, p. 125. And Dominique Carré, ed., *Berlin Tempelhof, Liverpool Speke, Paris Le Bourget*, Paris, 2000, p. 17.

7 Jérôme Peignot, *Air France Affiches 1933–1983*, Paris, 1988, pp. 41 f. See Amélie Gastaut, 'On Air – Une histoire d'Air France', exhibition brochure from the Musée de la Publicité, Paris, 2003, pp. 4 f.

8 Junkers Luftverkehrs AG was founded in 1924 but had already merged with Luft Hansa by 1926.

9 Michael Geyersbach, 'Wie verkauf' ich meine Tante?' *Corporate Design bei Junkers 1892 bis 1933*, ed. Design Zentrum Sachsen-Anhalt, Dessau, 1996, pp. 17–21.

10 Ibid., p. 62. Incidentally, the corporate emblem of the company Dornier was also created by a painter: Marcel Dornier, the brother of company founder Claude Dornier. In addition, Marcel furnished the Dornier Komet and the flying boat Delphin. See Eduard Hindelang, ed., *Marcel Dornier: Gemälde – Zeichnungen – Grafik*, Sigmaringen, 1983, p. 27.

11 Detlef Siegfried, *Der Fliegerblick – Intellektuelle, Radikalismus und Flugzeugproduktion bei Junkers 1914–1934*, Bonn, 2001, pp. 141 f.

12 The earliest example is the company AEG, which had commissioned the architect Peter Behrens in 1907 to rework and design products, printed materials and exhibitions for the company. See Tilman Buddensieg and Henning Rogge, *Industriekultur. Peter Behrens und die AEG 1907–1914*, Berlin, 1981. Junkers' decision to standardise the design of company propaganda was most likely motivated by two factors: On one hand, the company's various lines of business – aeroplane factory, body supply plant, engine construction and water heater factory – had to be visually recognisable as belonging to one and the same company. On the other, Junkers planes were also being sold abroad in large numbers. The international dissemination of its aircraft certainly helped foster the desire for a uniform corporate image.

13 See F. Robert van der Linden, *Airlines and Air Mail*, Lexington, 2002.

14 Janet R. Daly Bednarek, *America's Airports. Airfield Development, 1918–1947*, College Station, pp. 14 ff.

set oneself apart from other airlines by means of design. Nevertheless, this period saw the creation of the first airline logos, some of which continue to exist to the present day, albeit with some modifications. As advertising director for the Deutsche Luft Reederei, the architect Otto Firle designed the company symbol of a soaring crane in 1918 (**197**). When the company merged with the newly formed Luft Hansa in 1926, the stylised bird emblem was taken over. It has continued to represent the German airline to the present day. KLM, founded in the Netherlands in 1919, used an emblem created by the architect Dirk Roosenburg, a friend of the company's founder Albert Plesman. The intersecting letters KLM were set in a hexagon supported by two wings and capped with a crown (**199**). The right to use the symbol of the crown and the name Koninklijke Luchtvaart Maatschappij was bestowed on the company by Queen Wilhelmine.[6]

In 1933, Air France took on its emblem from Air Orient, one of the four companies that merged to form the new airline. The winged seahorse, originally designed by Couallier, was meant to symbolise strength and speed while also referring to the flying boat tradition of Air Orient (**198**).[7]

One of the most highly stylised design marks created in this period was the 'Speedbird' by the English graphic artist Theyre Lee-Elliott. Designed for Imperial Airways the year of its formation in 1924, the dynamic, modern, arrowhead-like Speedbird was adopted fifteen years later by the British Overseas Airways Corporation (BOAC) when it took over from Imperial Airways. Lee-Elliott continued to design posters for BOAC into the 1940s featuring the design mark he created (**205**).

A high degree of abstraction also characterises the company symbol designed in the mid-1920s by expressionist painter Friedrich Peter Drömmer for Dessau-based Junkers AG and its division Junkers Luftverkehr AG.[8] The figure of the 'flying man' was reduced to basic geometric forms, its outspread arms giving it a certain resemblance to a three-blade propeller (**200**).[9] Junkers' example stands out in that its efforts to shape visual

communication went further than other companies at the time. In his capacity as artistic advisor and advertising director from 1923 to 1933,[10] Drömmer also had the task of standardising the 'propaganda' of the corporation in trade fair presentations and advertising. Even the interior design of the Junkers planes, in particular the design of the lighting conditions and visibility, fell within his area of responsibility.[11] Junkers was thus one of the first companies that sought to create a uniform image.[12]

Beginnings in the United States

While European air transport was directly subsidised in many countries by the respective national governments, state support of the airlines in the United States occurred only indirectly through the awarding of airmail routes.[13] Postal service and the military fostered the construction of airports in communities across the nation.[14] As in Europe, variations in routes offered initially provided sufficient grounds for distinction among the airlines in the United States. Yet when United Airlines, American Airlines, and TWA began in 1930 to offer scheduled transcontinental flights, then lasting 30 to 40 hours, it set the stage for competition.[15] Up to this point, a number of the U.S.-based airlines still each operated with different types of planes, for many of them were contractually bound to certain aircraft manufacturers and their models. Yet when the new Douglas DC-3 was introduced in the fleets of the 'big four' almost simultaneously in the mid-1930s, it marked the beginning of a gradual standardisation of the fleets. It was thus seen as high time for the airlines to find other ways to set themselves apart and create a unique image.[16] From this point on, American Airlines called its aeroplanes 'Flagships', Eastern Air Lines flew the 'Great Silver Fleet', and TWA went under the name 'The Lindbergh Line'.[17] In 1936, United Airlines had commissioned the architect Zay Smith to design a logo in the form of a coat of arms with block stripes in patriotic red, white, and blue (**201**, **202**).[18] Starting in 1940, the airline had its 'Mainliner' fleet uniformly painted white and blue.[19] Pan American

197 With the founding of Luft Hansa in 1926, at Berlin Tempelhof Airport the new name was combined with the symbol of the crane, already designed by Otto Firle in 1918.

198 A 1947 Air France ticket, showing the Air France 'sea horse' design mark. Adopted by the airline in 1933, it was developed earlier by the graphic artist Couallier for Air Orient.

199 KLM's first logo, designed by the architect Dirk Roosenburg in 1919.

198

197

199

200

201, 202 The United Airlines logo, originally designed c. 1936 by the architect Zay Smith, in two variants, on the body of a Douglas DC-3 in the 1940s and on a ticket from 1955.

201

202

15 Competition ensued despite the fact that the airlines used different routes for their coast-to-coast flights well into the 1950s. American Airlines flew the southern route (via Nashville, Dallas and El Paso), United Airlines shuttled between New York and San Francisco via Denver, and Transcontinental and Western Air operated on the route planned by Lindbergh via Pittsburgh, Columbus, St. Louis, Kansas City, and Albuquerque. Davies, *A History of the World's Airlines*, p. 245.
16 Ibid., p.135.
17 Starting in 1928, the popular aviation pioneer Lindbergh had assisted the predecessor company of TWA, Transcontinental Air Transport, in establishing postal and passenger service from coast to coast. Geza Szurovy, *Classic American Airlines*, Osceola, 2000, p. 87.
18 See John Zukowsky, 'Introduction', *Building for Air Travel: Architecture and Design for Commercial Aviation*, Munich and New York, 1996, p. 23. The United Airlines logo made its inaugural appearance in 1936 in the 'Official Aviation Guide', an international index of flight plans. See reprint of the 'Official Aviation Guide', July 1936, p. 17, in Robert J. Serling, *Birth of an Industry*, New York, 1969.
19 Peter M. Bowers, *Boeing Aircraft Since 1916*, London, 1989, p. 208.
20 Szurovy, *Classic American Airlines*, p. 109.
21 Hollywood produced films like *China Clipper* (Ray Enright, 1936) starring Humphrey Bogart and *Bombay Clipper* (John Rawlins, 1942), the fashion industry designed Clipper clothing with a South and Central American flair. William E. Brown Jr., 'Pan Am: Miami's Wings to the World', *The Journal of Decorative and Propaganda Arts*, 23 (1998), p. 154 ff.
22 See Davies, *A History of the World's Airlines*, p. 149. See Duden. *Das Fremdwörterbuch*, Mannheim, 1990.
23 Davies, *A History of the World's Airlines*, p. 398.
24 See Kenneth Hudson and Julian Pettifer, *Diamonds in the Sky: A Social History of Air Travel*, London, 1979, p. 129. In their presentation folder for Lufthansa's corporate design, Otl Aicher and the Entwicklungsgruppe 5 from the HfG Ulm point out this fact: 'Should a company be widely identified with its country of origin due to its standing and global charisma or should it take it upon itself to represent its country, the corporate design is elevated to the level of a cultural mirror.' Hochschule für Gestaltung, Entwicklungsgruppe 5, corporate design of Lufthansa as commissioned by the airline, No. KV 2/420226-9, October 1962, HfG Archive Ulm.
25 Davies, *A History of the World's Airlines*, pp. 112 and 303.

Airways, then the company with the largest route network, christened all its passenger planes with the name 'Clipper', starting with the Sikorsky S-40 flying boat (1931).[20] Pan Am's promotional efforts with the Clippers were so pervasive that 'clipper' – originally a type of sailing vessel from the nineteenth century – became a fashionable term in the 1930s.[21] Just as Pan Am was long regarded in other countries as the American airline, 'clipper' continues to be used as a synonym for an 'American long-range aircraft utilised on overseas routes'.[22]

The Post-War Era: State Airlines as National Representatives

Post-war Europe saw the establishment of new national airlines, like Portugal's Tap (1945) and Italy's Alitalia (1947), as well as the nationalisation of existing ones, like Air France (1945), Finnair (1946), and Swissair (1947). In face of the rising acquisition costs for the ever larger and faster planes, state support was increasingly needed to secure the continued existence of the airlines. Sweden, Norway, and Denmark even allied themselves to form the Scandinavian Airlines System in 1946 as a joint Nordic airline. Having a national airline meant being connected to the world and served as an important national symbol of technological progress. Aviation historian R. E. G. Davies identified admission to the United Nations and establishment of a national airline as the most important prerequisites for a nation's recognition in the world community.[23] The image of an airline was therefore given great significance.[24] One of the first airlines to realise this was the British Overseas Airways Corporation. As the successor to Imperial Airways, it operated the intercontinental routes beginning in 1946, while the newly established subsidiary British European Airways flew the routes within Europe (203, 204).[25]

British Overseas Airways Corporation

'Good design is invisible [...] The employment of a designer is not just a whim of an arty-crafty business

house [...] but a plain fundamental necessity.'[26] This progressive view of design was espoused by BOAC already shortly after the war. The airline saw itself as the representative of its country and its aeroplanes as 'flying industrial fairs'.[27] In a special edition of the magazine *Art and Industry* (May 1947), the airline's design committee presented the new corporate identity policy. The model was the look of London Transport, the city's public transport system, which had set the standards for graphic design in the preceding decades.[28]

For its corporate logo, BOAC took over Lee-Elliott's Speedbird and combined it with the company acronym in the Cyclone font (205, 206).[29] The position of art director in the airline's advertising department went to the graphic artist FHK Henrion, who later also designed the corporate identities of KLM and British European Airways. The colouring of the aeroplane interiors, like that of the Avro Tudor II, was chosen for its suitability for all the destinations within the Empire: dark blue seats and carpeting for 'a comfortable warm feeling' in 'wintry conditions', combined with contrasting white and subdued shades of grey meant to 'give a sensation of refreshing coolness' in the tropics.[30] In-flight tableware, glasses, and cutlery were developed in collaboration with British designers and companies. Here the focus was on practical considerations such as stackability and light weight. Artists designed passenger menus and lunchboxes.

The new design guidelines also affected employee uniforms, the marking of the buses on the tarmac, as well as the waiting rooms in the airports outfitted with furniture especially designed for BOAC. Blue and gold were the predominant colours used. Due to postwar shortages, however, BOAC had to improvise in some areas and was not able to fully implement all its plans.

Swissair

A very different approach to coming up with a new image was taken by Swissair, founded in 1931. In February 1952, the airline held a competition, open to members of the Association of Swiss Graphic Designers

it's a small world by Speedbird

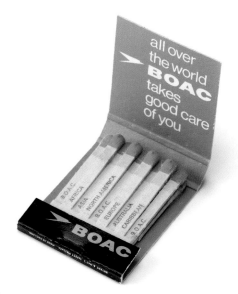

203 A luggage sticker from British European Airways, which in 1946 was founded as a subsidiary of British Overseas Airways Corporation (BOAC). The design mark, 'The Key to Europe', was probably designed by the graphic artist Theyre Lee-Elliot, also the creator of the 'Speedbird'.

204 Ticket, British European Airways, 1957.

205 The Speedbird, the design mark of BOAC, designed by Theyre Lee-Elliot for Imperial Airways in 1924. The trademark is here shown on a 1947 poster by FHK Henrion, the art director of the advertising department at the time.

206 Matchbook, BOAC, late 1960s. Design mark and logo were revised by the Swiss graphic artist Karl Gerstner in 1964. BOAC and BEA would later merge to form British Airways in 1974.

26 Kenneth Holmes, 'Design for Air Travel Service', Art & Industry, special B.O.A.C. issue, 42.251 (May 1947), pp. 148 and 152.

27 Viscount Knolly's, 'Foreword', Art & Industry, ibid., p. 129. See also Frank Jackson, 'The New Air Age: BOAC and Design Policy 1945–60', Journal of Design History, 4.3 (1991).

28 For instance, the London Underground logo as a red circle with a blue bar or the route map for the tube system designed by Harry Beck (1933), which has remained a model for such orientation aids to the present day.

29 Holmes, 'Design for Air Travel Service', p. 144 (see note 26). The logo was updated in the mid-1960s by the Swiss artist and graphic designer Karl Gerstner. See Manfred Kröplien, Karl Gerstner. Rückblick auf 5 x 10 Jahre Graphik Design etc., Ostfildern-Ruit, 2001, p. 147.

30 Holmes, 'Design for Air Travel Service', p. 132.

31 Typescript of the competition announcement, 9 February 1952. Rudolf Bircher Archive.

32 Swissair Propaganda Division, 'Competition for Emblem and Logo for Swissair. Minutes of the Jury Meeting from 16 May 1952', Zurich, 20 May 1952. Rudolf Bircher Archive.

33 Swissair Propaganda Division, 'Competition for Emblem and Logo for Swissair. Minutes of the Jury Meeting from 2 July 1952', Zurich, 5 July 1952. Rudolf Bircher Archive.

34 Bircher's design is notable in that the silhouette with the wings tucked back already corresponds to the form of a jet, years before such aircraft took up regular service in passenger air transport. With the propeller planes standardly flown at the time, the wings were still mounted on the fuselage at almost a right angle.

35 Interview with Rudolf Bircher, 12 December 2003, Zurich.

36 A good overview of Swissair's corporate design is contained in Wolfgang Schmittel, Design Concept Realisation, Zurich, 1975, pp. 197–224.

37 'IFliegt die Swissair richtig?', idee… Zeitschrift für angewandte Kreativität, 5/80, unpag.

38 Robert A. M. Stern et. al., New York 1960: Architecture and Urbanism Between the Second World War and the Bicentennial, Cologne, 1997 (first edition New York, 1995), pp. 381–85.

39 The tenants sharing the building were TWA, United Airlines, Pan American Airways, Eastern Airlines, and American Airlines. David Brodherson, '"An Airport in Every City": The History of American Airport Design', Building for Air Travel, ed. Zukowsky, p. 78.

and a number of personally invited participants, for the creation of a new symbol and a new company logo, Although there were few set specifications, the competition guidelines did stress that the aeroplane was a modern means of transport and that this should be conveyed in the design. Entrants were furthermore instructed they could integrate the Swiss cross in the design.[31] Of the 104 designs submitted, five were anonymously selected for the short list,[32] with the entry from graphic designer Rudolf Bircher eventually being chosen in July.[33] His arrow-like symbol won over the jury with its simplicity and multiple meanings: It could be read as an aeroplane silhouette, as a direction indicator and a symbol for speed while also evoking the Swiss cross (207).[34] Bircher's logo for Swissair picked up on its predecessors. The clear font was also easily legible from some distance, such as on aircraft as they taxied down the runway. It was furthermore easy for repair workshops abroad to correctly apply the lettering to the aeroplane fuselage thanks to the simple design specifications, with the upper and lower edges of the letters running parallel and curvatures appearing as segments of a circle. For the coloured marking of the aeroplanes, Bircher personally took the measurements of the planes on the tarmac himself (208).[35]

Bircher worked over 25 years for Swissair. His efforts encompassed not only the look of printed materials and advertising but also the design of the personnel insignia and the interior furnishings of ticket offices.[36] The arrow logo endured until 1978 when it was replaced by a new design from the Swiss painter and graphic artist Karl Gerstner, whose advertising agency GGK had already been handling the airline's advertising campaigns for a number of years. In a survey, the old logo was still recognised two years later by 85% of the Swiss interviewed.[37]

Ticket Offices

In the 1950s, architecture and interior design began to play an important role in the external presentation of the airlines. The ticket offices were the first point of contact for potential customers, and represented the airlines in cities, especially for the then still predominant portion of the population that had not yet flown in an aeroplane and were at best familiar with airports from Sunday outings to the flight observation deck. In their city centre offices, the companies not only pushed their own services but also promoted tourism in the country they represented. The interior design was frequently handled by renowned architects and designers and was talked about in architecture and interior design magazines. Although the first ticket offices had been opened here and there starting in the 1930s, such as those for Lufthansa, it was only now that a worldwide network of branch offices began to proliferate. One of the most important locations was New York, for the transatlantic connection between the United States and Europe was the prestige object for many airlines. In 1946, Air France was the first non-American airline to open an office in the American metropolis, followed two years later by KLM, Swissair, and BOAC. In 1952, Pan Am was the first American airline on the prestigious Fifth Avenue with an office outfitted by the architects Carson & Lundin.[38]

Back in the 1940s, the five largest American airlines still shared the premises of a building called the 'Airline Terminal', built by John B. Peterkin (1937–1940).[39] Now the ticket offices of the airlines spread along Fifth Avenue to such an extent that an entire section of the boulevard was renamed Airline Alley.[40] Whether El Al (Dvora and Yeheskiel Gad, 1957)[41], Aeronaves de Mexico (Jack Freidin, 1958),[42] or Pakistan International Airlines (Space Design Group, 1962),[43] airlines from all over the world were represented here. An interior design magazine noted in 1968:

Manhattan's most delightful unofficial design competition rages among the foreign airline ticket offices in Fifth Avenue. Strung out between 42nd and 57th Streets like the world's booty on a chain, they strive to outdo each other in eye-pulling bravado and exotic atmosphere, tugging without mercy at the wanderlust urge. The taste is remarkably high for such a showy genre.[44]

207 Layout guide for printed matter for Swissair, using the firm logo designed by Rudolf Bircher, 1950s.

208 Body markings of a DC-8, designed by Rudolf Bircher.

207

208

209 Japan Airlines Office on New York's Fifth Avenue, designed by Antonin Raymond and L.L. Rado, 1958.

210 The interior of Alitalia's New York office, designed by Gio Ponti, 1958.

211 Interior of Air France's London office, designed by Charlotte Perriand, 1957.

212 Plans for the façade and interior of the SAS's Amsterdam city office, c. 1958.

209

210

211

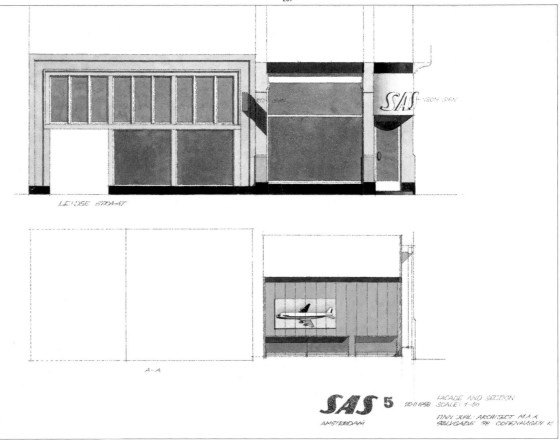

212

In the branch office opened by Japan Airlines in Rockefeller Center in 1958, Antonin Raymond and L.L. Rado installed a gridded backlit wall into which they inserted large-format Japanese landscape shots. Opposite the wall of photos they put up the silhouette of a jet plane with a superimposed drawing of the airline's route network. In the middle of the room, they placed a Japanese table fountain by the artist Junzo Yoshimura (**209**).[45]

The same year, Alitalia commissioned Gio Ponti, the designer and editor of the magazine *Domus*, to handle the interior finishing of their New York office. Ponti primarily employed ceramic elements, which he saw as a material typical of Italy. Tiles in three shades of blue covered the floor, laid out in geometric patterns, with terracotta figures by Fausto Melotti serving as ornamentation and Ponti's elegant Legerezza chairs provided for customers (**210**).[46]

In addition to such individual commissions, some airlines also worked with a particular designer on an ongoing basis to give their offices around the world a uniform appearance. Lufthansa had the architect Rambald von Steinbüchel furnish a number of its ticket offices in the 1950s.[47] And TWA worked with Raymond Loewy, who handled the company's overall corporate design in the period around 1960.

In 1957, Charlotte Perriand received the commission to outfit Air France's London ticket office, having already furnished an entire building for the airline in Brazzaville (1952) in collaboration with Jean Prouvé. Perriand now used a large set of shelves she had designed as a room divider, filling the compartments with handicrafts from Air France destinations around the world (**211**). Two years later she was asked to do the interior furnishing of the office in Tokyo where Perriand mounted a backlit wall-sized photo showing an aerial perspective of the North Pole[48] – an aesthetic allusion to the Air France route between Paris and Tokyo that crossed over the North Pole.

In 1956, SAS commissioned the Danish furniture designer Finn Juhl to design its ticket offices in Europe and Asia. From 1957 to 1961, he was responsible for the furnishing of over 30 SAS offices, providing interiors as

well as refurnishing existing offices (**212**). Here Juhl not only utilised his own mass-produced furniture pieces but also created new office elements. Much to his regret, his proposal to issue a binding handbook for office design was not pursued by SAS,[49] nor was his idea to exhibit works by internationally renowned artists in the airline's branch locations.[50]

Other airlines commissioned works of art especially for their offices. For KLM's New York office, Gyorgy Kepes created an 'electrified wall painting' made of blackened and perforated back-lit aluminium plates meant to convey the look of a metropolis at night from a bird's eye perspective.[51] Along with other artists like Josef Albers, Kepes was also selected to produce a site-specific piece for the lobby of the Pan Am Building in New York, completed in 1963. With the giant Pan Am logo emblazoned on its façade high above New York, the skyscraper put the airline above its peers with regard to self-presentation. The ground floor contained a check-in counter for Pan Am passengers while helicopter service to local airports was offered from the roof through 1977. At the Copenhagen SAS Hotel (built 1955–1960 by Arne Jacobsen), guests were also able to check in right in the middle of the city before being ferried to the airport in courtesy buses.

Finally, another high point in the airlines' self-presentation through architecture was New York's Idlewild Airport (today John F. Kennedy Airport), where the five biggest American airlines had their own terminals built. This solution served to raise the profile of TWA and Pan Am thanks to their spectacular structures, but ultimately proved impracticable for both passengers and the coming airport expansion.

Design for the Jet Age

Between 1951 and 1966, commercial aviation was the fastest growing economic sector in the United States.[52] The field of aviation saw rapid proliferation in Europe as well. With the international expansion of route networks, the establishment of city centre offices

40 Stern et. al., New York 1960, p. 381. See 'Showmanship with Light', *Architectural Forum* 115 (August 1961), p. 12.
41 'Showcase for Travel and Tourism', *Interiors* (June 1957), pp. 102 f.
42 'Aeronaves de Mexico Ticket Office, New York', *Interiors* (September 1958), p. 96.
43 'A Symmetry of Angles and Curves', *Interiors* (November 1962), pp. 120–23.
44 J. A., 'New Accent on Fifth Avenue', *Interiors* (October 1968), p. 130.
45 'Ticket Offices', *Progressive Architecture* 39 (February 1958), p. 158. Betsy Darrach, 'Foretaste of Flight and Destination: Junzo Yoshimura's Ticket Office for Japan Airlines', *Interiors* (June 1957), pp. 106–08.
46 Gio Ponti, 'La nuova sede dell'Alitalia a New York', *Domus* 354 (May 1959), pp. 7–11. See also Lisa Licitra Ponti, *Gio Ponti. The Complete Work 1923–78*, Cambridge, 1990, p. 178.
47 *Lufthansa Nachrichten*, 21 July 1955.
48 'Offices for Air France, London', *Architectural Review*, 124.741 (October 1958), pp. 251–53. Exhibition catalogue of the Musée des Arts Decoratifs Paris, *Charlotte Perriand. Une art de vivre*, Paris, 1985, p. 55.
49 Esbjorn Hiort, *Finn Juhl – Furniture, Architecture, Applied Art*, Copenhagen, 1990, pp. 82 f.
50 Ibid., p. 19 f.
51 'An Office Building Reborn', *Architectural Forum* 112 (January 1960), pp. 119–121.
52 John Mecklin, 'U.S. Airlines: Into the Wild Blue What?', *Fortune* (May 1961), p. 147.

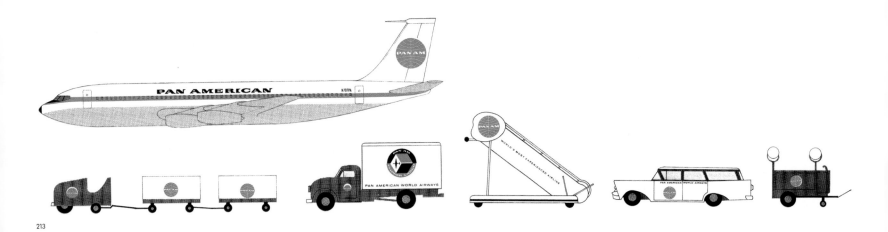

213

around the globe and the tremendous growth in fleet size, airlines increasingly sought to coordinate aspects of design to signal unity and cohesion on an aesthetic level. A further reason for the growing importance of distinctive corporate identities was that the service offerings in international aviation were becoming more and more similar.[53] In the United States, for instance, the domestic routes of the airlines were regulated by the state-run Civil Aeronautics Board up to 1955. The allocation of routes was still partly determined by the so-called 'Grandfather Rights' from the 1930s. When they were finally lifted, this led to a surge in competition among the American airlines.[54] Finally, in the mid-1950s the Jet Age was just around the corner. And many European and American airlines felt it was time for a change in the way they presented themselves, and the lead here was taken by Pan American Airways.

Pan Am

Unsatisfied with its visual identity, Pan American World Airways turned in 1955 to the architect Edward Larabee Barnes as a design consultant.[55] Barnes began with a highly systematic analysis of the status quo: for six months he documented all elements of the company's image encountered by passengers during their travel preparations and the flight itself. Barnes was assisted in this effort by the architect Charles Forberg, who taught product design at Chicago's Institute of Design. The fact that Pan Am entrusted two trained architects with the task of creating a new image shows how new this field of work still was at the time. Nowadays international agencies have long specialised in this area.

Barnes and Forberg replaced the old logo – a winged globe showing the continents – with a stylised light blue globe on which only the degrees of latitude are still suggested as a white lined grid (213). According to Barnes, the symbol was meant to convey 'an impression of space and speed'. The transformation of the company logo over the years can also be seen as a reflection of the development of the airline. In its

inaugural years from 1927 to 1928, the logo was an arrow piercing the letters PAA, an allusion to the pioneer spirit of early aviation. Next, from 1928 to 1944 when Pan American Airways was the only American airline with connections to South America, it was represented by a winged globe showing the landmasses of North and South America. After the route network had been further expanded, the continents of Europe, Africa, and Asia were added as well starting in 1944.[56] Now 'the world's most experienced airline', as its slogan went, finally flew worldwide.

Given that the old company colour, a dark blue, had meanwhile become widespread in air transport, Forberg and Barnes decided to lighten it by a few shades. The company initials PAA, standing for Pan American Airways, were replaced by the catchier Pan Am by which it had long been commonly known. The famous logo was now set in an upright typeface instead of italics. Little by little, these changes were transferred to all printed materials, the fleet of 141 aircraft, and the airline's 153 ticket offices.[57] The check-in area of the Pan Am Building was handled by Barnes and Forberg personally in 1963. Here they created an organically shaped island with elegantly curved walls and a large relief-type map of the world.[58] The furnishings, done in white and light grey, contrasted with the semicircular visitor's benches in a vivid shade of orange.[59]

The exterior and interior design of the new jets – with the chief motivation for the design overhaul having been the entry into the Jet Age – was likewise handled by Barnes and Forberg. In updating the seats for the Boeing 707, they changed small but important details of the upholstery and the footrests. For the design of the seat covers, they commissioned the textile designer Jack Lenor Larsen. Pan Am passengers could henceforth be seen sporting the new logo on specially produced canvas bags and vinyl luggage. The endurance of the logo design attests to its modernity; the logo lasted over thirty years with only minor changes, until 1991 when the airline ceased operations in the wake of passenger air transport deregulation.[60]

53 See Henrion, The Image of a Company, The Hague, 1990, p. 43.
54 Davies, A History of the World's Airlines, 1964, p. 247.
55 B. D., 'Pan American Expresses a new Personality for a New Kind of Travel', Industrial Design (March 1959), p. 32. It was not the trained architect's first contact with aviation, for he had already worked on the cabin design of a Consolidated Vultee aeroplane in the latter half of the 1940s in the office of Henry Dreyfuss. See Russell Flinchum, Henry Dreyfuss. Industrial Designer, New York, 1997, pp. 90 f. (see also the article by Barbara Hauß in this catalogue.
56 'PAA Identification Program', unpag. Pan Am Archive, Otto Richter Library, Miami University, box 213, file 16.
57 'Pan American Gives Itself a "New Look"', press release from Pan American Airways, 20 January 1958. Pan Am Archive, Otto Richter Library, Miami University.
58 Stern et. al., New York 1960, p. 366.
59 Olga Gueft, 'Pan Am's Ticket Office in the Pan Am Building', Interiors 124 (November 1964), pp. 90–93.
60 Zukowsky, Building for Air Travel, p. 135. In 1971, the Pan Am logo was changed to a sans serif typeface and positioned next to the globe. Clipper, 22.16 (16 August 1971).

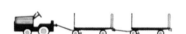

Reisedokumente
Travel Documents

Lufthansa

Cabin

217

214 Ticket, Lufthansa, c. 1961.

215 Baggage sticker, Lufthansa, c. 1960.

216 From the project study 1400 for Lufthansa's corporate image, designed by Otl Aicher and the Entwicklungsgruppe 5, Hochschule für Gestaltung, Ulm, 1962

217 Luggage sticker and ticket, Lufthansa, c. 1970.

218 Project Study 1400, proposed corporate image for Lufthansa, Otl Aicher and the Entwicklungsgruppe 5, Hochschule für Gestaltung, Ulm, 1962. The final markings retained the old white rudder with parabolic field (see 216), and were then replaced in 1967 by a blue rudder with a yellow circular field containing the blue Lufthansa crane.

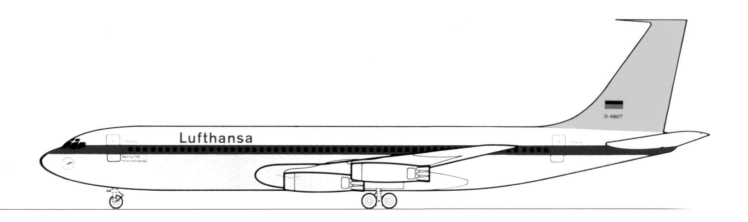

218

159

61 'Lufthansa Corporate Design Rückblick', Deutsche Lufthansa AG, Corporate Design Division, FRAU EC/C-3, October 2001, p. 4. For more information on the history of Lufthansa's corporate design, see also the main topic 'Lufthansa', *Design Report 9* (January 1989), pp. 12–20.
62 See Bernd Franck, '…und wie man sich zeigt, so ist man', *Form Spezial, 2* (1998), p. 69.
63 See 'Erscheinungsbild der Lufthansa', *Ulm – Zeitschrift der Hochschule für Gestaltung*, no. 10/11 (May 1964), pp. 38–49.
64 Otl Aicher, 'Analyse '80', typescript, Hans (Nick) Roericht Archive. Thanks to Hans (Nick) Roericht for referring me to this information.

Lufthansa

The same year that Barnes and Forberg began their work for Pan Am, Lufthansa resumed operations in Germany. Visually it was still represented by Otto Firle's crane, which now soared on a yellow parabola set on a blue background (214, 215). The Lufthansa logo was set in capital letters in shadow italics on aeroplanes, in shadow normal on other vehicles. Created by an anonymous designer this look was nonetheless already consistently implemented from the tail unit to the service vehicles up to the flight ticket and ashtrays for passengers (216).[61] With its entry in the jet era, Lufthansa saw the time had come in the early 1960s to modernise its corporate appearance. The commission was given to Otl Aicher and the Entwicklungsgruppe 5 at the Ulm Hochschule für Gestaltung. In the initial presentation of their concept in 1962, the group – featuring Tomàs Gonda, Fritz Querengässer, Hans 'Nick' Roericht and Alfred Kern – explicitly pointed to Pan Am's corporate design as a model. Bircher's Swissair symbol, then already over ten years old, was also cited by the group as a successful contemporary emblem. The term '*Erscheinungsbild*' as a German equivalent for 'corporate design' – literally 'image of appearance' – was presumably coined at the time by these designers. They defined the term as 'the visual counterpart to the company's own image' – in other words, as a reflection of how the company saw itself. According to their definition, corporate design consisted of the following elements: 'company colours, pictograms, logos, typeface, formats, graphic and typographic rules and norms, style of photography, quality of the carrier materials, packaging, exhibition systems, characteristics of the architecture, forms of the interior décor and equipment, style of the work clothes and uniforms', a definition that was quite far-reaching and comprehensive for its time.

In the new symbol, the soaring crane was enclosed by a circle to emphasise its significance as a brand. Lufthansa clung to the blue-yellow parabola on a white tail unit until 1967 when this was replaced with a crane in a yellow circle on a blue tail unit. The upper part of the aeroplane fuselage was now painted white while the lower half was kept as brightly polished metal, with a blue row of windows in the middle. The new word/design mark was developed using the Helvetica Demibold font and took the place of the old logo with serifs (217, 218).[62] The in-flight tableware was created by Nick Roericht, with menus designed by Otl Aicher.[63]

Aicher's approach was notable in that he explained the outdatedness of the corporate design in light of technological and cultural advances. For instance, he compared earlier corporate emblems to the changing shapes of the aeroplane fuselages and, looking at the tapered silhouette of future supersonic aircraft, concluded that only an arrow logo was suitable as an up-to-date representation of an airline. Yet Lufthansa held on to the crane. When Aicher was commissioned by Lufthansa to evaluate the existing corporate design in 1980, he proposed 'high-tech' as the new cultural model and cited corresponding examples from architecture and design. Silver was the colour of technology, he said, concluding that Lufthansa aeroplanes should henceforth be painted all silver.[64]

Cabin design

With the Boeing 707 and the Douglas DC-8 on long-distance flights and the French Caravelle on short routes, jet planes began to dominate air transport worldwide in the early 1960s. Their international dissemination soon led to a high degree of standardisation among the airline fleets. As the use of jets was primarily profitable on long hauls, airlines that had previously only offered national connections now began to offer international service as well. Jets thus fostered the expansion of route networks, which inevitably brought about greater overlaps in service. In face of such diminishing distinctiveness, airlines increasingly sought to set themselves apart from the competition through individually designed cabin interiors. The possibilities, however, were limited in this regard:

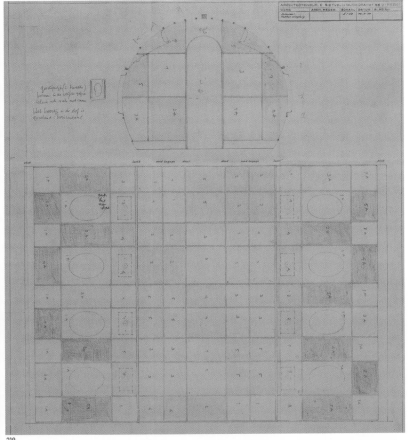
219

219 A colour scheme for the cabin of the Fokker F.27 Friendship, designed by Gerrit Rietveld.

220 Study, colour design of the lounge in KLM's Lockheed Electra, Gerrit Rietveld, no date [1957].

221 Study, colour design of the seats in KLM's Douglas DC-3, Gerrit Rietveld, 1958.

222 Interior, model Fokker F.27 Friendship showing Gerrit Rietveld's colour scheme.

223 Study, colour design for a dividing cabin wall in KLM's Douglas DC-8, Gerrit Rietveld, no date [1958].

222

220

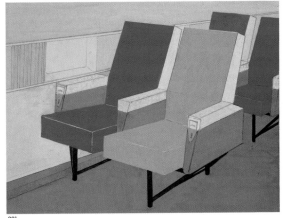
221

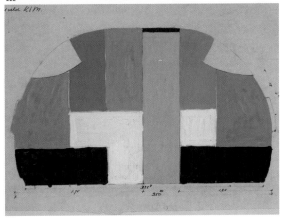
223

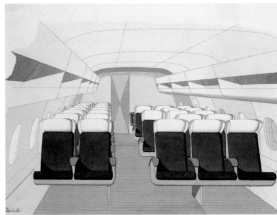

224

225

226

An an unalterable given was not simply the narrow, elongated shape of the cabin, which left little room for experimentation. From the luggage rack up to the seats, the design of the fixtures was largely determined by the manufacturer. Most designers thus primarily focused on the colour scheme of plane interiors.

KLM led the way here. Starting in the mid-1950s, the Dutch considered equipping all their fleet's planes with colour-coordinated interiors.[65] In 1955, the architect and designer Gerrit Rietveld was commissioned by the Dutch aircraft manufacturer Fokker to develop a colour scheme for the Fokker F.27 Friendship (**219**). To mute the tube effect of the fuselage, the wall and ceiling covering were articulated by a grid of rectangles in alternating colours. He employed the same colours for the covers of the seat backs. Based on several colour variants Rietveld had proposed, a mock-up of the cabin was built followed by a prototype of the plane (**222**). At approximately the same time, Rietveld was commissioned by KLM to present proposals for the interior colour scheme of the Lockheed Electra (**220**), and the Douglas DC-3 (**221**), DC-7C, and DC-8 (**223**). Here as well, he experimented with various colour schemes: using coloured lozenge and kidney-shaped patterns for the lounge of the Lockheed Electra and geometric patterns reminiscent of DeStijl for the cabin partitions of the DC-8. Unfortunately these ideas never progressed beyond sketches and draft drawings.[66]

In contrast, more tangible results were achieved by the cooperation between SAS and Finn Juhl who, as mentioned above, also outfitted the ticket offices of the airline. About the same time, he received the commission to design the interior of the first SAS DC-8 jets. In December 1956, he travelled to the Douglas plant in the United States with Rune Monö, the airline's artistic advisor since 1946, to view a mock-up of the DC-8 cabin.[67] Juhl planned to replace Douglas' standard seats with special revolving units to enable a flexible seating arrangement. Based on his design, SAS had twelve samples produced and installed in a cabin mock-up. Due to lack of time and details that were not

65 Wells, 'KLM – A History of the Future', p. 125 (see note 6).

66 Ludo van Halem, 'Kleur tussen hemel en aarde. De vliegtuiginterieurs van Gerrit Rietveld (1955-58)', *Jong Holland* (February 1995), pp. 44–61 (English summary, p. 87).

67 Rune Monö had designed the cabin interior of the Douglas DC-7, described in a magazine article as 'pleasantly Scandinavian'. 'Interiors contract series '57', *Interiors* (June 1957), p. 121.

68 Hiort, *Finn Juhl – Furniture, Architecture, Applied Art*, pp. 84 f.

69 Tuula Poutasuo, 'Futurism and Everyday Goods', in Marianne Aav , ed., *Tapio Wirkkala – Eye, Hand and Thought*, Porvoo, 2000, p. 201. For information on Tapiovaara's proposals for the exterior colour schemes, see John Wegg, *Bluebirds*, Helsinki, 1985, p. 65.

70 Ibid., p. 201. Illustration in John Wegg, *The Art of Flying since 1923*, Helsinki, 1983, p. 136 f. The Aero Oy logo on the fuselage was superseded at the time by a blue cross on a white background. The new logo – a stylised aeroplane whose tail fin formed an F – was created in 1968.

71 See the essay in this volume by Joanne Entwistle.

72 P. G., 'Multi-Colored Fly-By Look: A Labyrinth of Luxus', *The News*, Mexico City. (10 November 1965).

73 'Braniff Reports Record Revenues and Traffic', *B-Liner*, 17.2 (February 1966). See 'The Airlines Striking Figures', *Fortune* (15 June 1967), p. 287.

yet fully developed, however, such as the integration of the ventilation nozzles, reading lamps and fold-down trays, the seats did not go into production. Juhl was left to handle the design of the galley, closets, toilets, and the lounge in First Class (**224, 225**).[68]

In its work with Robin Day, BOAC also selected a renowned native designer as a style advisor. He outfitted the lounge of the BOAC Stratocruiser, designed a new colour scheme for the Comet 4 in 1961, and reworked the interior furnishings of the Super VC10. While his work on these models was primarily limited to the colouring, he was also able to influence seat design for the VC10 (**226**).

Finnair placed the design of the interiors and fuselage markings of its first Caravelles in the hands of the Finnish interior designer Ilmari Tapiovaara.[69] The first of Finnair's Douglas DC-8 planes were christened *Jean Sibelius* and *Paavo Nurmi* and put into service in 1969 on the Helsinki–New York transatlantic route. It was likened to a flying exhibition of Finnish applied art: the interior and fuselage markings, textile place mats and seat covers were all from Finnish designers. For the flight attendants, Kari Lepistö designed 'space-style' uniforms.[70]

Braniff International Airlines

The most radical and comprehensive visual makeover was pursued by U.S.-based Braniff International Airlines, which flamboyantly heralded in 1965 'The end of the plain plane' (**227**). Deeming planes with silver or white fuselage monotone and outdated, the slogan issued from Mary Wells, who had conceived the accompanying campaign and soon thereafter rose to become the most prominent female advertising professional in the US. It was the leitmotif for the work of the designer Alexander Girard (**229**). The trained architect had the aeroplanes of the Braniff fleet – the entire fuselage, except for the wings and the tail unit – painted in one of seven different colours: two shades of blue, two beige tones, yellow, orange, and mint (**228**). The colourful jets immediately caught the eye on the

runway and led the company to proudly announce: 'You can fly Braniff International seven times and never fly the same color aircraft twice!' For the markings on the aeroplanes, for tickets, luggage stickers, menus, and stationery, Girard developed an elegantly curved font; the letters 'BI' in this font constituted the new logo (**231**). The 'Golden Bird' Girard had originally envisioned for the logo was utilised for flight attendant lapel pins and on the company stationery (**230**).

In the aeroplane interior, the seat covers picked up the respective exterior colour of the plane and provided variety through the use of complementary colours and six different patterns. Here Girard was able to draw on his experience as artistic director for the textile division of furniture producer Herman Miller.

Girard's work did not, however, remain limited to aeroplanes and printed materials for the company. He also designed the interiors of Braniff's waiting rooms and furnished them with handicraft pieces from his personal collection whose origins alluded to the airline's South American destinations. Similar motifs were used on advertising posters for the airline. In addition, Girard designed sofas and armchairs for the Braniff lounges (**232**). The chair shells swing upward on both sides and then turn out, wing-like, parallel to the floor. The manufacturer Herman Miller later made them available for sale to the general public.

Another significant coup for Braniff was engaging the Italian couturier Emilio Pucci to design the new flight attendant outfits.[71] To even further boost the easy recognition of the airline at airports, ground personnel and mechanics were given new uniforms as well (**228**).

The advertising campaign, for which Braniff doubled the annual budget, today seems to be an early forerunner of event marketing. For the unveiling of the new corporate identity, 120 journalists were flown to Acapulco where they were wined and dined for several days.[72] The effort paid off. From coast to coast, the American dailies ran stories on the extravagant airline for the new jet set, contributing to a 58% rise in the company's stock value that year.[73]

227 Braniff International promoted its new image in 1965 using advertisements designed by Mary Wells.

228 Braniff's New Look. The photograph shows ground personnel in new uniforms by Emilio Pucci as well as service vehicles and a plane in the new colours.

The end of
the plain plane.

227

229 Alexander Girard presenting the new logo of Braniff International, 1965.

230 The Golden Bird, designed by Girard for Braniff, was used as a lapel pin.

231 The tickets were also designed by Alexander Girard. The checkerboard pattern was repeated in the seat coverings in the aeroplanes and lounges.

232 Braniff's lounges were outfitted with furniture especially designed for this purpose by Girard.

229

230

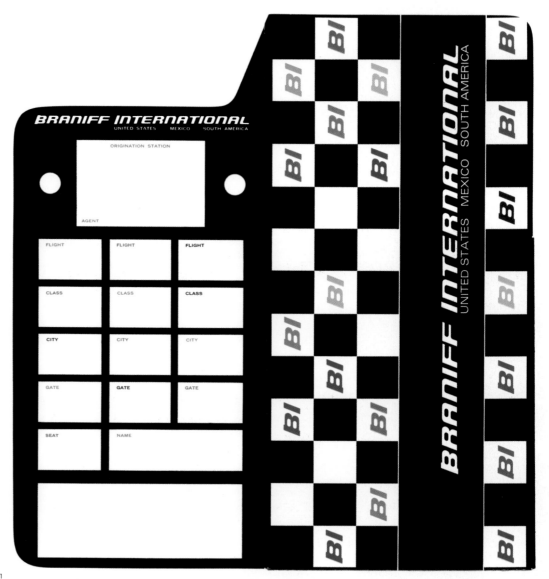

231

74 'Design News from Loewy Associates', undated (October 1960), Hagley Museum & Library, Acc. 225, Lot 212, Box 31A, File TWA 1960. See Hans Weckerle, 'Typographer as Analyst', *Design*, 240 (December 1968), pp. 42 f.

75 For the airline's new logo, he took the block letters TWA, lightened the colour and superimposed them on two golden interlocking globes.

76 'Eastern Airlines' New Look', *Industrial Design*, November 1966, p. 45.

77 'New Look for the Astrojets', *Astrojet News*, (21 April 1969), p. 12. Henry Dreyfuss Papers, Cooper-Hewitt, National Design Museum.

78 Wells, 'KLM – A History of the Future', p. 127.

79 Henrion, *The Image of Company*, p. 28.

80 Jackson, *Robin and Lucienne Day. Pioneers of Modern Design*, p. 182.

81 For information on F. H. K. Henrion's design for BEA, see Galerie Intergraphic, ed., *Design Systeme für Internationale Unternehmen – Henrion Design Associates London*, exhibition brochure, Munich, 1971, unpag.

82 Back in 1946, Rune Monö designed the first SAS symbol with the emblems of the three founding nations, superimposed by the letters SAS. See Knut Hagrup, *The Making of SAS – A Triumvirate in World Aviation*, Stockholm, 1973, fig. 2. The exterior design of the planes was also handled by Monö.

83 Kröplien, *Karl Gerstner. Rückblick auf 5 x 10 Jahre Graphik Design etc.*, p. 147 (see note 29).

84 Gastaut, 'On Air – Une histoire d'Air France', p. 12 (see note 71).

Word and Design Figurative Marks

As previously shown emblems can be divided into word and design marks. Word marks convey the company name as a characteristic logo and have the advantage that they simultaneously constitute the brand name. Design marks, on the other hand, represent the company by means of an image that has to be familiar to viewers to be associated with the company name. The advantage of design marks is that they are usually quicker to grasp visually and capable of conveying multiple meanings.

A small number of iconographic motifs predominate among the airline design marks: the globe as a symbol for the worldwide network of the airlines (TWA (**234**), Pan Am); the arrow as an expression of speed (Swissair, the early logos of TWA (**233**) and Pan Am); and finally the bird expressing the idea that 'flying is our nature' (the American Airlines eagle (**237**), the Eastern Airlines falcon (**235**), the Lufthansa crane, the BOAC Speedbird). Comparing the design marks of the airlines and their transformation over the decades, an increasing abandonment of figurative motifs and a tendency toward abstraction and simplification can be seen: 'The bird, arrows, clouds, planes appeared repeatedly. Interestingly, the more literal, the more realistic the interpretation of these devices the less powerful its impact. For example, the least successful bird symbols showed the entire bird with feathers and eye and beak in almost photographic representation; the most impressive reduced the bird to a bird-symbol, a wing perhaps, and reduced the bird-symbol to a simple graphic or stylistic form.'[74] When Raymond Loewy made this statement, he had himself just developed a new corporate design for TWA.[75] His hypothesis is borne out by such examples as the development at Eastern Air Lines, whose falcon was replaced by the agency Lippincott & Margulies in 1966 with an abstract, arrow-like symbol framed in a blue oval (**236**).[76] The American Airlines eagle was also due for a replacement, according to Henry Dreyfuss who worked on the airline's new image in 1969. Yet after protests by numerous employees, it was retained – albeit in stylised form (**238**).[77]

The move toward the simplification and reduction of logos was based on the assumption that people abridge everything they see to simple basic forms when stored in their memory:[78] the simpler the form, the more memorable the logo. To modernise design marks, it was therefore common practice in the 1960s to take out-of-focus photos of them and use that to develop the simplified form from the blurred contours. Such was the method adopted by FHK Henrion when creating the new crown for KLM, which has endured to the present day (**239**).[79] The simplified forms were also supposed to guarantee optimal recognition when seen from a distance and in motion. This was important above all for plane markings on the runway. In photos and especially in the new medium of television, the design marks had to likewise be easily recognised.[80]

To establish their company names as a word marks as well, many airlines developed their own fonts that, despite their individual distinct character, were also subject to the typographic fashions of the time. Initially favoured were italic typefaces, with a slant making them appear more dynamic – such as in the case of KLM, BOAC, or BEA (**240, 241, 242**).[81] The SAS logo developed by Rune Monö in the 1950s was also slanted (**243**).[82] In the 1960s, the italicised fonts were gradually discarded in the word marks: The windswept letters of Pan Am were straightened, Karl Gerstner gave BOAC a non-italicised bold typeface in 1964 (**206**)[83] and Henrion shifted KLM upright. For Air France, Roger Excoffon developed the font Antique Olive.[84] At the same time, Antiqua fonts were increasingly being replaced by sans serif grotesk typefaces. A particular favourite was Helvetica, which the Entwicklungsgruppe 5 had introduced at Lufthansa; this font was also adopted by American Airlines in the 1960s and Pakistan International Airways and British Airways in the 1970s.

Airline Corporate Design Today

History shows that there is a fine line between the trademark modernisation and the loss of visual

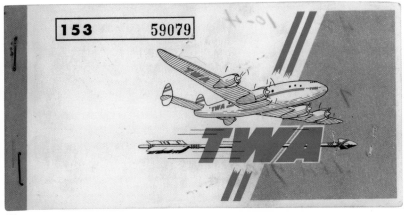

153   59079

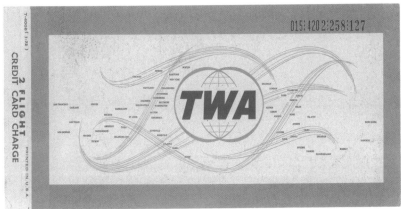

233

233 A 1946 TWA ticket with the arrow logo, which dates from the pioneering years of the company.

234 A 1978 TWA ticket with the firm logo designed in 1960 by Raymond Loewy.

235 Eastern Air Lines luggage sticker, 1960s.

236 Eastern Air Lines logo by Lippincott & Margulies, 1966.

237 Luggage sticker, American Airlines, 1960s.

238 American Airlines logo with stylised eagle, Henry Dreyfuss, 1969.

234

235

236

EASTERN

237

238

239

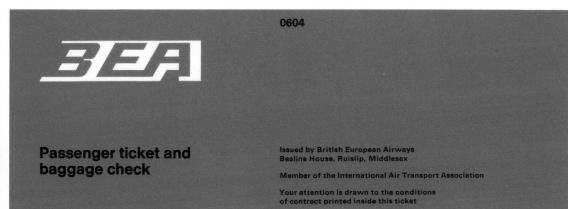

0604

BEA

**Passenger ticket and
baggage check**

Issued by British European Airways
Bealine House, Ruislip, Middlesex

Member of the International Air Transport Association

Your attention is drawn to the conditions
of contract printed inside this ticket

240

BEA
cabin baggage

BEA
Sovereign Service

cabin
baggage

BEA

cabin baggage

241

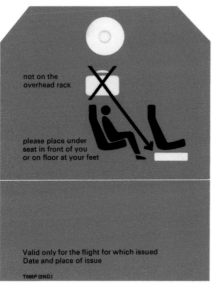

not on the
overhead rack

please place under
seat in front of you
or on floor at your feet

Valid only for the flight for which issued
Date and place of issue

T666P (2ND)

BEA

**Flugplan
International**   13

**Deutsche Ausgabe Winter 1972/73
1. November 1972 — 31. März 1973**

242

240 In 1967, Henrion Design Associates also designed the new corporate image of British European Airways, using the font Helvetica.

241 Samples of BEA baggage tags from the corporate design handbook, Henrion Design Associates.

242 German flight plan, BEA, 1973. The logo was also the work of Henrion Design Associates.

243 Rune Monö, sketch for the body markings of a Convair CV-440 Metropolitan, introduced in 1956 at SAS.

244 Stockholm Design Lab's body markings for the Boeing 730-600 at SAS, 1998.

243

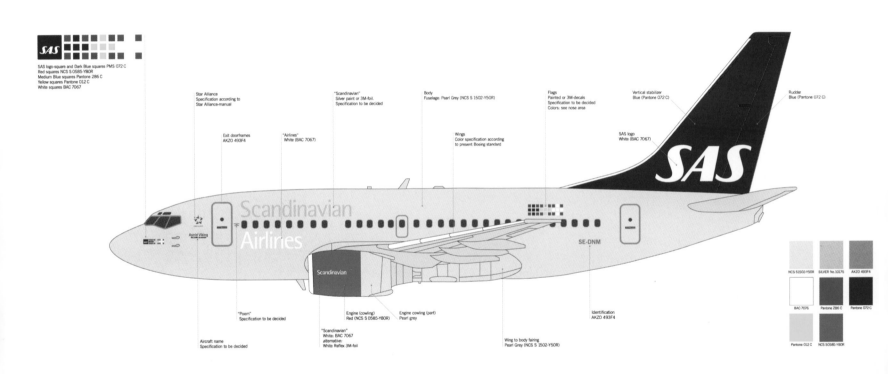

SAS logo-square and Dark Blue squares PMS 072 C
Red squares NCS S 0585-Y80R
Medium Blue squares Pantone 286 C
Yellow squares Pantone 012 C
White squares BAC 7067

Star Alliance
Specification according to
Star Alliance-manual

Exit doorframes
AKZO 493F4

"Airlines"
White (BAC 7067)

"Scandinavian"
Silver paint or 3M-foil.
Specification to be decided

Body
Fuselage: Pearl Grey (NCS S 1502-Y50R)

Wings
Color specification according
to present Boeing standard

Flags
Painted or 3M-decals
Specification to be decided
Colors: see nose area

SAS logo
White (BAC 7067)

Vertical stabilizer
Blue (Pantone 072 C)

Rudder
Blue (Pantone 072 C)

Scandinavian
Airlines

Astrid Viking

Scandinavian

SE-DNM

"Poem"
Specification to be decided

Aircraft name
Specification to be decided

"Scandinavian"
White: BAC 7067
alternative:
White Reflex 3M-foil

Engine (cowling)
Red (NCS S 0585-Y80R)

Engine cowling (part)
Pearl grey

Wing to body fairing
Pearl Grey (NCS S 1502-Y50R)

Identification
AKZO 493F4

NCS S1502-Y50R | SILVER No.10175 | AKZO 493F4

BAC 7076 | Pantone 286 C | Pantone 072 C

Pantone 012 C | NCS S0585-Y80R

244

245

246

245 The business class seating on Swiss International Air Lines, designed in 2002 by the Swiss product designer Patrick Lindon and the textile designer Caroline Flueler.

246 Tyler Brûlé and his agency Wink Media designed the logo for the newly founded Swiss International Air Lines in 2001.

85 See Claire Dowdy, 'Join the Mile High Club', Design Week, 11.4 (26 January 1996), p. 8. And Dowdy, 'Davies Baron's Aviation Jobs Reach Dizzy Heights', Design Week, 11.20 (17 May 1996), p. 8.
86 Jocelyn Thompson, 'Airline Distinctions', Design, 327 (March 1976), p. 48.
87 SAS Identity Manual, 1 June 1999.
88 'The SAS Lounges', undated SAS brochure. See also Stephanie Schmidt, 'Duschbad in der Business-Lounge', Design Report (February 2002), p. 70 f.
89 See Andreas Spaeth, 'Die Marke soll nicht trendy sein', interview with Tyler Brûlé, Design Report (April 2002), pp. 60 f.
90 Chris Winteler, 'Neue Foulards und mehr zu essen', Tages-Anzeiger, 27 (March 2002), p. 35.
92 Claire Dowdy, 'New Budget Airline to Boldly Go', Design Week, 13.5 (6 February 1998), p. 8.
93 Ibid. Only the budget airline JetBlue, founded in 2000, aims to set itself apart from the competition 'through its image and not through ticket prices'. Steffan Heuer, 'Economy Class', brand eins, 4.1 (February 2002), p. 33.

individuality. In the 1970s, the greater abstraction of the logos led to an increasingly similar look among some airlines, making it harder and harder to tell them apart. A reason for this tendency may have been that corporate designs were being developed more and more by internationally active agencies like Landor Associates, Negus & Negus, and Wolff Olins, with client lists including various airlines.[85] For instance, Landor Associates developed the corporate design for British Airways (1973) as well as for AirEurope, Alitalia, British Midland, Canadian Airlines, Delta, and Varig.

Formed by airlines for economic reasons since the 1990s, the international alliances have also contributed to the loss of distinctiveness in the visual identities. The airline ticket offices that played such a big role in the golden age of aviation have become almost irrelevant. Bookings are made online, over the phone, or directly in the travel agency as part of a package offer. At airports, airlines have limited possibilities for staging their corporate identities. Starting in the late 1960s, airports began placing more weight on uniform interior design and stringent orientation systems, and developed corporate design programmes of their own. Nowadays the only place where airlines can present a comprehensive image is in their lounges for First and Business Class passengers. On the runways, the planes are supplied by the service vehicles of the respective airport. The marking of the aeroplanes is subject to stringent IATA regulations regarding the dimensions of the lettering and the paint's degree of reflection.[86]

The tickets, which were still individually designed into the 1970s, now all possess the same computer-generated appearance, and those who book over the Internet or fly last minute just get handed the boarding card at the airport. Gone are the days of lovingly designed ticket pouches that, in addition to the flight ticket, also contained information on itinerary and destinations as well as currency exchange tables and airmail stationery with the airline's emblem.

Despite all these limitations, recent years have seen some positive examples of newly developed corporate design programmes. For the current corporate image of SAS, Stockholm Design Lab alluded to the tradition of Scandinavian design, characterised by simplicity and informal elegance. The graphic look is correspondingly clear and orderly. The design team worked with a combination of text and photos by renowned Scandinavian photographers, chiefly featuring landscape shots and nature motifs. Selected printed matter, products, and the aeroplane fuselages are imprinted with couplets somewhere between poetry and pathos, intended to build a personal connection with the customer (244).[87] The bright, comfortably furnished lounges are characterised by natural materials like wood and stone. Here the airline even exhibits pieces of contemporary art in a collaboration with the Stockholm Moderna Museet.[88]

Switzerland's new airline Swiss International Air Lines, which began operating flights in March 2002, commissioned Wallpaper magazine founder Tyler Brûlé to develop its inaugural corporate image.[89] With his agency Wink Media, Brûlé put the focus on elegance, understatement and 'Swissness'. Two red squares with the white logo and Swiss cross constitute the new design mark (246). The aeroplane fleet is painted white except for the Swiss cross on a field of red on the tail unit. Next to the English 'Swiss', the word appears in the four Swiss national languages.[90]

With many of the budget airlines like Ryan Air or Air Berlin that have operated with growing success in recent in years, corporate image no longer plays much of a role. Tickets are almost exclusively booked via Internet. There are no sales offices of bricks-and-mortar. Many of these airlines were founded by entrepreneurs with a highly pragmatic perspective on the topic of corporate design. With easyJet.com, the garish orange word mark created by company founder Stelios Haji-Ioannou thus simultaneously indicates where the airline can be found on the Internet.[92] Referred to as 'no frills airlines', this focus on the basics is also communicated by their design, intentionally keeping passenger expectations low regarding comfort and service. Here, the design of the price is all that matters.[93]

FASHION TAKES FLIGHT: THE AIR STEWARDESS AND HER UNIFORM

JOANNE ENTWISTLE

By taking up this challenge, my desire is to invent a new universe, a cross between two worlds which are strongly associated with dreams, the world of flight and the world of fashion.

— Christian Lacroix, speaking about his contract to design Air France's uniform in 2003[1]

Fashion is a child of modernity, concerned with incessant change and modification. While on the one hand playful, frivolous and fickle, it can also be loaded with meaning: fashion speaks of the desires and characteristics of a modern life that is restless and always in flux. It thus does not usually feature as an aspect of business or corporate culture, which is characterised by a seriousness of purpose and an inherent conservatism. However, fashion has been a feature of airline uniforms (as well as other aspects of airline design) since the 1940s and 1950s, and since then numerous airlines have called upon prominent fashion designers to design uniforms for their airborne employees.

Why have airline companies called upon fashion so consistently, and what does this use of fashion have to say about the way these companies represent themselves? In particular, why is it that whenever airlines feel they need to 'update' their image, this image is always embodied by the female flight attendant in her fashionable new uniform? The simple answer is that it makes good business sense for both designers, who find the relationship very lucrative, and airlines, obtain company cachet and status by using a named designer. For a more complex answer to the question, however, one can turn to Lacroix's words above for some clues. As he eloquently puts it, the two worlds of flight and fashion are very 'strongly associated' in that they capture the dreamlike nature of the modern world. Considering that there is hardly a business more emblematic of modernity than the airline industry, the marriage of fashion to flight makes sense in terms of the similar cultural associations of glamour, adventure, and romance that both enjoy. Thus, an analysis of fashion

and flight needs to examine the historical and cultural context within which they have developed and look at the meanings their union has produced over the course of twentieth century modernity.

From its very beginnings, air travel has captured the imagination, with Hollywood films such as *Air Hostess* (Al Rogell, 1933) and *Flying Hostess* (Murray Roth, 1936) playing to audiences in the early years of popular cinema.[2] The latter film deals quite accurately with the process by which airlines chose and trained their stewardesses, an indication, perhaps, of an early fascination with the young women whose jobs it is to serve passengers on aeroplanes. However, it was during the period from 1945 to the present that both fashion and air travel grew exponentially and came to be more and more intimately linked. The post-war era was a golden age of air travel during which time not only were more people travelling by air, but the idea and *image* of air travel took hold to become associated with all the glamour and romance of twentieth-century modernity.

It was over this same time period that fashionable clothing became widely available to more people than ever before and came to represent a slice of glamour and sophistication that could be readily purchased by all. In this way, the second half of the twentieth century provided the conditions for the marriage of fashion and air travel, in which fast developing mass consumerism, aided by processes of globalisation and increasing media saturation, stimulated consumer desire for modern adventure and experimentation. Indeed, it was not just in the *consumption* of air travel and fashionable clothing that this version of modernity manifested itself, but in the forms of *production* they generated. Both fashion and air travel opened up a new occupation and new opportunities for young women, and with these associations of glamour and excitement.

Two iconic figures, namely the fashion model and air stewardess, came to represent the new freedoms of post-war modernity for women and were especially significant in the 1960s. These occupations were the

1 Christian Lacroix quoted in Spring 2003, www.vogue.co.uk/daily/story/story.asp?stid=7963&sid=102.
2 James H. Farmer, *Celluloid Wings. The Impact of Movies on Aviation*, Shrewsbury, 1984, pp. 92 and 96.

3 Trudy Baker and Rachel Jones, *Coffee, Tea, or Me? The Uninhibited Memoirs of Two Airline Stewardesses*, New York, 1968, p. 8.
4 Alice Hughes, 'Stewardesses Pert and Pretty', *Muncie Indiana Star*, 21 August 1959.
5 This was true for other branches as well who tried to use the glamour of air travel and the stewardess for their advertising. In 1965 more than 20 different companies incorporated the name Lufthansa or the Flying Crane into their campaigns, including manufacturers of women's hosiery who had the photo model Heide Rose dress up as Lufthansa-Stewardess to advertise its 'Arwa Vita 2000', much to Lufthansa's chagrin. 'Lufthansa: Bis zur Taille', *Der Spiegel* 44 (27 October 1965).

aspiration of the new 'Swinging' generation, demanded youthful good looks, a slender figure, grace, and poise, and were featured heavily in popular representations of young women. By the 1960s they had become an important factor in society; perhaps not in sheer numbers – although the population of airborne labour certainly did rise astronomically with the expansion of flight – but certainly in the symbolic and cultural value invested in them, as they came to play a central role in magazines, newspapers, films and advertisements at the time. The 1967 bestseller *Coffee, Tea or Me?: The Uninhibited Memoirs of Two Airline Stewardesses* brought together all the elements of the 1960s stewardess: glamour, freedom, and uninhibited sexuality, associations that were captured by her portrayal in a sexy, revealing uniform. The following description, supported by Bill Wenzell's sexy iconographic cartoon images, vividly captures the air of frivolity central to this wildly popular book:

We turned to see the flashing white teeth, flaming red hair and remarkable upthrust bosom of Betty O'Riley, better known to her classmates at stewardess college as Betty Big Boobs. Betty bounced and jiggled over to us, her smile as programmed and precise as roadway neon sign. 'My flight's been cancelled 'causa weather in Atlanta.' She kept smiling and whispered, looking around to insure privacy, 'But ah'm goin' to dinner with the captain. He models for cigarette commercials, sometimes.'[3]

1960s films repeatedly underscored the link between the stewardess and cosmopolitan fantasies of sexuality, sometimes for the purposes of comedy. In the Hollywood film *Boeing Boeing* (John Rich, 1965) a journalist (Tony Curtis) maintains love affairs with three stewardesses of different airlines (247, 248). When faster airliners are introduced, his 'flight schedule of love' begins to get out of hand, and his friend (Jerry Lewis) needs to help out. In another example, Francois Truffaut's *La Peau douce* [*The Soft Skin*] (1964), a well known publisher (Jean Desailly) has an affair with a stewardess of Pan American Grace Airways while on business trips (249). With their high cultural status, ability

to dress fashionably, travelling careers, and regular contact with affluent men, who in turn saw them as 'trophy wives', these young women were also in a position to 'marry well'. Thus, both careers opened doors to the lucrative end of the marriage market: as one journalist summed it up, 'Two careers which, more than any others, are said to catapult girls into marriage, are those of fashion models and air stewardesses'.[4] This theme also inspired many films of the period. In *Come Fly With Me* (Henry Levin, 1963) three stewardesses, Donna, Bergie and Carol of flight 403 from Paris to New York, each find an admirer in a pilot, a baron, and a millionaire, and after all sorts of confusion, in the end a man for life (250). In the romantic comedy *Ein Engel auf Erden* [*Angel on Earth*] (Geza von Radvanyi, 1959) Romy Schneider plays a double role. Acting as the guardian angel of race driver Pierre Chaillot (Henry Vidal), she tries to convince him not to marry his rich but mean fiancée, but rather fall in love with a stewardess who is secretly in love with him (251). It is, therefore, hardly surprising that during the 1950s and 1960s the occupation of air stewardess became almost as desirable as any job on offer to women at the time. It afforded the appearance, if not quite the reality, of a life of glamour and sophistication, combined with a promise of freedom from the restraints of family and tradition and travel to far-flung places, offering up a whole world of new and potentially exotic (even erotic) experiences.

All of this was captured in the iconography of the stewardess and contributed to making her a figure of considerable desire. Not only was she a figure of aspiration for many young women and a sexual fantasy for many men, she was also a marketable commodity for airline companies. Indeed, airlines were quick to tap into the iconic power of the 'air stewardess' (or 'hostess' as she was sometimes called) and her gendered characteristics, namely her supposedly 'natural' feminine abilities to calm and care for people, as well as her polish, glamour, sexuality and beauty; these became crucial selling points in a competitive market.[5] As sociologist Arlie Hochschild has argued forcefully in her detailed

247, 248 Stills from John Rich, *Boeing Boeing*, 1965.

249 Still, François Truffaut, *La Peau douce* [*The Soft Skin*], 1964.

250 *Illustrierte Film-Bühne* advertising the German release of Henry Levin's *Come Fly with Me*, 1963.

247

248

249

250

251 Still from Geza van Radvanyi,
Ein Engel auf Erden [An Angel on Earth], 1959.

251

study of air stewards entitled *The Managed Heart,* airline corporations have always invested heavily into the bodily attributes of their employees who are on the 'front-line' between the company and the customer.[6] In various combinations, the attributes of the flight attendant – her smile, good manners, charm, and sex appeal – have served to embody the service itself rather than being incidental to it.

However, in a culture that places greater emphasis upon female embodiment than the male body, it is the physical appearance of the female flight attendant that has been and continues to be seen as a commodity by airlines, and images of her rather than her male counterpart are still more frequently used in advertising iconography. She must, therefore, work to manage her appearance along with her emotions to project the appropriate image for her job. The smile, face, and body that so often epitomise the marketing campaigns of airlines serve to personify the airline and are used to project its image.[7] The changing nature of her uniform and its particular relationship to fashionable dress of the day tells the story of how the stewardess has been represented. How have these themes of femininity, sexuality, and service informed the design of her uniform?

If in the early inter-war years of commercial air travel, the air stewardess only played a small walk-on part, after 1945 she would become the major character, if not the star. Not pilots, but stewardesses in their smart and fashionable uniforms provide some of the most enduring iconic representations of air travel in the post-war era. It is in the heady days of post-war aviation that all the ingredients for the stereotype of the air stewardess, that still linger today, were first laid out.

Throughout the 1920s, passenger service was provided exclusively by male stewards or even co-pilots. The first women began working on board aeroplanes in the 1930s, but the early, inter-war years of commercial aviation produced an image of the stewardess quite different to that of today. When in 1930 Boeing Air Transport Company, later amalgamated into United Airlines, was persuaded by Ellen Church, a young nurse, that someone with her training might better serve passengers on board their aeroplanes, a new career took flight for women. Church was employed with seven other nurses, and other airlines quickly followed suit (United Airlines).[8] In Europe Swissair hired Nelly Diener as the very first stewardess in 1934. These nurses-as-stewardesses initially embodied the message of safety and care that the new airlines wanted to project in order to promote air travel, their presence possibly helping to generate a psychological comfort zone for the newly travelling public. This assurance was also conveyed in their dress. A close association between war and early aviation was established by the idea of a uniform that was a serious affair, almost military in style, usually dark and formal and finished off with a cape not unlike that of a nurse. The only concession to femininity was in the darting of the jacket and the ubiquitous skirt, since women wearing trousers, especially so publicly, was still not quite 'respectable' until beyond the 1930s.

In contrast, the uniform of the 1950s stewardess projected an image of sophisticated femininity. Although it was not until the mid-1960s that uniforms became high fashion or couture garments, most famously in the shape of Pucci's designs for Braniff International, the air stewardess of the 1950s wore the smart, tailored garb characteristic of then current women's fashions. Over the 1950s and 1960s, these uniforms became ever more closely tied to everyday fashions in womenswear, to the point when in Pucci's hey-day they appeared not to be uniform-like at all, but as fashionable as anything a young woman might wear to a nightclub (Braniff International).

Subsequent designs have reined in this tendency towards high fashion, and the activities of stewards unions have served to render a more professional (hence uniformed) appearance. However, the use of fashion designers has been a constant, from Cristobal Balenciaga's (1969), Carven and Nina Ricci's, (1978) and Christian Lacroix' designs for Air Fance (Air France)

6 Arlie Russell Hochschild, *The Managed Heart: Commericalization of Human Feeling,* Berkeley, 1983.
7 See also the article by Mathias Remmele in this volume.
8 William Garvey and David Fisher, *The Age of Flight: A History of America's Pioneering Airline,* Greensboro, 2002, p. 69.

9 See Hughes, 'Stewardesses Pert and Pretty'.
10 The uniforms designed for Lufthansa by Ursula Tautz are an important exception. The airline's chief stewardess until 1961, Tautz was responsible for their 'New Look' in 1965. See Lufthansa Pressedienst, 6 April 1965.
11 'Trans World: Hostess uniforms', Design News from Loewy Associates, 11 July 1960 (Draft), p. 1, Accession 2251, Raymond Loewy Archives, Hagley Museum and Library.
12 Ibid., p. 2.
13 Ibid.
14 In 1961, a stewardess of Air France sued the airline for their 'illegal and immoral ordinance' prohibiting flight attendants from getting married. She lost the case. 'Glamour Girls mit hartem Job', Die Zeit, 30 June 1961.

to Carven's (1967), Christian Dior's (1971), and Calvin Klein's (1983) designs for SAS (SAS), to name just a few examples. As the stewardess became increasingly important to the experience of travel, the design of her uniform became a major feature of airline marketing, with constant relaunches of new uniforms helping to keep an airline's profile high.

It is noteworthy airline companies almost invariably drew on male designers. One journalist, writing about the launch of United Airlines and Pan Am uniforms in 1959, explained the preponderance of male designers in the following way: 'These stewardess costumes, designed by men, make the girls happy and hopeful they will be observed by other men.'[9] In this historical context at least, men were assumed to know best how to dress a woman to make her attractive and sexy to other men.[10]

While fashion and aesthetics featured as an aspect of the uniform, it was but one part of it. Other features, particularly functionality, also have to be borne in mind and have played a more or less important role, depending on the period. For example, when TWA was putting together its 'New Look' in 1960, design consultants at Loewy Associates were concerned not to be 'pressured by the fashion approach' but put together a look that is both 'feminine and efficient' (TWA).[11] In the news briefings at the time, Loewy Associates described how the look of the uniform was important, but so too the other design considerations of 'durability, consistency of appearance, ease in use, ease in maintenance, quality, versatility.'[12] Thus, almost in the manner of earlier 'time and motion' studies, the designers were employed to observe the stewardesses at work on a typical flight to see what clothes would support the constant stretching, bending, stooping, and straightening that the job entailed. The result was a uniform with durability and flexibility: 'a loose box jacket without confining seams or set-in sleeves' and 'A skirt, straight but not pencil slim', all of which allowed for 'sufficient freedom of action'.[13] Some airlines, such as Eastern, for example, employed committees and sub-committees made up of management

and stewards to approve new uniforms, often with the effect of frustrating the designers themselves, as was the case when Bill Blass designed his uniform for American in 1974. Design by committee runs quite counter to the normal artistic freedoms enjoyed by fashion designers and perhaps demonstrates the difficulties of marrying fashion with corporate culture.

In design terms, the thought behind the uniforms of flight personnel both assumed and imposed a gendering of the air travel experience. The 'flight attendant' or 'air steward' in today's gender-neutral parlance was almost always assumed to be female. This gendering of the role was quite solid, although stewards could sometimes be male. In contrast, the pilot, flight engineer, air traffic controller were always assumed to be male and despite years of hard won sexual equality, even to this day, men dominate in these occupations. It is interesting to note, in addition, that the appearance of male stewards was rather obscured by their dress. The male flight attendant of the late 1950s and 1960s was frequently dressed in the exact same uniform as the pilot and flight crew, giving him an appearance of greater importance and status compared to his female counterpart (Lufthansa). However, crucially, in the iconography of the age, the customer was always assumed to be male and with this gendered universe informing the marketing of commercial aviation, the classic image of a beautiful young stewardess happily serving male customers became the staple diet of airline advertising campaigns.

Throughout the 1950s, the stewardess' role was to perform 'femininity' through her appearance, manner, and sensibility. She had to decorate the aircraft, keep it clean and tidy, and remain constantly attentive to the needs of her customer; all the while – and sometimes under considerable pressure from generally unwanted male attentions – she was to remain polite and charming. In sum, her role was much like the 1950s housewife; ironically, however, she had to be unmarried, since it was not until the later 1960s and early 1970s that the marriage bar was lifted.[14] Thus, when Pan Am and

United 'engaged highly qualified male designers' (Raymond Loewy at United and Don Loper at Pan Am), 'it was with the aim of rigging out the stewardesses in a manner to look "irresistibly pleasing"'.[15] The result was that Loewy designed a more 'feminine' attire: in contrast to the usual browns and beiges that stewardesses had worn before, he came up with a 'rose-beige tone, flattering to blondes, brunettes and redheads'.[16] At Pam Am, Don Loper created a light blue uniform that similarly aimed to turn their stewardesses into something more pleasing to the (male) eye. Hence, the design of the uniform was about the total commodification of the stewardess, both as a marketing tool for the airlines in their battle to attract male customers, and as a commodity in the marriage market, wherein her 'true' feminine identity (as housewife) could eventually be realised.

Not only were the terms for describing air travel gendered, the very idea of flight itself has often been charged with sexuality, as was the stewardess/male customer relationship, and this association became firmly established in the 1960s. The excitement of 'taking off', the leaving behind of the familiar for some exotic location, the close physical proximity of bodies in a confined space, all helped to add a frisson to the interactive nature of the stewardess' work. Thus, the very abilities that made her so appealingly 'feminine', her service and feminine care, once within the confines of the plane, as opposed to the familiarity of home and hearth, were the source of sexual excitement and danger. Since the stewardess tended to the needs of men who were not her husband, she was not, in fact, quite the typical housewife and by the 1960s, the marketing campaigns of airlines, capitalising on the new sexual freedoms of the age, played up associations of stewardesses with sexuality. In a 1962 campaign for the Brazilian airline Varig,[17] the airline, its services, and the appeal of the 'lovely girl from Brazilian society who wears high fashion clothes instead of a uniform and is absolutely covered with charm' are depicted as a challenge to the harmony of matrimony, since the husband receives far better service from the stewardesses than from his wife. These themes of beauty, charm and fashionable dress were continued by Varig in the European edition of their *Interline Traveller* magazine. Here, the stewardess is described as having 'the poise of a popular debutante, the beauty of a "Miss America" contestant, the intelligence of a feminine doctoral candidate, the vivacity of a comedienne, and the keen eye for detail of a physicist' who, 'wearing the latest fashions instead of uniforms […] add the ultimate touch of elegance'.[18] This strategy, part of a marketing strategy in which 'each passenger is greeted by name', has the airline personified by the steward in her fashionable dress which appears to signify the informality of the service that the airline wants to promote. Fashionable clothing also seems to act as a marker of her particular attractiveness, sex appeal and femininity.

Thus, by the 1960s, a gradual loosening of sexual mores began to have its impact upon the representation of the stewardess. In contrast to the homely but attractive housewife, the stewardess became a sexual figure to the men she served on board; she was the 'mistress', or at a very least, a non-suburban, exotic, and glamourous cosmopolitan, a theme captured in numerous representations from the decade in which air stewardesses epitomise the sexual, non-domestic woman. The strict recruitment requirements, with tight limitations on age and weight, insured that air stewardesses were chosen for their supposed physical attractiveness; this in turn reinforced the association of stewardesses with a youthful sexuality. This trend reached its apotheosis when Emilio Pucci was brought in by Mary Wells to redesign Braniff International in 1965 (**Braniff International**). As she put it, in *Business Week* in 1967, 'When a tired businessman gets on an aeroplane, we think he ought to be allowed to look at a pretty girl' and indeed, the Braniff stewardesses were noted for their considerable good looks.[19]

15 Hughes, 'Stewardesses Pert and Pretty'.
16 Ibid.
17 'Each Passenger is Greeted by Name. Unique among World Airlines…Varig Executive Hostess Program,' *Varig Interline Traveller, European Edition* (June 1962).
18 Ibid.
19 Mary Wells quoted in www.2wice.org/issues/uniform/stew.html. For images and commentary on Braniff and Pucci's designs, see http://www.braniffinternational.org.

I'm naming Varig in my divorce

I'm not being vindictive, you understand. I'm just putting the blame where it belongs. Varig Airlines, that's who caused all the trouble. All right, so my husband has to fly to Brazil every month on business . . . . I don't mind that. Business is business. But flying Varig is something else again. Why can't they just be like any ordinary airline?

Don't they know what that kind of service does to a person? Every time he comes back from a trip on Varig, he can't talk about anything else. First he starts with the food. Why can't we have fresh beluga caviar and blinis for hors d'oeuvres. Or at least jellied trout in chablis sauce. Imagine! Then he actually suggests that I try to get the recipe for suprême de poularde au champagne from the Varig chefs. (Apparently one chef on a flight isn't good enough for Varig. They have to have two chefs to prepare his dinner. Not to mention a wine steward, heaven forfend he should choose the wrong wine!) Well, I ask him, what am I supposed to do? Hire a staff to

serve your dinner and supervise them personally? Why not, he says. Varig has an Executive Hostess to do just that, he says. A lovely girl from Brazilian society who wears highfashion clothes instead of a uniform and is absolutely covered with charm. She chats graciously with him, attends to his comfort and sees that his drink is mixed properly.

Well! Maybe you think that was the last straw—but oh, no. It was when he looked at our table and asked why we couldn't have exquisite china and lovely linen and six different kinds of crystal stemware, like they do on Varig's planes! Now, that's more than any woman can be expected to put up with!

I ask you, what right does an airline have to spoil a man with luxury like that? Is it good for him? Is it good for me? I don't know, but I'll tell you one thing—if I ever do get that divorce, I'm going to get it in South America. And I'll give you one guess which airline I'm going to fly!

EUROPEAN OFFICES 6 Frankfurt/Main Germany Am Hauptbahnhof 2 Tel. 338681/82 Sita: frarrrg Telex: 13313 Cables: VARIGLINES
Zurich Switzerland Nuschelerstr. 31 Tel. 27 67 67 Sita: zrhrrrg Telex: 52657 Cables: VARIGLINES
London S. W. 1. England, 46, St. James's Place St. James's Street Telephone: Hyde Park 4207/8 Telex: 24686
Sita: lonrrrg Cables: VARIGLINES London

252

Pucci's designs, beginning in 1965 with the 'Gemini 4' Collection helped achieve this by throwing out the old idea of the uniform and bringing couture fashion into commercial aviation. In her Pucci clothes, the Braniff stewardess signified high-class glamour; she represented the stewardess as jet setter. The clothes themselves, layers of soft printed jersey silk and gabardine in the characteristic Pucci palette, a colourful incarnation of pink, plum, electric blue, turquoise and purple, came in four combinations of trousers, mini-skirts, shifts and jackets, and were accessorised with scarves, pillbox hats and striking plastic bubble helmets. The Braniff stewardess also heralded the era of the stewardess as sex symbol that was to become a common feature of many subsequent figures in popular culture. Indeed, this very theme was captured by the Braniff 'Air Strip' campaign, which referred to the way in which these layers of clothes could be shed like veils throughout the flight according to weather conditions.

All of this was finished off with the famous Pucci headgear. Although ostensibly designed to preserve the hairstyles of the stewardesses, it primarily served the purposes of aesthetics rather than functionality. Part of this aesthetic was the dream of space travel that so dominated the decade and could be found in the work of other designers at the time, like Pierre Cardin and Paco Rabanne, and was captured in popular representations of the day such as *Barbarella*. The air stewardess, with her freedom to travel, her youth and beauty and her fabulous couture clothes, had never looked so good, nor had she ever looked so fashionably informal.

Pucci went on to design five collections for Braniff, introducing shift dresses and pants suits to the range. His designs stand out in the history of aviation not only for their sheer imagination and inventiveness, but also because they discarded with the normal conventions of uniforms, replacing the standard dark colours, severe lines, and formality of tailored uniforms with softer flowing fabrics and vibrant colour.[20]

However, as the confidence and optimism of the 1960s gave way to the deep global recession and social unrest of the 1970s, such inventiveness and futurism receded. The traditional uniform made its comeback with Bill Blass and Ralph Lauren reintroducing the classic tailored look at American Airlines and TWA (TWA). The re-establishment of a more conventional uniform came alongside growing discontent with working terms and conditions, as well as the sexist and sexy imagery that had become so commonplace. A burgeoning feminist agenda and growing unionisation at the end of the 1960s saw 'flight attendants' challenge the sexism that had been so widely accepted within the industry, with age and weight requirements, the bar on marriage and children, offensive scrutiny of employee dress, all finally lifted.[21] In the USA In 1973 the Association of Flight Attendants became an independent, self-governing affiliate of the Air Line Pilots Association. The previous year a number of flight attendants had founded the Anti-Defamation Defense League.[22] With it came calls for a more 'professional' image for the work, incompatible with associations of sexuality that had been so much a feature in the past.

While fashion frequently celebrates sexuality and exaggerates sexual difference, professional wardrobes and uniforms aim to diminish sexuality or at the very least, keep it under control. Thus, fashion and flight appeared to be more at odds with one another than ever before, although as the 1980s progressed and so-called 'power dressing' became a widespread style, there was, in fact, some considerable congruence. Tailored dress, especially the tailored jacket and knee-length skirt became popular at a time when the 'career woman' – the professional or business woman – was making a prominent appearance. Not a uniform as such, it became a 'technology' of dressing for the aspiring career woman. As such, it borrowed elements from the male suit, its strong contours and structured design, signifying 'professionalism' right down to the female equivalent of the tie, the scarf or pussy cat bow knotted at the neck and worn under the collar of the

20 The exception to this was Southwest Airlines, one of the earliest 'cheap' airlines based in Texas that had their stewardesses don high heeled leather boots and hot pants until the early 1980s and who now wear casual attire (polo shirts and khakis).
21 See for example, Jay, Matthews, 'Stewardesses Map Airline Rules Fight', *The Washington Post*, 28 February 1973.
22 Laurie Johnston, 'Airlines Assailed by Stewardesses. Sexism of Employees and Flying Public is Scored', *The New York Times*, 8 December 1972. See also: 'Women's Rights Reach New High – With Wings', *The New York Times*, 3 December 1973.

23 John T. Molloy, *Women: Dress for Success*, London, 1980.
24 Ibid.
25 Charlie Porter, '"Sexy" uniform for cabin crew meets union disapproval: British Airways tells Givenchy designer to tread carefully', *Guardian Online*, 17 May 2001: www.guardian.co.uk/uk_news/story/0,3604 ,492298,00.html.

blouse. These elements found their way into the design of many stewardess' uniforms around the same time with the aim of signifying professionalism as opposed to sex appeal (**Alitalia**).

This is not to say that uniforms cannot be sexualised, since they most certainly are the focus of intense sexual interest. Indeed, there is a clear tension between the aims of power dressing, as outlined by John T. Molloy and other dress consultants of the 1980s, to try to devise a standard of dress to diminish sexuality and bestow authority on the wearer, and the overall effect which can and indeed was highly sexualised.[23] Moreover, Molloy's rules of dress would always retain some elements of 'femininity' through the use of accessories such as scarves, and his rule that skirts are preferable to trousers comes down to the fact that 'men like to see a woman's legs', ensure that at least some element of sex appeal is retained.[24] Power dressing and the spin-off uniforms it influenced in the 1980s were never meant to be asexual, and the emphasis upon the sexuality of the stewardess were still evident in numerous airline campaigns of the period.

Today, after attempts by stewards to professionalise their work, the uniforms have become a much more sober affair, tailored, smart, and often in fabrics like polyester that are hardly renowned for their sensual properties. Indeed, even the very overtly sexist campaigns that typified the 1960s and 1970s in particular, have gone from most airlines, although they can still be found in the campaigns of Far East airlines, such as Singapore Airlines (**Singapore Airlines**). Here, images of beautiful young Asian women play into the exoticist fantasies of Western men and draw on the repository of cultural associations between Eastern women and servitude.

However, sex remains a continual theme in the meanings that both fashion and flight have accumulated. Moreover, it is not hard to understand their relationship when one considers that over the twentieth century sex became increasingly commodified. Thus, the uniform itself has become an object of sexual interest, the focus of intense sexual attention on the part of some fetishists. Type the word 'air stewardess' into an Internet search engine and some of the first sites to come up are fetish sites in which one can find stories and chat about every aspect of the stewardess' uniform. In this respect, her uniform is just those of other professions – police, nurse, or soldier – that have long been fetishised. Thus, while today's flight attendants may try to shake off the associations with sexuality, the fact remains that the changing nature of the images of stewardesses, as well as the changing nature of her uniform as it takes on elements of contemporary fashions, are the embodiment of this commodification of sex, harnessed by the airlines in their marketing campaigns.

For one, the 'classical' figure of the 1960s stewardess has of recent reemerged in a nostalgic mode. One quite prominent example of this is the DreamWorks film, *Catch Me if You Can*, starring Leonardo DiCaprio as Frank Abagnale, Jr., the teenage fraud who passed himself off as a pilot (as well as a doctor and lawyer) in the early 1960s. Abagnale's choice to pose as a pilot had everything to do with the associations of glamour and sophistication that this occupation carried in the 1960s and the images in the film capture how evocative air travel was at this time. Shots of DiCaprio striding through the airport lounge with half a dozen glamourous stewardesses on his arm draw on the common stereotype of the (normally blonde) air stewardess as manicured and immaculate in her smart uniform.

This kind of return to the supposedly 'glamourous' past of airline labour also has real impacts on current uniform design. So, for example, when Julien McDonald was brought in recently to re-design BA's uniform, he claimed that his aim was to make them 'sexy' again (**British Airways**). More particularly, he said, 'I want to bring glamour back into travel. The girls will look very sexy and the men will look like strong heroes'.[25] This met with some resistance from the stewards and the Transport and General Worker's Union representing them, who declared, 'We would like BA to distance itself from comments made by the designer. For us,

26 Ibid.

cabin crew are safety professionals, not marketing tools for BA'.[26] However, whatever the objections that stewards and unions have to this sort of sexualisation, it would seem to be almost inevitable that it occurs when fashion designers are brought in to redesign their uniforms. Fashion has always had an obsession with sex and designers constantly play with the markers of sexuality and sexual difference, however much flight attendants protest their sexualisation.

253 Winter uniform, 1954–62, Georgette de Tréze | 254 Summer uniform, 1963–68, Christian Dior | 255 Winter uniform, 1963–68, Christian Dior | 256 Summer uniform, 1969–77, Cristóbal Balenciaga | 257 Winter uniform, 1969–77, Cristóbal Balenciaga | 258 Uniform, 1978–87, Carven and Nina Ricci | 259 Summer uniform, 1987–98, Louis Ferraud and Nina Ricci

260 Uniform, 1998–2005 | 261, 262 Sketch proposal, 2005 uniform, Christian Lacroix | 263 Summer uniform for Concorde, 1976, Jean Patou | 264 Summer uniform for Concorde, 1986, Nina Ricci

265

265 Uniform, 1969, Mila Schön | **266, 267** Uniform, 1991–98, Giorgio Armani

266

267

AMERICAN AIRLINES

268 Uniform, c. 1934–37 | 269 Summer uniform, 1937 | 270 Uniform, 1937–40 | 271 Summer uniform, 1945–59 | 272 Winter uniform, 1945–59

273 Summer uniform at the start of the jet age, around 1960 | 274 Graduation from the stewardess training program, American Airlines, c. 1960 | 275 Uniforms from the 'American Beauty Line', 1967–68 | 276 Uniforms from 'Great American Look', 1969–71

277

278

279

277 The photograph from Braniff International's 'Air Strip' campaign showing Emilio Pucci's first collection for the airline, Gemini 4 (1965) | **278** The 1966 Pucci II collection served as a complement to Gemini 4. The fur coat was only needed on the routes to the military bases in Greenland and Iceland. | **279** The Pucci II-Collection, together with Gemini 4

280

281

282

283

280 Pucci's third collection for Braniff, 1968 (third from left) | **281** Pucci's fourth Braniff uniform, 1971. The 747 Collection came in two colour variations. | **282** Pucci's last collection for Braniff: Pucci V and Pucci VI, 1974 | **283** Uniform, 1977, Halston

284 British European Airways Uniform, 1950s (Photo c. 1960) | 285 British European Airways Uniform, 1960 | 286 British Overseas Airways Corporation Uniform, c. 1970

287

288

289

287 British European Airways Uniform, 1972, Hardy Amies | 288 British Airways Uniform, end of the 1970s | 289 Sketches for British Airways uniforms, Julien MacDonald, 2003

290

291

290 Uniform, 1959 | **291, 292, 293** Summer uniform, 1971–75 | **294** Winter uniform, 1971–75 | **295, 296** Winter uniform, 1975–82

292

293

294

295

296

LUFTHANSA

297 The first stewardesses of Lufthansa began service in 1938. | **298** Uniform, 1938–45 | **299** Summer uniform, 1955–65 | **300** Winter uniform, 1955–65 | **301** Summer uniform, 1965–70, Ursula Tautz

302 Winter uniform 1965–70, Ursula Tautz | 303 Uniform, 1970–79, Werner Machnik | 304 Uniform, 1979–87, Jobis | 305 Uniform, 1987, Jürgen Weiss | 306 Uniform up to 2001| 307 Uniform, 2001, Strenesse

308

308 Uniform 1966–75, Pierre Cardin

SCANDINAVIAN AIRLINES SYSTEM (SAS)

309

310

311

312

309, 310 Summer uniform 1967–83, Carven | **311** Winter uniform, 1971–83, Christian Dior | **312** Winter uniform 1983–99, Calvin Klein. The grey summer uniform was discontinued after the Boeing 767 went into service, since it did not harmonise with the plane's grey interior.

SINGAPORE AIRLINES (SIA)

313

313 Designed by Pierre Balmain in 1968, the uniform is still worn by stewardesses of Singapore Airlines today

314 Uniform, 1973 | 315 Uniform, 1996

316 Nelly Diener, the first stewardess in Europe. She died in a plane crash on July 27, 1934 |
317 The later stewardesses (c. 1936) wore a uniform that was reminiscent of their additional training as a nurse

TRANS WORLD AIRLINES (TWA)

318 The first uniform in 1935 | **319** Uniforms, 1944 | **320** Summer uniform, 1960, Raymond Loewy and Don Loper | **321** Uniform around 1965, Pierre Balmain | **322** Winter uniform, 1968 | **323** Uniform, 1971, Valentino | **324** Uniform, 1978–2001, Ralph Lauren

325 On 15 May 1930 the first eight stewardesses in the world began service for Boeing Air Transport, a predecessor of United Airlines | **326** Uniform, 1933 | **327** Summer uniform, 1939 | **328** Uniform, 1940

329 Summer uniform, 1941–48 | **330** Stewardess doing the 'Chic Check', 1951 | **331** Uniform, 1957, Raymond Loewy | **332** Uniform, 1960 | **333** Jean Louis, surrounded by United Airlines stewardesses in the uniform he designed, 1968 | **334** Uniform, 1968, Jean Louis

335

336

337

338

339

335 Uniform, 1973, Jean Louis | **336** Uniform, 1976 | **337** Uniforms, 1980 | **338** Uniforms, 1992 | **339** Uniforms, 2002

DINING ALOFT

JOCHEN EISENBRAND

Translation by Brian Currid

With a Picnic Basket into the Skies

Four water glasses, four paper cups, two bottles of mineral water, two bottles of wine, a thermos with a litre of coffee, ten paper napkins, twenty rolls, four packets of butter, two pounds of ham and sausage, chicken in aspic and roast beef, fifteen oranges, bananas, and apples, two pounds of grapes, chocolate, and zwieback. What now sounds like the culinary preparations for a day in the countryside was the usual Lufthansa in-flight food service during the 1930s. The delicacies were brought on board in wicker baskets as sustenance for the passengers.

This picnic atmosphere during mealtime prevailed not only on European airliners, but on American airliners as well, because the narrow, tubular aeroplane cabins did not yet provide space for a galley. An exception to this were the spacious flying boats, in which well-heeled travellers could feel as if they were in a flying restaurant. The galley of the Boeing B-314, for example, which took up regular service in 1939, was equipped with a water tank, an ice box, an electric heated thermos, and a heated aluminium cabinet.[1] 200 porcelain plates and 350 sets of cutlery could be securely stored. The dinner menu read as follows: 'Celery and olives, fresh shrimp cocktail, turtle soup, filet mignon, mashed potatoes, asparagus hollandaise, alligator pear salad with lemon oil dressing, bisquit tortoni, petit fours, coffee or tea, and mints'.[2] The passengers on the Dornier Do-X, which went on its first international demonstration flight as the largest aeroplane in the world in 1930, also dined from china plates. The meals were prepared on hot plates or in pots with electrical heating coils (340). In the board bar, the passengers could 'successfully fight off any possible "weakness" with the obligatory whisky or their favourite cocktail', as one brochure put it.[3]

But until the mid-1930s, passengers on regularly scheduled flights usually had to be satisfied with cold meals. On the Ford Tri-Motor flown by Transcontinental Air Transport, for example, which flew the United States coast to coast linking New York and Los Angeles, the passengers were served cold roast meats, sandwiches, and fruit compote. The airline prided itself on having prepared the meals according to a nutritionist's recommendations to prevent 'airsickness'. At lunchtime, a small aluminium table with tablecloth and napkins was placed before the seat of each passenger. The plates and cutlery were made of gilded aluminium: noble in appearance, but still light in weight.[4]

The First Galley in Airline Service

The first warm meals in regular international airline traffic were served in 1929 by Imperial Airways on the London to Paris route.[5] In the Handley Page HP 42, a complete galley was positioned at the wings, between the fore and rear decks. During the flight over the channel, which lasted two hours and fifteen minutes, the stewards served a five-course meal.[6]

In the mid-1930s, American aeroplane manufacturers, airline companies, and engineers began to concentrate on developing airliner galleys.[7] At the same time, food preparation on the ground was also professionalised. For this purpose, United Airlines opened the first ground kitchen for in-flight service in 1936 in Oakland, California. The meals prepared here before take-off were wrapped in paper while still warm, placed in cardboard boxes, and then brought on board. There, they were stored in an insulated cabinet until serving, for there was still no way to heat, never mind cook meals during flight.[8] In *The Official Aviation Guide*, which contained the flight plans of international airlines, United Airlines advertised hot à la carte meals and breakfast in bed for the first time in 1937 – naturally served by a stewardess.[9] In the same year, Willard J. Marriott, the founder of the hotel chain, opened a catering service in Washington, D.C that served Capital, Eastern, and American Airlines. Only five years later, American Airlines followed United's example, founding Skychefs, their own in-flight caterer. In order to offer their passengers something special, the airline even had its own cutlery made, with the handles formed to

1 M. D. Klaás, *Last of the Flying Clippers. The Boeing B-314 Story*, Atglen, 1997, pp. 34 f.
2 Ansel E. Talbert, 'Research in Food for Air Travelers Insures Choice Meals for Passengers on Atlantic Flight', *New York Herald Tribune*, 28 May 1939.
3 E. Tilgenkamp, 'Erläuterung zu den Bildern', ed. Emil Schaeffer, *Do-X. Das größte Flugschiff der Welt*, Zurich, 1931, p. 13.
4 Grace Williamson Willett, 'From Coast to Coast by Airplane', *Harper's Bazaar*, October 1930, p. 132.
5 Talbert, 'Research in Food'.
6 Eric Niderost, 'Handley Page's Slow and Stately H. P. 42', http://preview.thehistorynet.com/aviationhistory/article/2000/0700_text.htm.
7 The vice-president and chief engineer of Douglas Aircraft Corporation argued in a 1936 lecture that a device was needed for keeping food warm or cooking during flight. The general picnic atmosphere would, he suggested, soon be replaced by a dining car ambience. See Arthur E. Raymond, 'Designing to Please the Air Traveller', transcript of a speech held at the National Aircraft Production Meeting, Society of Automotive Engineers, Los Angeles, 15–17 October 1936, p. 3. Archive of the National Air and Space Museum, File FO-094030-20.
8 William Garvey and David Fisher, *The Age of Flight: A History of America's Pioneering Airline*, Greensboro, 2002, p. 136. See also Suzrovy, *Classic American Airlines*, Osceola, 2000, p. 57.
9 At a congress of the Society of Automotive Engineers, a representative of United Airlines referred to these innovations: 'More elaborate meals are served aloft than heretofore, consisting usually of a hot meat, a hot vegetable in addition to salad, breads cakes, ice cream, hot beverages, nuts and mints. The meals are served on real china plates, and silverware and cloth napkins are provided.' H. O. West, 'Interior Finish and Arrangement of Transport Airplanes', transcript, speech held before the National Aeronautic Meeting, Society of Automotive Engineers, Washington, D.C., 11–12 March 1937, p. 2. Archive, National Air and Space Museum, File FO-094030-20.

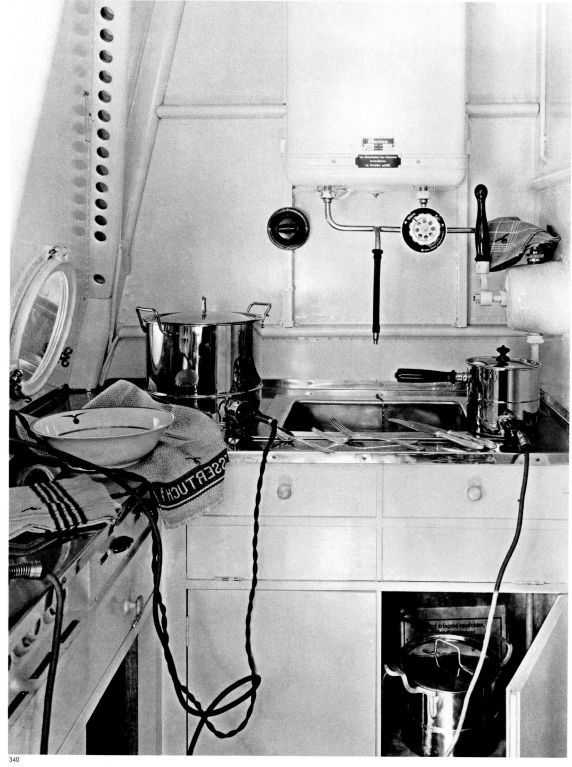

340 Galley, Dornier Do-X, around 1930.

341 Galley, Boeing B-377 Stratocruiser, c. 1946.

342 Around 1950, in the Boeing B-377 Stratocruiser a further development of the galley was installed, designed by industrial designers van Doren, Nowland & Schladermundt.

341

342

model the shape of the fuselage of one of its flagships. They are still to this day popular collector's items.

Free food and drink established itself in passenger air travel from the very beginning and was used in airline advertising as an argument against the competition of the train. But this competitive advantage and concern for the physical well-being of the passengers were not the only motives for the free service. Into the 1950s, the advertising photographs showing dining passengers served to emphasise both the luxurious character of air travel as well as its safety: if you could dine on a turkey leg in peace and quiet, no turbulence had to be feared. Up until today, meal times on long flights serve to distract the passengers. Especially on long trips, they are an important way of dividing up the flight into manageable lengths of time.

By the mid-1930s, engineers had realised that airliner galleys had to be constructed in a modular fashion. This alone could ensure that the units and equipment for food storage and preparation could be individually removed and readily cleaned or refilled.[10] Since the first galleys, like that on the DC-3, did not yet have a separate entrance, the food had to be brought through the passenger aisle on board,[11] an awkward and time-consuming process. The galley, on the DC-3 still at the front of the aeroplane, was now placed in the rear on the DC-4, where it could take up more space. Now it was also possible to heat meals on airliners.[12]

By the introduction of the Boeing B 377 Stratocruiser to passenger service in 1947, manufacturers had begun to specialise in producing airliner galleys with all the required equipment (341, 342). Using motion studies on kitchen tasks and the stewardess' movement through the cabin, the designers established the elements needed and their required placement. One manufacturer would ultimately not only offer the necessary galley equipment, including Whirlwind ovens, but also the pre-cooked meals.[13]

Around twenty-five years later, in the second generation of jet aeroplanes like the Lockheed L-1011 and the Boeing 747, the galleys, which with their completely planar and flush surfaces had come to look like the interior of spaceships, were moved from the passenger cabin to the lower deck (345, 346). This made it easier to load and also created additional seats for paying passengers. With small cargo lifts, the trays could be transported to the passenger level.[14] Trolleys were introduced in the 1960s, when the increased passenger numbers on the large jets made the distances too long for the stewardesses to serve individual trays.

Design Parameters for In-Flight Tableware

Into the 1950s, it was usual on airline flights to balance meals on a pillow placed on the thighs, since the integrated tray tables on the seatbacks had not yet been invented.[15] Thus, for the United Airlines DC-3, Henry Dreyfuss designed a lunchbox combined with a tray. At mealtime, its cover was removed and turned over, serving as a pedestal for the tray. When eating, the passengers then placed the construction on their laps.[16] In some aeroplanes, a folding table could be inserted into the armrests during meal times. The rest of the time, these were stored in the cabin, taking up valuable space. In propeller planes like the British Vickers Viscount (1948), the Italian Breda-Zappata (1951), or the American Lockheed L-188 Electra (1957), the first seat models that integrated tray tables into the armrests were introduced.[17] With the beginning of the jet age and planes like the Boeing 707 or the Douglas DC-8, this became the industry standard.

Since then, the measurements of the tray tables as well as the service trays have determined the dimensions of tableware systems, giving industrial designers little room to manoeuvre. When working for the British Overseas Airways Corporation (BOAC) in 1968, Robin Day would find out how restricting and complex the design of onboard tableware could be. 'This was an interesting exercise in logistics […] as economy of space and weight in even the smallest things are crucial to the economics of operating passenger aircraft. Relation-

10 West, 'Interior Finish', p. 5.
11 Walter Prokosch, 'The Planning of Cabin Interiors for Transport Aircraft', typescript, speech at the National Aeronautic Meeting, Society of Automotive Engineers, New York, 3–5 April 1946, p. 4. Archive, National Air and Space Museum, File F0-094030-25.
12 Garvey and Fisher, The Age of Flight, p. 136.
13 Society of Industrial Designers, U.S. Industrial Design 1949/1950, New York 1949, p. 118.
14 Barbara Allen, 'Mess Halls in the Air', Industrial Design, May 1968, pp. 28–33.
15 'There is, at this time, no really satisfactory tray holder available. Numerous schemes have been tried, but we are still using the pillow, since of all methods it is the most practical scheme yet proposed. Obviously, there is a very definite need for a good tray holder. Some designs have been tried with a rack which slides out of the arm of the chair. […] If tables are used, the stowage problem is a serious one.' Albert P. Elebash, 'Passenger Aircraft Facilities: Design and Operation', typescript, speech held at the National Air Transport Engineering Meeting, Society of Automotive Engineers, Chicago, 2–4 December 1946, p. 9. Archive, National Air and Space Museum, File F0-09403025.
16 Helen E. McLaughlin, Footsteps in the Sky, Denver, 1994, p. 224. Delta and Continental also used lunch boxes in the 1940s. See also pp. 63 and 73.
17 See Industrial Design, October 1957, p. 89; Giulio Minoletti, 'Interno di un velivolo', Domus, 261 (1951), pp. 38–39.

343 Galley, Boeing 707, c. 1959, in which up to 168 meals could be prepared.

344 Dining on board a Boeing 707, c. 1959.

345 Kitchen equipment and supplies of a British Airways Boeing 747.

346 Lower deck galley of a Boeing 747, c. 1970.

347 Henry Dreyfuss, plan for a clap tray, c. 1970.

343

344

345

346

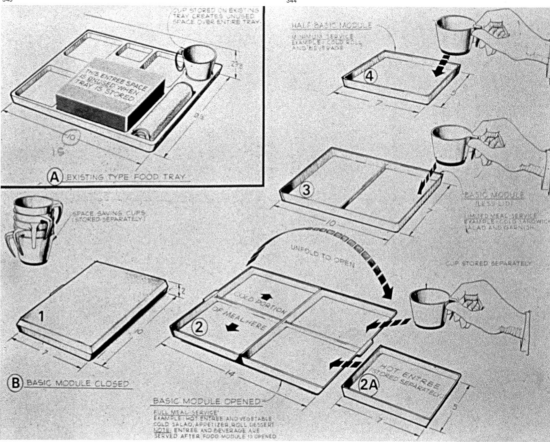
347

348 Plates of KLM's in-flight tableware, melamine, designed by Andries Copier, 1948. Pieke Hooghoff Collection, Amsterdam.

349 KLM in-flight tableware, 1952, melamine, designed by Andries Copier. Pieke Hooghoff Collection, Amsterdam.

350 KLM in-flight tableware, 1952, melamine, designed by Andries Copier. Pieke Hooghoff Collection, Amsterdam.

351 KLM in-flight tableware, 1963, melamine, designed by Van Niftrik. Pieke Hooghoff Collection, Amsterdam.

352 Pan Am in-flight tableware, melamine, 1960s.

348

349

350

351

352

353 Cumulus flatware for Finnair's DC-8, steel, designed by Tapio Wirkkala, 1968. Beginning in 1971, this tableware was also available on the consumer market in silver and alpaca.

354 In-flight tableware for Finnair's Caravelle, melamine, designed by Tapio Wirkkala, 1960.

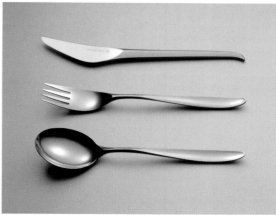

353

354

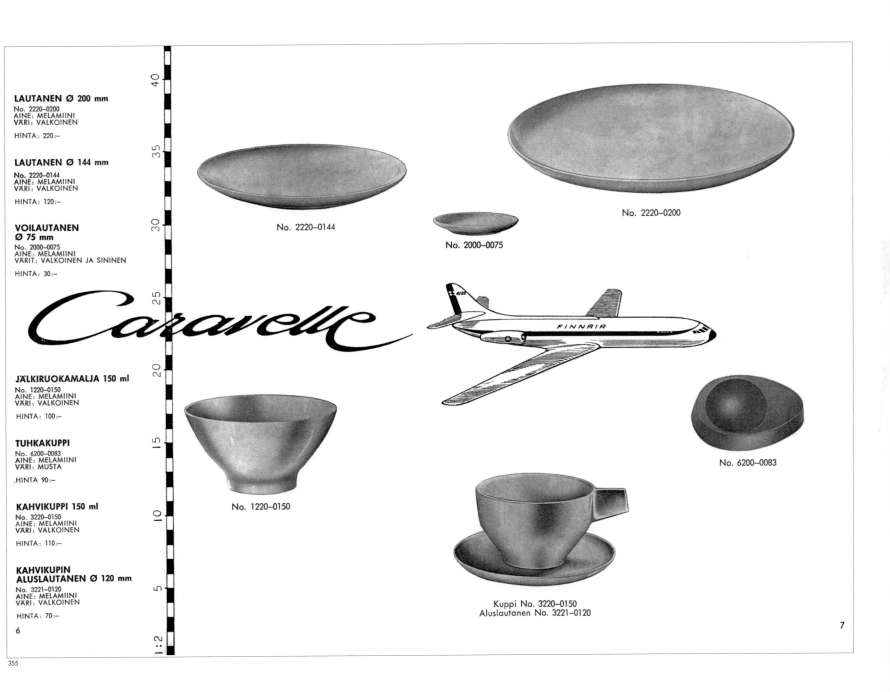

LAUTANEN Ø 200 mm
No. 2220–0200
AINE: MELAMIINI
VÄRI: VALKOINEN

HINTA: 220:–

LAUTANEN Ø 144 mm
No. 2220–0144
AINE: MELAMIINI
VÄRI: VALKOINEN

HINTA: 120:–

VOILAUTANEN Ø 75 mm
No. 2000–0075
AINE: MELAMIINI
VÄRIT: VALKOINEN JA SININEN

HINTA: 30:–

JÄLKIRUOKAMALJA 150 ml
No. 1220–0150
AINE: MELAMIINI
VÄRI: VALKOINEN

HINTA: 100:–

TUHKAKUPPI
No. 6200–0083
AINE: MELAMIINI
VÄRI: MUSTA

HINTA 90:–

KAHVIKUPPI 150 ml
No. 3220–0150
AINE: MELAMIINI
VÄRI: VALKOINEN

HINTA: 110:–

KAHVIKUPIN ALUSLAUTANEN Ø 120 mm
No. 3221–0120
AINE: MELAMIINI
VÄRI: VALKOINEN

HINTA: 70:–

6

No. 2220–0144

No. 2220–0200

No. 2000–0075

No. 1220–0150

No. 6200–0083

Kuppi No. 3220–0150
Aluslautanen No. 3221–0120

7

355

356

ships of dimensions and stacking were essential on several levels: firstly, the compact fitting of vessels and implements of trays; secondly, the exact accommodation of trays on mobile trolleys; and thirdly, the accommodation of this equipment on the galley, on the airfield and in the airport.'[18] The in-flight tableware to which he was referring was intended for the tourist class of the Boeing 707. Since the individual elements were produced by different manufactures, and each had to be coordinated with one another, development dragged on for more than 18 months.

Dreyfuss, mentioned earlier, and Day were by no means the only prominent industrial designers commissioned by an airline to find the ideal form for in-flight tableware. Most of them came with prior experience in designing domestic tableware for well-known porcelain manufacturers. For many, their work in the air travel industry was their first experience in using plastics.

Plastics and Porcelain

American Airlines already used trays, bread plates, salad or soup bowls made of plastic in the 1930s.[19] In Europe, melamine, a durable plastic that after hardening no longer changes form, established itself as a new material for airline tableware in the 1950s and 1960s. Sturdier and more resistant to cuts than many other plastics, it is also heat resistant and is pleasant to the touch. Still today, kitchen equipment and camping plates are sometimes made of melamine.

The Dutch glass artist Andries Dirk Copier, who was associated with the Glasfabriek Leerdam for more than five decades, was one of the first to design a melamine in-flight tableware system. His designs for KLM, including a hexagonal plate bearing the airline's logo, were first made in 1948 (348). Copier was also responsible for the two subsequent light blue melamine tableware systems realised in 1952 and 1959 (349, 350). The plastic tableware was manufactured by the Dutch melamine producer Van Niftrik (up to 1952 IKI, Kornelis), which

presumably also developed the fourth generation of KLM post-war tableware in 1963 on its own (351).[20] Its bowls and cups, thanks to progress in production capabilities, were now two-tone: the inner surface was white, while the outside was blue.

Like Copier, the Finnish designer Tapio Wirkkala had made a name for himself through his work with glass; but he was also well known for his work in wood and porcelain before being commissioned by an airline to confront the characteristics of plastic. For Finnair's first flights of the Caravelle in 1960, Wirkkala developed an in-flight tableware system with a coffee cup and saucer, a small and a large plate, a dessert plate as well as a streamlined ashtray (354). The unusual form of the cup holder was similar to the Caravelle's tail unit. The elegant, gracefully swung steel cutlery was named Cumulus (353). Up until 1972, the Caravelle tableware was also produced for household use by the company Strömfors. The manufacturer advertised that the tableware had its origins in air travel in order to ameliorate the poor reputation of plastic tableware (355).

Some years later, Wirkalla took on another commission from Finnair, designing in-flight tableware for both tourist and first class on the DC-8. Beginning in 1969, the 'tourists' ate from pine green tableware, manufactured by the Finnish company Fiskars in the plastic material Luran. Finnair commissioned Rosenthal to produce the tableware for first class. This time the tableware was adorned with a Finnair logo designed especially by Wirkkala for this system. Ultima Thule, the elegant glasses that went with the first class tableware system, are still in production today.[21]

In 1966–67, the Swedish industrial designer Sigvard Bernadotte created an all-black in-flight tableware for SAS (356). While he used melamine for the plates, cups, and bowls, he had the trays made of polycarbonate, a lighter material. The emphatically flat stainless steel cutlery could be stored in a manner that was particularly economical with space, using precise angles that allow the pieces to be stored flush next to one another.[22]

18 Robin Day in a letter to Lesley Jackson, quoted in: Lesley Jackson, *Robin and Lucienne Day. Pioneers of Modern Design*, New York, 2001, p. 138.
19 United Airlines used it on flights of the Boeing 247 and the DC-3. See the United Airlines website: http://www.ual.com/page/article/0,1360,2312,00.html.
20 The information about the KLM tableware and the collaboration with Copier was provided by Pieke Hooghoff. See also Pieke Hooghoff, *Plastiks in het huishouden*, Zaltbommel, 2001, pp. 69–71.
21 Tuula Poutasuo, 'Futurism and Everyday Goods', ed. Marianne Aav, *Tapio Wirkkala – Eye, Hand and Thought*, Porvoo, 2000, pp. 200–03.
22 See Nationalmuseum Stockholm, ed., *Sigvard Bernadotte*, Stockholm, 1997. My thanks to Cilla Robach for pointing this out.

357 Sketch for 'Linea 72,' an in-flight tableware for Aitalia's economy class, designed by Joe Colombo, 1970.

358 Joe Colombo's 'Linea 72', melamine tray.

359 Sketch for the first class version of 'Linea 72'.

360 'Linea 72' in the first class china version, 1970.

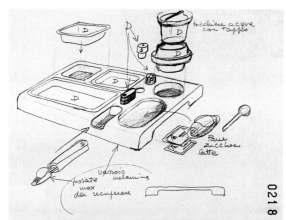

357

358

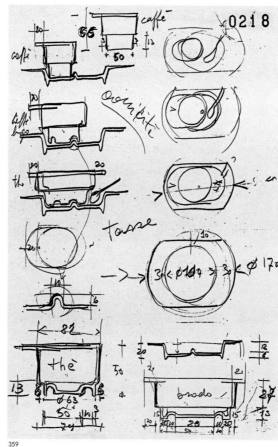

359

360

361 Lufthansa in-flight tableware, melamine, designed by Wilhelm Wagenfeld, 1954–55, melamine. Wilhelm Wagenfeld Stiftung, Bremen.

362 View through a cabin window into the interior of a Vickers Viscount showing Wagenfeld's in-flight tableware, 1958.

361

362

Around the end of 1960s, melamine tableware was sometimes replaced with disposable articles in economy class. For this purpose, Joe Colombo designed Linea 72 for Alitalia in 1970: this tableware system featured disposable plastic containers that could be precisely fitted into a melamine tray (**357, 358**). Colombo's porcelain plates for first class, in contrast, had grooves on the base, allowing the tableware to be placed on horizontal raised ridges on the trays to prevent them from shifting during flight (**359, 360**).[23]

Tableware at Lufthansa

Promptly with the start of Lufthansa's new flight service on 31 March 1955, the new tableware that Wilhelm Wagenfeld had designed for the airline was ready for use. In October of the previous year, the industrial designer had established contact with the plastic manufacturer Buchsteiner, which had ties to the airline due to the planned production of melamine in-flight tableware. Wagenfeld had fundamental doubts about the use of plastics, but let himself be convinced of the qualities of melamine.[24] In November 1954, his office began to develop a tableware system according to Lufthansa's specifications.[25] Although the airline at first planned black trays and yellow plates, they then turned to the colours suggested by Wagenfeld.[26] The tray was thus made of yellow nylon, while dinner and desert plates, two side-dish bowls, and a coffee cup were made of blue-grey melamine. Wagenfeld's associate Heinz G. Pfaender based the form and scale of the small, clear polystyrene salt and pepper shakers on a small pile of West German ten penny coins. Adorned with the Lufthansa crane, these two disposable items were conceived as passenger souvenirs (**361, 362**).[27]

At the beginning of the 1960s, the new Lufthansa, which by now had established itself in international air travel, built a two story building for its own in-flight catering at Frankfurt Airport. The building was designed for the daily production and storage of 10,000 meals: warm, cold, or deep-frozen.[28]

23 See also Ignazia Favata, *Joe Colombo and Italian Design of the Sixties*, London, 1988, pp. 50 ff.
24 Heinz G. Pfaender, *Meine Zeit in der Werkstatt Wagenfeld. Tagebuch 1954–57*, Hamburg 1998, p. 15. My thanks to Beate Manske for pointing out this publication.
25 Ibid., p. 37.
26 Ibid., p. 57.
27 Ibid., p. 61. According to Nathalie Heinke, Wagenfeld's tableware was made a year later with Luran, since melamine had proven too heavy. See Nathalie Heinke, 'Förmlich abgehoben. Berühmte Designer entwerfen das Lufthansa-Geschirr', *Frankfurter Allgemeine Sonntagszeitung*, 24 February 2002, p. 66.
28 Otto Apel and Hannsgeorg Beckert, 'Das Lufthansa-Borddienst-Gebäude auf dem Flughafen Rhein-Main', *Baukunst und Werkform*, 15.2 (1962), pp. 91 f.

363 In-flight tableware for Lufthansa's economy class, designed by Nick Roericht. This Luran tableware system went into service in 1967.

364 At the EXPO 67 in Montreal, Roericht's in-flight tableware for Lufthansa was shown in a design exhibition held in the German Pavilion.

363

364

When Otl Aicher and the Entwicklungsgruppe 5 at the Hochschule für Gestaltung Ulm a year later began work on a new image for Lufthansa, Hans (Nick) Roericht, a member of the group, was entrusted with the design of the in-flight tableware. Roericht was predestined for this task, since at the academy he had designed a stackable tableware system, TC 100, as a graduation project; this system was later produced by Rosenthal. Like Wirkalla's later tableware system, this in-flight tableware was made of Luran; coloured 'snow-violet', it weighed only 650 g with the black tray.[29] Disposable coffee cup holders and eggcups were made of cardboard. A second, smaller tray was intended for the less extensive meals. This tableware could not only be stacked, but thanks to its coordinated dimensions could also be combined in multiple ways (363).[30] The plates and bowls were made in just the right size to provide mutual stability on the tray when combined, making ridges in the tray, as in Wagenfeld's design, unnecessary.

At the Expo 67 in Montreal, the tableware that was now in design terms part of the airline's image was introduced at the German Pavilion (364).[31] In March 1968, it was used officially for the first time, only two years after Lufthansa had founded its own catering service for air travel: Lufthansa Service GmbH (LSG). Originally the tableware was only intended to be used in the economy class of the Boeing 727, which began service in Spring 1964, but it gradually came to be used serve all Lufthansa flights.

Roericht continued to experiment in the following years with the arrangement of in-flight tableware for successor models; he made a number of suggestions until 1975. Tableware that could be stored at 45 degree angles next to one another, plates and bowls with rounded, wave-shaped outlines or disposable cutlery, in which the user could punch out a knife, fork, and spoon from a plastic form, in a sense as a freshness seal. These designs, however, did not go into serial production (365, 366).[32]

Like Finnair, Lufthansa commissioned an industrial designer who had worked for major porcelain manufacturers to design the first class porcelain tableware and cutlery. The in-flight tableware system with cobalt ornamentation designed by Hans Theo Baumann in 1963 was produced by Rosenthal as of 1964 (367).[33] The subsequent set of first class tableware was manufactured by Hutschenreuther beginning in 1976 (368).[34]

Baumann based it on his Rastergeschirr 2298, a geometric tableware system for which he won the West German national design prize in 1973. Now the round plates and bowls of the first generation of tableware were replaced with almost rectangular plates with rounded corners, that could be more easily arranged.[35] Stackable tableware systems with conforming sizes, like those of Roericht and Baumann, are used largely in gastronomy. For air travel, the plate rims need to have different height: they must be high enough to prevent meals from overflowing, and low enough to fit into the filled tray cart.

At the beginning of the 1980s, Lufthansa invited seven designers to submit proposals for a new in-flight tableware system. Including all containers that were necessary for serving, it was to comprise 120 articles of porcelain, plastic, glass, metal, textiles, and paper. From among the seven competitors, two were chosen, each independently receiving a development commission. In 1984, Wolf Karnagel finally triumphed over Dieter Rams; two years later, his tableware took off for the first time (369).[36]

Lufthansa's newest economy class tableware, designed by the office of Topel und Pauser Industrial Design, is called Wing and was introduced in 2001 after a development period of three years (370). The bowls made of the plastic SAN are alternatively concave and convex, and fit together in a flush manner. In order to ensure easier handling of the trays on the trolleys, the designers developed trays with specially grooved edges, and as the designers proudly reported, this enabled them to save an additional 0.8 centimetres of space. The design of airline tableware remains the work of millimetres.

29 Lufthansa Pressemitteilung, 23 January 1967, Lufthansa Archiv, Cologne. Luran was chosen since the Entwicklungsgruppe 5 at the Hochschule für Gestaltung previously was to produce a colour chart for plastics for BASF, and supposedly there learned of the advantages of the new BASF product. Private conversation of the author with Prof. Nick Roericht, Ulm, 18 September 2003.
30 Ulm. Zeitschrift der Hochschule für Gestaltung (10/11), May 1964, p. 44.
31 Lufthansa Pressedienst, 23 January 1967.
32 Private conversation with Prof. Hans (Nick) Roericht, 18 September 2003. See also 'In-Flight Meal Equipment', Domus 561, August 1976, pp. 42 f.
33 Hans Theo Baumann and J. Mehlin, H. Th. Baumann Design, Maulburg, 1979, p. 9. Baumann had already designed a series of stackable glass goblets in 1959. Like the tableware, in 1964 it went into production for Lufthansa IIbid., pp. 120 and p. 1671.
34 Ibid., pp. 42 f. The tableware is now again offered by the mail-order company Manufactum.
35 Hans Theo Baumann designed in 1987–87 a further in-flight tableware system, which was produced by Rosenthal beginning in 1989.
36 'Flugbegleiter', April 1985, p. 14. Lufthansa Archiv Köln. Dieter Rams' proposal is illustrated in Dieter Rams, Weniger aber besser, Hamburg, 1995, p. 111.

365, 366 These prototypes for Lufthansa in-flight tableware were developed between 1961 and 1975 by Nick Roericht in collaboration with Michiko Asaka and Franco Clivio.

365

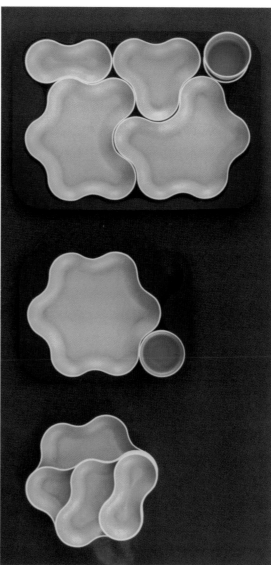

366

367 Lufthansa in-flight tableware, designed by Hans Theo Baumann in 1963, produced by Rosenthal beginning in 1964. Private collection, Hans Theo Baumann, Schopfheim.

368 In-flight tableware system, designed by Hans Theo Baumann in 1971, produced by Hutschenreuter beginning in 1976. Private collection, Hans Theo Baumann, Schopfheim.

369 Lufthansa tableware system, designed by Wolf Karnagel, 1985. Neue Sammlung, Staatliches Museum für Angewandte Kunst, Munich.

370 Wing, Lufthansa's current in-flight tableware system, developed by Topel and Pauser Industrial Design in 1998, went into service in 2001.

371 In-flight tableware for Air France, Radi Designers, 2000.

367   368

369

370

371

37 See on this Wolfgang Schepers, 'Unterwegs zu Land + Luft', *Kunststoff auf Reisen – Essen Unterwegs*, Solingen and Düsseldorf, pp. 32–43. My gratitude to Ellen Kreutz from the Kunststoff-Museums-Verein for pointing out this book.

In-Flight Catering: Between Quantity and Class

A large portion of today's airline tableware comes from the design centre of a single company. As one of the market leaders in this area, DeSter delivers its products to 350 airlines around the world.[37]

Collaborations between airlines and designers not from the air travel industry, like that between Air France and Radi Designers for economy class tableware in 2000, are today fairly rare (**371**). Rare as well is the pleasure to be had flying SAS business class: after a first course of cold cuts of elk and reindeer with cream cheese and lingonberries served on porcelain plates created by the Danish designer Ursula Munch-Peteresen, one can cut the smoked salmon on tomato-hollandaise-basil sauce with cutlery by Bo Bonfils into delicious morsels, and then with desert drink a 1997 Sauternes from glasses devised by the Swedish designer Gunnar Cyrén. For the creation of their menu, the airline hired Scandinavian top chefs. Like other airlines, SAS advertises that they have their own sommelier, who in his choice of wines keeps in mind the altered sense of taste at 10,000 m.

Apart from such exclusive exceptions, the huge market of airline catering is divided between the two market leaders Gate Gourmet and LSG Skychefs. The latter emerged in 1993 with the fusion of the Lufthansa Services Group and Skychefs, founded more than 40 years previously. Together the two leaders produce more than 500 million on-board meals a year. At www.airlinemeals.net, you can let the Internet community and the cooks know what you think of their culinary art.

AN INVITATION TO FLY: POSTER ART IN THE SERVICE OF CIVILIAN AIR TRAVEL

MATHIAS REMMELE

Translation by Brian Currid

Promoting Airlines and Tourism

Stewardesses with charming smiles, Hawaiian girls with leis and flowers in their hair, images of the breathtaking skyline of Manhattan, aeroplanes racing at lightning speed, romantic sunsets on palm covered beaches, as well as abstract paintings or stylised maps of the word: no matter the motif, if printed on a poster and equipped with the name of an airline, they ultimately serve the same goal: an invitation to take to the skies.

In the 'golden age' of civil aviation, air travel posters were a key advertising tool for airlines. They are rightly considered the most important public emblem of the airlines, in addition to advertisements in the print media, often similar to the posters, and ticket sales offices. This is especially true of countries with a highly developed poster culture, like Switzerland and France, where for decades the national airlines entrusted leading graphic artists with designing their posters. The innovative designs that resulted from this collaboration were often considered exemplary around the world, and played an important part in influencing poster design in general.

In surveys of poster art, air travel posters are usually subsumed under the more general rubric of travel posters.[1] This has its justification, for their primary task is to inform the viewer and to awaken a desire to travel. In addition, most air travel posters advertise using the destinations served by the airlines, whereby the representation of the tourism locations does not differ from other kinds of tourism advertising either in form or content. But even if air travel posters do not represent an entirely independent genre with a characteristic visual language, it is still worth taking a separate look at them: only in this way can we show how these posters reflect the technical, social, and economic development of civilian aviation as well as the history of poster art in terms of printing techniques and design. Aviation posters provide insight into travel possibilities and interests, collective dreams and visual worlds, as well as the artistic trends of their time. Making no claim to completeness, the following essay will attempt to grasp the essential aspects of this subject.

Beside the undeniable clear parallels to the graphic design used to advertise tourism in general, two aspects are important to consider in order to understand the air travel poster. Firstly, in almost all countries except for the United States the airlines were completely or partially owned by the state, and as the bearer of the national colours, they soon became national status symbols. Accordingly, in their advertising they not only promoted themselves but also their country – either as a tourist destination or simply in a more general sense. The obvious synergies between the promotion of national airlines, tourism promotion, and the strengthening of the country as a place to do business manifested themselves not least in the shared foreign offices of airlines and tourism boards.[2]

Secondly, the aeroplane has always been in competition with other means of transport: initially the railroad and sea traffic, and after the Second World War, in the course of a drastic increase in individual motorisation and large-scale highway construction, the automobile as well. Today, the aeroplane is only unchallenged as the preferred means of transport over long distances and intercontinental traffic. But even in this market segment, where aeroplanes could take full advantage of their superior travel speeds, it took a surprisingly long time for the majority to come to have faith in aviation. Only at the end of the 1950s did the number of Atlantic crossings with the aeroplane surpass those by ship. The posters thus not only played a role in competition between airlines, but also served to popularise flying in and of itself. This is made clear in some of Lufthansa's early posters, like the poster *Fliegt! [Fly!]*, which shows a Junker tri-motor plane rising behind a Lufthansa banner (**372**). Even in the poster designed by Hans Vogel ('Fly to the seaside!') – a beach scene with two sunbathing young women, one of them joyfully waving to the plane flying overhead – the promotion of flying itself clearly stands in the foreground (**373**).

1 Up until now, only the posters of Air France have been treated in a monograph, Jérôme Peignot, *Air France Affiches/Posters 1933–1983*, Paris, 1988. A useful overview of the history of travel posters is provided by an essay by Corinna Rösner in the catalogue *Reiselust. Internationale Reiseplakate. Von der Jahrhundertwende bis heute*, ed. Florian Hufnagel, Munich, 1995, pp. 6–50. On the tasks of the travel poster, see Willy Rotzler, 'Das Touristikplakat', *Das Plakat in der Schweiz*, eds. Willy Rotzler, Fritz Schärer, and Karl Wobmann, Schaffhausen, 1990, pp. 119–23.

2 For example, Swissair opened an office in 1951 together with the Swiss Tourist Board and the Swiss Bank Association in New York's Rockefeller Center. On this, see *Remember Swissair 1931–2002*, Zurich, 2002, p. 20.

372 Eduard (Edo) Freiherr von Handel-Mazetti,
mid-1930s.

373 Hans Vogel, c. 1927

374 Paul Lawler, late 1930s

372

373

374

375

376

233

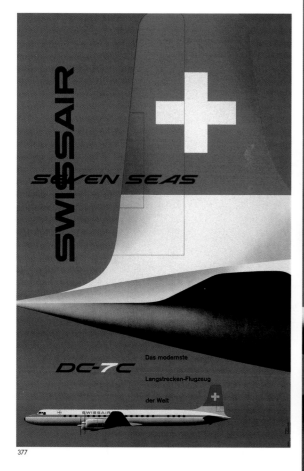

From among the huge number of air travel posters and the wide variety of motifs used, we can isolate a number of thematic complexes to help classify and describe the material. The message of the posters presented here played a decisive role in their selection. In a few cases, the aesthetic quality of the designs will be explored in detail.[3]

Aeroplane Types

For civil aviation, the development and introduction of new types of aeroplane had a significance that could scarcely be overestimated. Until airline fleets became by and large identical due to the process of consolidation in the aeronautics industry, the aeroplane model used was an important subject in poster advertising. The aeroplanes shaped the image of the airlines; they were a sign of modernity and technological competence and were presented with great pride.

Posters advertising a particular type of aeroplane began in the 1930s. Pan Am and the British airline Imperial Airways in particular understood how to show their enormous flying boats in an impressive light (374). At around the same time, the airlines presented their machines by means of drawn cross-sections. In this way, for example, the DC-3 turned up on Swiss Air and Pan Am posters (375, 376). But only in the years after the war did the posters with which the aeroplanes were advertised reach their height. At first the illustrations were merely drawings, but in the 1960s colour photography became dominant. The most convincing designs are from Switzerland and France, like the posters Kurt Wirth designed in 1956 for Swissair (377, 378).[4] In the foreground, he placed a detailed view of the aeroplane, chosen with a sure sense of visual effect. On a much smaller scale, a side-view of the aeroplane can be seen in the image background. The print, reminiscent of a construction plan, is cool, objective, and yet elegant, and emphasises the aeroplane's technological brilliance. Manfred Bingler's Coronado poster from 1962 also deserves some

attention. Bingler uses a photograph of the topside of an aeroplane and frames the image so that the aircraft seems like a large arrow (379). A more abstract execution characterises the BEA poster *Fly Viscount* from the same year, done by Josef Müller-Brockmann (380). The most striking element are the arcs marking the movement of the propeller; the plane, off-centre, slightly tilted and frontally directed towards the viewer gives the poster an almost dramatic sense of dynamism. Mary Vieira's 1957 DC-7 poster for Panair do Brasil, where nothing is left of the aeroplane but a small, white ring symbolising the rotating propeller, marked a radical reduction for the period (381). Jean Colin used a totally different, less strict form of reduction for his 1959 Caravelle poster for Air France (382). His central motif is the striking, organically shaped cabin window of this jet plane, which provides the framework for a miniature representation of the aeroplane's elegance. The Caravelle posters for Sabena and Finnair (383) seem comparatively conventional in contrast, showing an aeroplane somewhat inexplicably combined with a woman's face.

After the introduction of large jet planes, posters advertising particular aeroplane models were hardly used. The awkward looking giants were considered quite clearly of little use for posters. One last high point of the aeroplane is the Concorde poster, designed by Charles Brunswick in 1976 for Air France. Before a blue background, it shows a photograph of the underside of the elegant plane, pointing like a huge arrow towards the sky.

Speed

In terms of travel velocity, the aeroplane still far surpasses all other means of transportation. The further the distance, the more positive the effect on travel time. Already in the 1930s, speed emerged as a topic of air travel posters. Thus, Lufthansa advertised using the catchy motto '*Luftverkehr — Schnellverkehr*' ('Air Travel-Fast Travel') showing an aeroplane race across the image with an amazing dynamism that could be sure of attracting the attention of the audience (384). But for a

3 There are of course cases in which the thematic categorisation of posters is not so clear cut. Overlaps are unavoidable between the categories of 'aeroplane models' and 'comfort' as well as the categories 'route networks' and 'destinations'.
4 'Noblesse in der Werbung. Zu den Arbeiten von Kurt Wirth', *Gebrauchsgraphik*, 36.11 (1965), pp. 8–16.

To Europe by Swissair «Coronado»

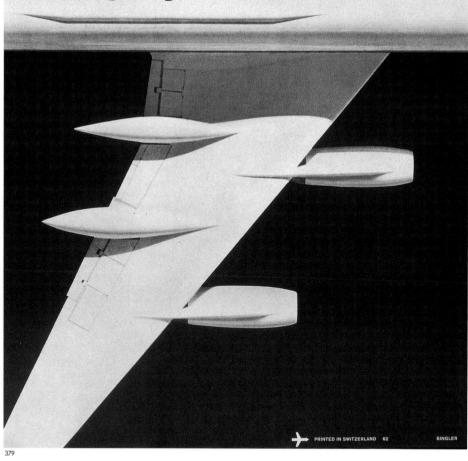

379

380

379 Manfred Bingler, 1962

380 Josef Müller-Brockmann, 1956

381 Mary Vieira, 1957

382 Jean Colin, 1959

383 Anttinen, 1959

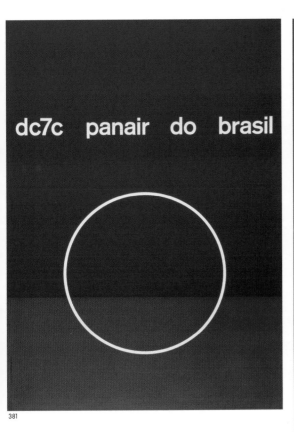

381

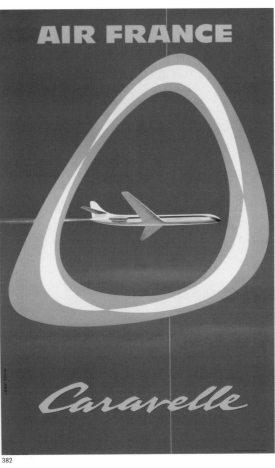

382

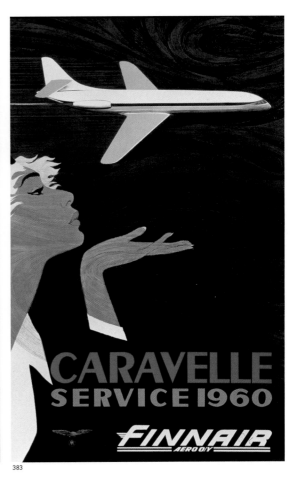

383

384 Albert Fuss, c. 1936

385 Theyre Lee-Elliot, 1936

386 Jan Lewitt, George Him, 1948

384

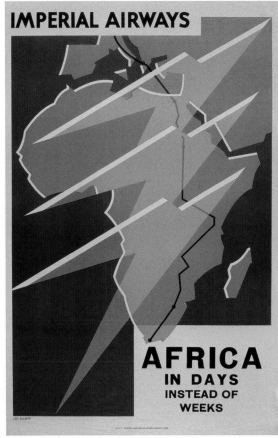

385

verkort uw reisduur

AMERICAN OVERSEAS AIRLINES

387 Hans Vogel, c. 1929

388 Anonymous, 1937

387

388

long time, graphic artists were at a loss when it came to finding a convincing way to represent the time saved through flight; textual information had to suffice. In the 1936 advertisements for their South Africa service, Imperial Airways used an abstract map showing the routes. Although the arrow-like birds – the 'speedbird' signet of the airline – gave some dynamism to the image, the actual message had to be put in words, using slogans like, 'Africa in days instead of weeks', or, 'For longer leave in England' (385). It took until 1948 for the graphic artists Lewitt and Him to design a poster for American Overseas Airlines (AOA) to use a viable visual depiction of speed, in a poster showing the vapour trails of two planes flying away from one another, stylised as rope tying up a map of the world (386). This symbolisation is certainly plausible, but because of the smallness of the details not particularly striking for capturing the 'shrinking' nature of the world through rapid flight connections.

Since the introduction of the jet plane around 1960, which once again significantly cut flight duration in comparison to the propeller plane, there has been no significant progress in terms of travel speed, except for the Concorde, which is now already out of service. It is thus not surprising that speed was soon to completely disappear as a poster subject after 1960.

Comfort

Until far into the 1950s, flying was an expensive pleasure, reserved for a well-heeled market accustomed to luxury. It was all the more crucial for the airlines to convince these customers of the comfort of air travel, since the luxurious ocean liners for a long time were their strongest competition in intercontinental travel.

Although the subject of Hans Vogel's poster *Auch im Winter* [*In Winter, Too*] is not luxury, it does point out an achievement absolutely necessary for comfortable flight: heated cabins. The poster shows the night flight of a Lufthansa plane before a snow-covered winter landscape (387). The view into the brightly-lit cabin windows shows the passengers warm and safe despite the icy outside temperatures.

Posters that convincingly depict the luxury on board aeroplanes emerged especially in the 1930s. The most interesting solutions were produced for the British airline Imperial Airways. A popular motif was a realistic depiction of the cross-section of an aeroplane, allowing a view of the complex interior life on board. In order to underscore the luxurious character of Imperial Airways' 'flying boats', this poster claims not only a separate 'smoking room', but also quite misleadingly a 'promenade deck' (388). The spurious techniques used in this advertising can be seen in the manipulated scale of the picture: in order to make the cabins seem as spacious as possible, the passengers were drawn the size of children.

Cyril Kenneth Birth succeeded in a comical, almost poetic representation of the theme of luxury. Using a cartoon-like style, the poster shows a steward with angel's wings hovering above the clouds carrying a serving tray before him; 'Travel comfortably', is the laconic slogan (389). Notable also is Steph Cavallero's poster designed in the style of Cassandre: 'By Air in Comfort'. In an art-deco style, the poster shows a passenger sunk in a voluminous club chair, and behind him the just recognisable silhouette of a steward offering a drink. Beside the writing, the soft, fluffy clouds are the only indication that the scene takes place on an aeroplane (390).

The Stewardess

The stewardess surfaced in the 1950s and 1960s as a poster motif. More so than pilots, usually invisible for the passengers, the young and always attractive women serve in a sense as the public face of the airlines and at the same time ambassadors of their country. Their appearance is fashionable, worldly, and naturally self-confident. On the posters they seem in a good spirits, dynamic, helpful, friendly, competent, and neat; a curious mixture of nurse and waitress. The uniform

389 Cyril Kenneth Bird (Fougasse), mid-1930s

390 Steph Cavallero, c. 1937

391 Anonymous, 1950s

392 Anonymous, c. 1967

391

392

5 Numerous examples can be found in Volker Duvigneau, ed. *Zwischen Kaltem Krieg und Wirtschaftswunder. Deutsche und europäische Plakate 1945-1959*, Munich, 1982, pp. 155f.
6 On Savignac's poster, see Jürgen Döring, *Plakatkunst. Von Toulouse-Lautrec bis Benetton*, Hamburg, 1994, pp. 146 f. as well as Martina Harms-Lückerath, ed., *Galerie der Straße. Höhepunkte der Plakatkunst von ihren Anfängen bis heute*, Heidelberg, 1998, pp. 136 f.

makes the stewardess into a person of respect, but at the same time these fashionable outfits tastefully emphasise the feminine charms of the young ladies.

In terms of design, the posters using stewardesses were not very innovative. More or less realistic illustrations were used during the 1950s, when such posters emerged for the first time, showing stewardesses placed usually at the centre of the image before the backdrop of an aeroplane or an airport scene (**391, 392**).[5] Never missing was a hat of some kind, a key emblem of the flight attendant. In the 1960s and early 1970s, photographs came to dominate, combined with the name and/or logo of the airline and perhaps a brief message, like Sabena's slogan, 'You're in good hands'.

Network

The density and extent of a flight network has always been an important element in airline advertising and self-representation. The network of flights is a kind of measure of the size, competence, and worldliness of an airline, and thus often surfaced as a poster subject. In particular Air France, for a long period in the post-war years the largest airline in the world, frequently used its dominant position and its global route network as a subject in its posters. Until the 1950s it was preferred to use maps of particular countries or world maps showing the routes and airports marked in colour. A paradigmatic example for this is the 1932 KLM poster advertising the route Amsterdam–Batavia (**393, 394, 395**). Such depictions can be informative but are not visually striking enough to be effective as a poster.

A second motif often used was the globe. At first, on the globe all routes were marked, in the 1950s a more abstract mode of representation began to establish itself, as in the 1956 poster by Jacques Nathan for Air-France, *le plus grand réseau du Monde*. At the centre of the poster, a globe is shown being bound up in a red-blue ribbon pulling like the vapour trail from the aeroplane pictured in the upper part of the image, symbolising the airline's global connections. The graphic

artist Perceval developed an alternative to the globe motif in 1954. The poster *Dans tous les ciel* shows before the backdrop of a lightly clouded sky sections of an aeroplane wing with motor, where there is a schematic depiction of Air France's logo at the time marked by the rotating propeller blades (**396**).

Raymond Savignac followed an entirely different visual conception.[6] At the centre of his famous 1956 Air France poster, before a dark backdrop a giraffe's head made of countless national flags can be made out. The friendly looking animal, depicted as drawn by a child, cranes its long neck to look longingly up at an aeroplane dipped in the French national colours. The Air France logo above the giraffe's head seems as if it were being pulled by the aeroplane like an advertising banner (**397**).

Interestingly, the essential elements of the poster had already emerged three years earlier in a poster designed by Paul Erkelenz for KLM (**398**). Although the astonishing formal parallels between the two works suggest that Savignac was inspired by the poster of his Dutch colleague, a comparison of the two posters shows the disparity in design competence between these two graphic artists. While Savignac succeeds in a few strokes to humanise the child-like, naïve-looking animal, immediately making it something to inspire warm feelings, the Erklenzian giraffe stares with a grotesquely distorted facial expression from huge blue (!) bulging eyes, full of wonder and horror for the KLM plane flying towards it, causing quite mixed feelings in the beholder. The graphic execution of the animal seems just as misguided. While the markings on the head remain naturalistic, they transform on the neck to become a partial map of the world, showing the area from Greenland to the southern Tip of Africa, and on closer inspection the 'Trans-Sahara Route', the subject of the advertisement. As notable as the idea of presenting a map using the markings of a giraffe might be, the result is not very convincing. Instead of recognising a map, the beholder is initially more likely to think that the poor animal is suffering from a pigment deformation.

393

394

395

396 Atelier Perceval, 1948

397 Raymond Savignac, 1956

398 Paul Erkelens, 1953

396

397

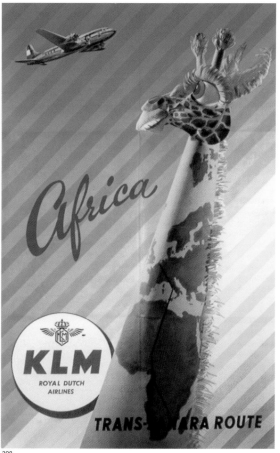

398

399 Amleto Fiore, 1956

400 Anonymous, 1950s

401 Anonymous, 1960

399

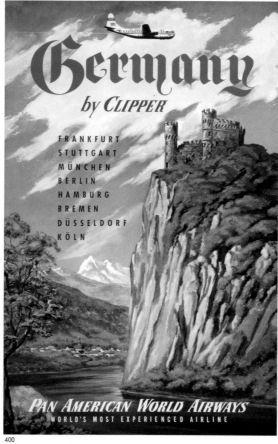

400

401

Destinations

As mentioned earlier, the posters with which airlines advertised their domestic and foreign destinations hardly differ from other tourism posters. Often they can only be identified as airline posters by the imprint of the name or logo of an airline or a small aeroplane placed in the image. Basically, in the 1930s primarily the routes were advertised, while in the post-war years it became more common to market primarily the service to tourist destinations.

As shown by the large number of examples, regardless of whether at issue are cities, regions, countries, or even continents, the same motifs were used over and over for marketing tourist destinations. Typical trademarks, as cliché-ridden as they might be, were simply endlessly repeated, and the only important differences between the posters lie in their graphic execution and their visual composition.[7]

Architectural monuments – the Eiffel Tower in Paris, Big Ben, or Tower Bridge in London – or landscape features like the Swiss Alps were often used (399, 400). A further popular image is the representation of persons in clothing typical for the country: Hawaiian girls wearing leis (401), Asian rice farmers with the coned hats, the torero in his richly ornamented costume, or the fiery Flamenco dancer.

But for a few exceptions, the most interesting examples of this kind of posters in terms of design come again from France or Switzerland. Notable are the series designed for Swissair at the end of the 1950s by Henri Ott (402, 403), Donald Brun (404, 405), and Fritz Bühler (406)[8] as well as the series by Guy Georget, influenced by cubism, for Air France at the end of the 1960s (407, 408).[9]

There are also a series of posters that avoid clichés or use them only in an ironic fashion. This is true for example of the Africa poster of Air India, for the poster pointing to Finnair's 'destination North' (409), a Finland richly blessed with water and fish, and especially for the series of posters that the Israeli graphic artist Dan Reisinger designed for El Al at the end of the 1970s.[10] Reisinger, who had already designed the airline's trademark, worked here with a formally reduced and thus all the more memorable visual play with images and letters. In the centre of the poster he placed the airline's logo, in which the L or the A was replaced with a strongly stylised symbol of the destination. For the destination Amsterdam for example, he chose a tulip, with a large red blood goblet – in the poster placed in the left upper corner – to catch the gaze of the beholder (410). The rigidly straight stem at the end, of which a single leaf swings at a right angle to the right side, then directs attention down to the airline's logo. The playfully formed letter L completes the logo. The tip of the dynamically swung leaf, pointed upwards, gives the impression that this upward motion is caused by the following letter A. On the lower margin, the destination is spelled out in narrow, sans serif large letters. To the left of this, an abstract aeroplane, turned to the right is shown: both an indication of the airline and – thanks to its triangularly formed wings (that almost evoke the Concorde) – a kind of arrow to the destination printed next to it.

Among the further highpoints of Reisinger's poster series are those advertising Paris and Zurich. In both cases, the letter A, the most prominent letter in El Al's logo, is replaced by an image, leaning on the following L, which is vertical. In the Paris poster, the Eiffel Tower stands in for the A (411). In contrast to Reisinger's otherwise geometric designs, the Paris trademark is here represented with a sketchy outline. This reference to the art centre allows the slanted representation of the tower to seem plausible. In the poster for Zurich, a mountain top forms the A, again asymmetrically formed (412). Rising steeply from the lower part of the image and crowned with a small Swiss flag, it towers far above the El Al logo. Two small jags just below the apex insure that the mountain, stylised as a white triangle, cannot be confused with a sail.

The use of the medium of photography allowed graphic artists to turn away from this clichéd visual language. Although Herbert Matter had already done

7 This is shown by the posters with which Air France, Swissair, and Pan Am advertised for their Germany flights. All three posters show a romanticised view of the German countryside, with the medieval castle as a central motif. In two cases, the castle towers over a romantic river valley – presumably the Rhine – and twice it is combined with typically 'German' half-timbered buildings. The one-sidedness of these images, in which the urban and contemporary in Germany had no place, is understandable considering the still fresh memory of the world war and Nazism.
8 See 'Swissair-Werbung', *Gebrauchsgraphik*, 32.11 (1961), pp. 2–13.
9 On Georget's posters, see Jérôme Peignot, *Air France Affiches/Posters 1933–1983*, pp. 74 and 90 f.
10 On Reisinger's poster series, see Klaus Popitz, ed., *Plakate aus Israel*, Berlin, 1985, pp. 121–26. For more on Reisinger, see FHK Henrion, *Top Graphic Design. Visuelles Kommunikationsdesign an Beispielen führender Grafik-Designer*, Zurich, 1983, pp. 126–33.

402 Henri Ott, 1950

403 Henri Ott, 1951

404 Donald Brun, 1958

405 Donald Brun, 1958 (?)

406 Fritz Bühler, 1958

407 Guy Georget, 1962

408 Guy Georget, 1963

409 Rolf Erik Bruun, c. 1959

402

403

404

405

406

AIR FRANCE

Guy Georget

grande bretagne

407

italie

AIR FRANCE

Guy Georget

408

FINNAIR

DESTINATION NORTH

FINLAND

409

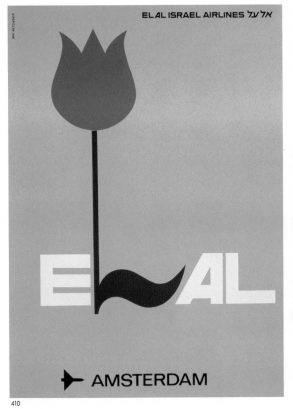

410

411

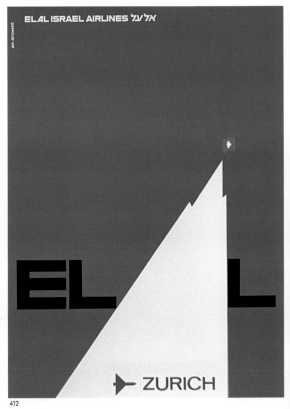

412

pioneering work in this area in 1935, using a coloured photograph collage, it would still take decades until this was again picked up (413).[11] As one of the first, Manfred Bingler in his 1964 series of posters rigorously explored the possibilities offered by photography.[12] Not only is the choice of motifs original, but also his selection and the way in which they were depicted, in order to achieve the greatest visual effect possible.

For the Japan poster, Bingler used a photograph of the rising sun taken with a powerful telephoto lens (414). The image, quite appealing in its aesthetics, brings about associations with Japan's flag, without in the least seeming tastelessly banal or forced. How brilliantly Bingler could work with the intelligently chosen images is exhibited in the poster *South America* from the same series. It shows before an orange red background a palm branch in the sunlight, with the leaf ends yellow in the sun (415). The palm branch bends, drawing a soft curve from lower left to the upper right across the entire poster surface, thus producing a dynamic upward motion. While the leaves, pointing right, pick up the direction of the stylised aeroplane on the lower right corner, the remaining leaves of the palm branch point upwards towards the sky. The motif, on its own terms quite ordinary, is here not only formally rich in tension. The palm branch seems like a feather, conjuring up not only sun and warmth, but also relaxation in the eyes of the beholder.

A completely different visual language is employed in the Africa poster, for which Bingler uses the motif of a black wooden mask (416). Again, both the subject, rich in associations, as well as the masterful execution are convincing. Based on aerial photographs by Georg Gerster, Emil Schulthess and Hans Frei created a further notable series of photographic posters for Swiss Air in 1971–72. They relied primarily on the astonishing aesthetic effect of aerial shots. The success of these posters is based on the quality of the photographs themselves and the sure feel for the graphic effect of the chosen section of the image. The Brazil poster, for example, shows the course of a river meandering through a rain forest (419), and a poster advertising the United States as a travel destination shows an elaborate web of highways that seem so well-composed, as if specially constructed for their striking visual effect (420).

A number of successful posters were also made for Lufthansa in the 1970s. The formal model of the Swiss Air posters cannot be overlooked, but in the selection of the pictures, the advertising division at Lufthansa took its own path. The idea of using a *Strandkorb*, a wicker beach chair typically used on the German North Sea and the Baltic, as a motif for a poster for Germany is certainly original (421).

A final benchmark in the development of photographic posters for civilian air travel was set by Odermatt and Tissi with their 1981 Swissair poster. As a motif they chose an everyday and yet always fascinating spectacle: at a great height, a four-jet plane leaves the traces of its movement on the blue sky, forming a characteristic white vapour trail (422). The aeroplane, which has almost crossed the entire surface of the poster from lower left to upper right, looks as it is about to leave the image in the next moment. The well-known dynamic effect of diagonals also applies to the Swissair logo, underlined with the vapour trail. The graininess of the photograph makes the aeroplane seem distant, removed from the world. The beholder might ask where the journey is leading, and will inevitably want to fly along.

Undoubtedly, the development of colour photography made possible the last great innovations in terms of iconography and graphic design. It should be noted that an important requirement for the legibility and thus the success of the photographic posters was the prior conditioning of a 'visually experienced' audience. Only when illustrated magazines and the visual media like film and television had in a literal sense provided a differentiated world image could the airlines do without the once omnipresent clichéd motifs of tourist destinations.

11 On Matter's poster, which was produced with at least three different texts, see Herbert Matter. *Foto-Grafiker. Sehformen der Zeit*, ed. Schweizerische Stiftung für die Photographie, Baden, 1995, p. 101; as well as Bruno Margadant, *Das Schweizer Plakat 1900–1983*, Basle, Boston, and Berlin, 1983, p. 303.
12 See on this Eberhard Hölscher, 'Swissair. Eine Neue Plakatfolge', *Gebrauchsgraphik*, 36.6 (1965), pp. 2–7.

413

414

415

Switzerland ✈

SWISSAIR

417

Mediterranean

SWISSAIR

418

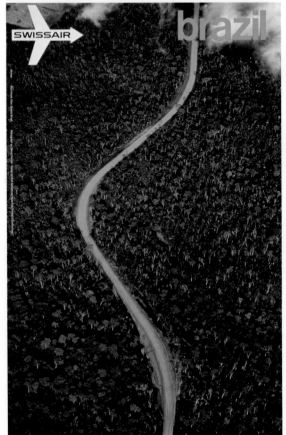

SWISSAIR ➤

brazil

419

SWISSAIR ➤

usa

420

417, 418 Manfred Bingler, 1964

419, 420 Emil Schulthess, Hans Frei,
Photograph: Georg Gerster, 1972

421 Anonymous, 1970s

422 Siegfried Odermatt, 1981

421

422

13 See on this Peignot, *Air France Affiches/Posters 1933–1983*, p. 104, as well as: Musée de la Publicité, ed., *On Air 1933–2003. Une Histoire d'Air France*, Paris, 2003.

14 The poster action was accompanied by exhibitions in Paris and Munich as well as a catalogue with texts by Carlu, André Maurois, and Jean Cocteau. See: 'Eine Plakataktion der Air France', in: *Gebrauchsgraphik*, 27.8 (1956), pp. 40–45.

15 See Hans Wichmann and Florian Hufnagel, *Künstlerplakate. Frankreich/USA. Zweite Hälfte 20. Jahrhundert*, Basle, Boston, and Berlin, 1991, pp. 46 and 108.

16 Quoted in: *Mathieu. 15 Plakate für Air France*, Air France brochure, 1967. (The French original was not available.)

17 Ibid.

18 More details on printing methods, colours, and paper qualities are contained in the brochure.

Artists' Posters

Posters not made by commercial graphic designers, but artists, are rare in air travel advertising, and at the same time a clear speciality of Air France. Far more than similar airlines in other countries, Air France understood itself from very early on as a cultural ambassador of the country – or was encouraged by the state to do so. The remarkable collaboration of the airline with the country's leading designers and couturiers will be discussed elsewhere in this catalogue.

In the design of their posters as well, Air France was always interested in the highest quality.[13] In 1956, the graphic artist Jean Carlu was commissioned to design a new poster series explicitly conceived to showcase French commercial graphic design. Carlu collaborated with famous colleagues like Jean Colin, Jacques Nathan, Guy Georget, and Raymond Savignac, who in the following years succeeded in conceiving a series of internationally respected designs.[14]

At the end of the 1960s, Air France decided to go a step further, commissioning fine artists with poster series design: in 1967 Georges Mathieu, in 1971 Raymond Pagès, and in 1980 finally Roger Bezombes. Little is known about the criteria for choosing these artists, but all three have often caused controversy with their works in the applied arts.[15]

Georges Mathieu, who in the 1960s was one of the most famous artists in France, is considered a leading artist of tachism or lyric abstraction. The theme of his poster series was again the various destinations served by Air France. Before a solidly coloured background, a sketchy abstract image develops, which is striking above all for the expressive and seemingly uncontrolled form of painting, typical for Mathieu. The images range from abstraction (like the Spain poster (423)) to relatively easy legibility (as in the Greece poster). Whether he succeeded in reaching his own goal, 'to bring such a multiple whole like the soul of a people into the language of lyric abstraction', to represent 'what makes up the most typical structural essence of a national character

to as many temperaments as possible', seems doubtful. 'To say the unsayable' – this is quite an ambitious goal, even for an artist.[16] In any case, Mathieu's visual inventions evidence a clearly subjective engagement with the issue at hand. Leaving aside more general aesthetic considerations, the subtlety and originality of his pictures might well be treasured; but their lacking legibility and the ambivalence of their statement can only be seen as problematic. A good example of this is the Germany poster, about which Mathieu himself remarked: 'The eagle, the traditional symbol. Example of an abstraction. Neither the eagle of Charlemagne, nor Otto, nor Bismarck, nor Hitler, but: mine. It is formed by the romanticism of Novalis, the authority of Frederick the Great, the majesty of a Beethoven symphony, Gothic longing for far away, the universality of Goethe.'[17] This quite vague explanation cannot blind us to the fact that the latent aggressiveness and threat of his eagle, in connection to the *Allemagne*, set in Gothic type, with the background of German history in the first half of the twentieth century, awakens quite different associations (424). The same can be said of his Spain poster, but in contrast the United States poster can be considered a successful creation, easy to grasp and yet rich in its play with meanings (425).

Great effort and expense was dedicated to realising Mathieu's poster series. Almost all printing techniques – off-set, deep print, lithography, and silk-screen printing – were used; sometimes multiple techniques for one and the same poster,[18] making production accordingly expensive. Special brochures were even printed to popularise the series, itself intended mainly to promote the image of the airline.

Raymond Pagès, who began designing posters in 1971 for Air France, also relied on country destinations for his themes. One is initially struck by the strict formal organisation of the posters. Before a neutral, usually white background, the actual image, each forming a precise square, takes up the upper half of the poster. Beneath this lies a great deal of white space, and then the destination written in outlines and the Air France

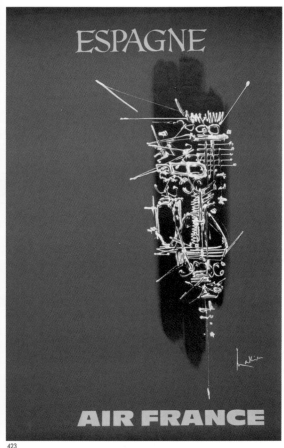

423

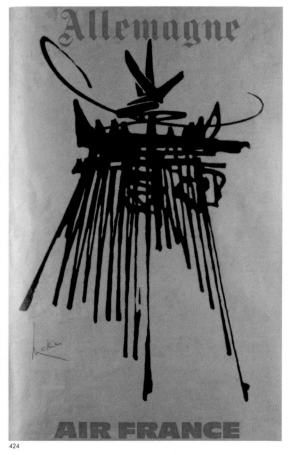

424

425

426

427

BRITAIN
AIR FRANCE

428

AIR FRANCE

429

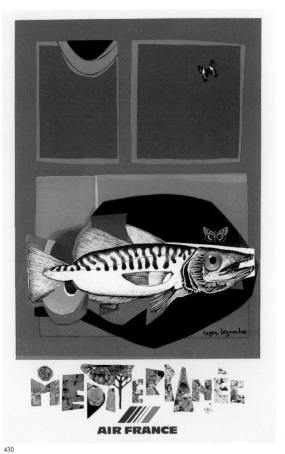

MÉDITERRANÉE
AIR FRANCE

430

19 See Wichmann and Hufnagel, *Künstler-plakate*, p. 46.
20 Quoted in *Raymond Savignac. Werke des französischen Plakatkünstlers aus den Jahren 1948 bis heute*, Munich, 1982, pp. 7 f.

logo. While many of his images, like those for France, USA (**426**), Brazil, and the Soviet Union remain entirely abstract, the posters for Great Britain and Spain present a strict collage pattern. The theme of the Spain poster is the bullfight, for the representation of which Page worked with parts of photographs, red and highly grainy photographs (**427**). For the Great Britain poster, he composed a large number of more or less easily deciphered colour photographs in a box – a kaleidoscopic, personal image of British everyday life and culture (**428**).

In contrast to Mathieu and Pagès, Roger Bezombes was given very unspecific thematic guidelines for his Air France poster series, *La vie du monde*.[19] He took advantage of this freedom to create a series of up-beat poetic collages with unusual titles such as *Ciel* (**429**), *Merveilles de la terre,* and *Liberté*. With works like *Mediterranée* (**430**) and *Orients*, in contrast, Bezombes also remained true to a classical theme of air travel posters. For the collages he used photographs, printed matter, and paintings in various degrees of abstraction. Stylistic borrowings from cubism are as clear as the inspiration of works of Henri Matisse. A strong, almost always amicable colourfulness is one of the essential trademarks of these posters which speak to and inspire the imagination of the beholder.

Air France's art posters did not find many imitators. Their usefulness as means of advertising is dubious, precisely due to their artistic character. Savignac offers an explanation for this, taking a clear position on the question of art and the poster. 'Like Cassandre, I believe there is no noble art in advertising. Free art and advertising can work together, but not mix. The poster must remain useful. One can in its realisation combine the useful with the pleasant, as Cassandre succeeded in doing, but not the reverse [...] The poster stands in the same relation to the fine arts as freestyle wrestling to good manners.'[20]

In the end, it was significant that the art posters emerged in a period when posters were beginning to lose their importance in airline advertising. At the latest since the 1970s, the poster began to be displaced as a part of airline marketing campaigns. Today, innovative design ideas in this area apparently no longer have any chance of being developed: the airlines' focus has long since shifted to print and the various electronic media.

THE INSPIRATION OF FLIGHT: DEVELOPMENTS IN ART, DESIGN, AND ARCHITECTURE SINCE THE 1930s

CHRISTOPH ASENDORF

Translation by Brian Currid

The organisers of the 1937 Paris World Exposition commissioned Robert Delaunay to design the Palais de l'Air. That this avant-garde artist was at all considered for such a task, intended for a mass public, could be attributed to the exposition's programme, which stood under the motto, 'Art and Technology'. As a kind of sketch proposal, Delaunay presented *Hélice et Rhythme* [*Propeller and Rhythm*], which synthesises various phases of his work. Already in his 1914 work *Hommage à Blériot* he had included a few aeroplanes, the Eiffel Tower, and coloured discs that seem to result from the movement of a large propeller, combining them to form a representation of the dynamism of modern life (**431**). In the following years, Delaunay returned again and again to these themes, perhaps more consistently than any other painter.

The commission for the Palais de l'Air was awarded in the mid-1930s, in other words, at a time of consolidation in the technology and infrastructure of air travel. Civilian air travel had developed slowly since World War I, and for many years only survived with the support of government subsidies. It was in the 1930s that financially independent air travel on a larger scale first emerged, along with aeroplanes with the size, robustness, and speed required. Beginning test flights in 1933, the most forward-looking of these aeroplanes – with its radically streamlined design – was the DC-3, which combined all three factors. In subsequent years, this plane would later be built thousands of times over. In addition, large airports were built, some of which are still in operation, like Berlin Tempelhof.

The pavilion that Delaunay ultimately realised in collaboration with architects was a large space in the form of a capsized zeppelin gondola. Behind a glass façade, inside the pavilion hung an aeroplane surrounded by orbits placed on different planes, and a walkway accessible to visitors (**432**). Delaunay had discovered a formal repertoire for the representation of air travel without resorting to direct mimesis. The orbits refer on the one hand to cosmic movement, the planetary orbits in the solar system. On the other hand, the arrangement also depicts the gimbal mounting of the gyroscopic compass, so important to air travel. On the walls of the pavilion, works by the artist couple Sonia and Robert Delaunay were hung. The entire space – which thrilled Le Corbusier – was an attempt to link painting, architecture, and technology. Delaunay was interested in crossing boundaries, an openness to all sides, an image of space in which direct, linear movements with a beginning and an end are replaced by a dynamic continuum.

Delaunay continued to develop the artistic language used in the Palais de l'Air in his painting. A perspective like that of Picasso, who exhibited his Guernica only a few metres away, remained foreign to him. Delaunay's fundamental point of view was deeply optimistic; he believed it was possible to synthesise nature, technological innovation, and art. This is expressed not only in the Palais de l'Air, but also in earlier works like *Hommage à Blériot*, and later series such as *Rhythmes sans fins* (**433**) and *Formes Circulaires*. As an expression of the period, as Delaunay put it, his art possesses an element of 'circular movement'.[1]

Le Corbusier's book on air travel was published almost simultaneously with the opening of Delaunay's pavilion; the book, simply titled *Aircraft*, appeared in 1935 as part of a series that also included Raymond Loewy's *Locomotive*. The publisher had inspired him to represent the changes resulting from air travel from his point of view. Unlike Delaunay, the architect and urban planner was interested in the topic more from the perspective of concrete possibilities of application. Le Corbusier did not write a continuous text, but included a total of 124 images treating various topics combined with 'titles' and brief texts, a *montage* charged with meaning. The images can be roughly divided into two groups: on the one hand, images of aeroplanes, including technical details and in part quite suggestively puzzling cross-section drawings (**435**), on the other hand aerial photographs, occasionally combined with drawings that Le Corbusier completed during or after his own flights (**434**).

1 Robert Delaunay, 'Zur Malerei der reinen Farbe', *Schriften*, ed. Hajo Düchting, Munich, 1983, p. 65.

431 Robert Delaunay, *Hommage à Blériot*, 1914.

432 Interior of the Air Palace (L'intérieur du pavillon d'air pour l'expo), 1937 World Exposition, Paris, designed by Robert Delaunay and Felix Aublet.

433 Robert Delaunay, *Rythme sans fin*, 1934.

431

432

433

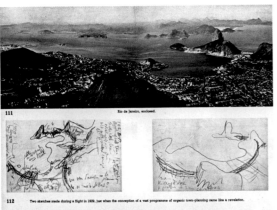

434

434 Page from Le Corbusier's *Aircraft* with a view of Rio de Janeiro and two sketches on urbanisation drawn during a flight in 1929.

435 Double page spread from Le Corbusier's *Aircraft*: the illustrations show details of various Imperial Airways aeroplanes (43 and 44: *Scylla*, 45: *Atlanta*, and 46: *Britomart*).

435

2 Le Corbusier, *Précisions sur un état présent de l'architecture et de l'urbanisme*, Paris 1960, p. 4.
3 Le Corbusier, *Aircraft*, New York, 1988 [1935], pp. 5, 12 f.
4 See Donald J. Bush, *The Streamlined Decade*, New York, 1975.
5 Walter Dorwin Teague, *Design this Day*, London, no year [1940], p. 143.
6 Norman Bel Geddes, *Horizons*, New York, 1977 [1932], pp. 3 ff.
7 Norman Bel Geddes, *Magic Motorways*, New York, 1940, p. 269. For more on the context, see Edward Dimendberg, 'The Will to Motorization. Cinema, Highways and Modernity', October 73 (1995), especially pp. 116 ff.
8 For more on this, see Christoph Asendorf, *Super Constellation – Flugzeug und Raumrevolution*, Vienna and New York, 1997, pp. 265 f.

Le Corbusier's interest in the constructive rationality of aeroplanes had already been expressed in 1923 in the programmatic text 'Vers une architecture', where the aeroplane represents a model of material economy and the optimal use of space. But in addition to an apparent pleasure in the plastic quality of streamlined figures, it was primarily the use of aeroplanes, the view from above, that inspired Le Corbusier. 'From the aeroplane, I have seen spectacles that could be called cosmic' – this ecstatic commentary after his first flights at the end of the 1920s[2] was concretised in *Aircraft*. From the air, Corbusier had been able to discover the large rhythms and contexts in nature, and at the same time the chaotic and dysfunctional growth of large cities: 'the aeroplane takes up the prosecution!',[3] as he now put it. New cities were to be built in a different form, on a generous scale and with the organic flow of all things in mind – just as nature presented itself to the air traveller.

Le Corbusier, then, was interested in a more natural form of organising life relations. As far as the easy transportability of people and things, Le Corbusier's considerations were in tune with a general trend of the time. In the United States, the 1930s are known as the 'Streamlined Decade' – culminating with the New York World's Fair of 1939 (**436**).[4] The central focus was on enabling the free flow of energy. This is true on the one hand for the world of objects. For Walter Dorwin Teague, for example, an aeroplane like the DC-3 was in every way a complete expression of modern design. In this plane, the connections between each individual element were worked out technologically as well as in terms of design to such an extent that all lines were clear and fluid. The DC-3 with its highly streamlined form could become the ultimate symbol of technical progress, since it united functional and emotional qualities, as Teague described, using as an example its characteristic outlines: 'This line, composed of a short parabolic curve and a long sweep, straight or almost straight, expresses force and grace [...] There surely is no more exciting form in modern design (**440**)'.[5]

Norman Bel Geddes went beyond such considerations on the individual object. His richly illustrated book *Horizons* appeared in 1932, at the start of the 'Streamlined Decade'. Soon after the start of the first chapter, 'We enter a new era', it quickly becomes clear that Bel Geddes is here presenting something like a model for society: not only things, but also social structures must be optimised in terms of design. The means for this are offered by technology.[6] His Futurama at the 1939 World Exposition carried out these ideas in a model: an America criss-crossed with superhighways and a dense network of air routes, where the difference between city and country is by and large sublated and the comfortable provision of commodities, services, and information is secured for the long term (**437, 439**). While Delaunay and Le Corbusier developed a new conception of space and/or a new scale for city planning based on the experience of air travel, at issue here was primarily the practical use of traffic technologies as a means of civilisational development. In *Magic Motorways*, a book published to accompany the exhibition (**438**), and thus appearing on the eve of the World War II, Bel Geddes described this new way of life: 'Living in such a world of light, fresh air, open parks, easy movement, the man of 1960 will more naturally play his full part in the community and develop in mind and body'.[7]

After the Second World War, under the leadership of the USA, the already long powerful notion of a world united by technology began to become reality. In 1943, the American politician and former presidential candidate Wendell Willkie published his book, *One World*. The title quickly became a buzzword, referring to a world in which the United States served as the future global guarantor of political and economic freedom and offering a common platform for the future direction of US policy in the post-war years.[8] Even a theory like that of the American philosopher John Dewey, who saw a world emerging where there are no longer fixed orders and borders, but processes of transformation and interaction, is fundamentally compatible with this kind of framework. When in the 1940s Siegfried

436

436 Aviation Building, New York World's Fair, 1939.
Designed by William Lescaze and J. Gordon Carr.

437 General Motors Pavilion, New York World's Fair, 1939.
Designed by Albert Kahn.

438 Aerial view of Norman Bel Geddes' vision of the 'City
of 1960', from Magic Motorways, 1940.

439 Norman Bel Geddes' Futurama, a vision of the 'City of
1960', General Motors Pavilion, New York World's Fair, 1939.

437

438

439

440 A double page spread from Walter Dorwin Teague's Design this Day, showing photographs of a Douglas DC-3 and the 'Bridge of Tomorrow' at the New York World's Fair, 1939. The photographs were taken by Margaret Bourke-White.

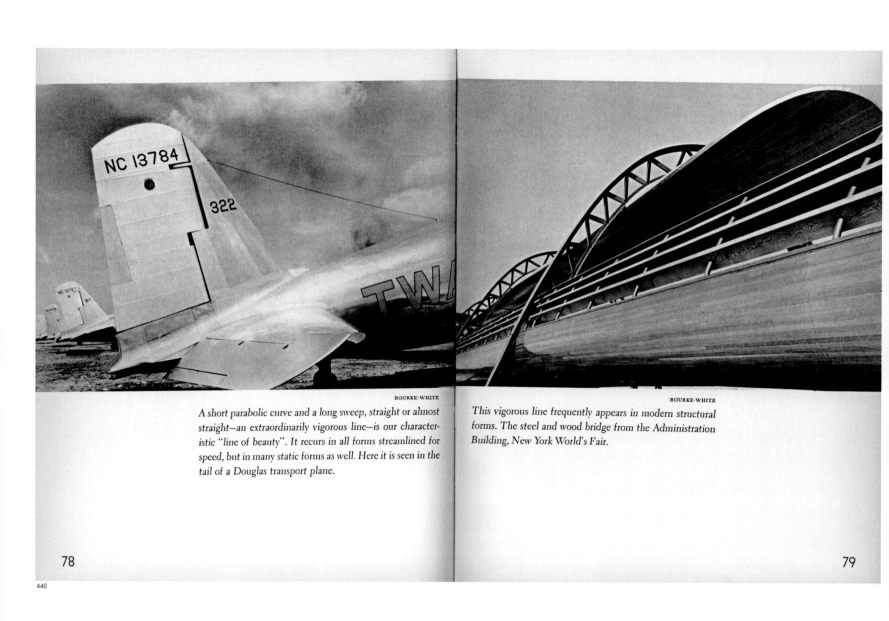

BOURKE-WHITE

A short parabolic curve and a long sweep, straight or almost straight—an extraordinarily vigorous line—is our characteristic "line of beauty". It recurs in all forms streamlined for speed, but in many static forms as well. Here it is seen in the tail of a Douglas transport plane.

BOURKE-WHITE

This vigorous line frequently appears in modern structural forms. The steel and wood bridge from the Administration Building, New York World's Fair.

78

79

440

Giedion, Alexander Dorner, and László Moholy-Nagy presented their great syntheses of modernism's *Kunstwollen*, they made reference to the conceptions of Dewey.[9] The three authors, who in the years between the two world wars had been leading representatives of the European avant-garde, had in the face of rising fascism emigrated to the United States, where their books were then published: first in 1941 Giedion's *Space, Time and Architecture* (**441**), then in 1947 Dorner's *The Way beyond 'Art'* and Moholy's *Vision in Motion*, and finally in 1948 Giedion's *Mechanization Takes Command*.

Dorner's book even includes a foreword by Dewey, where he emphasises that at issue is no longer the individual as a stable element, but the general life processes in which the individual takes part.[10] Of course, this also implies a permanent state of flux. Dewey explains further how he fundamentally shares Dorner's convictions, in particular a 'belief as to things common to artistic creation and appreciation, and all other vitally significant phases of human life.'[11] The brief reference to a world of experience that transcends separate spheres already leads to Dorner's central observation, that is, the presence of a 'supraspatial reality of pure energies'[12] that he (like Giedion in *Space, Time and Architecture*) sees in physics just as much as in the art of a Cézanne or Picasso. What needs to be the issue in the future, he argued, was 'integration on a dynamic basis'.[13] Absolute space and absolute time would lose their status as 'final truth' and would mutually influence one another.

The central figure in *The Way beyond Art* is Herbert Bayer, who according to Dorner developed a dynamic iconography for a world saturated with energies.[14] For Dorner's orientation towards the processual over the static, Bayer embodies the prototype of a new generation of designers who will shape a kind of behaviour adequate to a 'supraspatial' modern reality. During World War II, his works revolved in particular around two issues: spatial experience in the age of global air travel and the new science of electronics.[15] In both

cases, Bayer is interested in visualising the continuity of movement: the title of a 1942 informational brochure for General Electric reads *Electronics: A New Science for a New World*. Here, the history, function, and future applications of electronics are presented as a series of confidently composed double-page spreads. As a graphic element he often uses electron orbitals, which circle around an atomic nucleus as in the models of Rutherford and Bohr. Bayer exploits the model in all its dimensions; he shows electron paths in both the microcosm and macrocosm. They circle around people as well as planets, becoming the ultimate all-encompassing sign for energy (**442, 443**).

Bayer's paintings during this period are free artistic works that bear titles like *Interstellar Exchange* or *Celestial Spaces*: arrows illustrate the direction of heavenly bodies, showing constellations of energies or the constant penetration of meteorological phenomena into the earth's atmosphere. They are images of energies that are effective across space. He was awarded an important commission in 1943 by the Museum of Modern Art: the design of the exhibition Airways to Peace (**444**).[16] The general theme of the exhibition was how the view of the world was changed by the aeroplane, and the form and content of the exhibition were closely linked to one another. One of the central objects was a large, hollow globe, with the contours of the earth's surface painted on the interior, accessible to visitors (**445**). This inversion expanded the view of the concave surface: larger parts of the earth's surface could be grasped in one view. The mise en scène of this exhibition, its space-integrating design as much as the optical presentation of a future geography of global connections – still in the midst of the war – point to a spatial consciousness that no longer knows any bounds. At the same time, it becomes clear how Bayer sees the aeroplane: as an effective catalyst for the emergence of a civilisation marked by the idea of universal interaction.

As visible nature disappeared from the natural sciences, the arts also transformed themselves. In his influential 1954 work *Malerei im 20. Jahrhundert,* Werner

9 On Dewey's inspirational role in all three cases, see Stanislaus von Moos, 'Modern Art Gets Down to Business', *Herbert Bayer – Das künstlerische Werk*, Berlin, 1982, p. 100.
10 Alexander Dorner, *The Way beyond Art – The Work of Herbert Bayer*, New York, 1947.
11 Ibid., p. 10.
12 Ibid., p. 103.
13 Ibid., p. 103.
14 See the chapter on Bayer in *Herbert Bayer – Das künstlerische Werk*, a. a. O., esp. pp. 80 f., 90 f.
15 See Arthur A. Cohen, *Herbert Bayer*, Cambridge (Mass.), 1984, pp. 302 ff.
16 See on this Mary Anne Staniszewksi, *The Power of Display: A History of Exhibition Installations at the Museum of Modern Art*, Cambridge (Mass.), 2001, pp. 227–35.

441 The cover of Sigfried Giedion's *Space, Time and Architecture*, designed by Herbert Bayer.

442 Cover of the advertising brochure for General Electric 'Electronics – A New Science for a New World', designed by Herbert Bayer.

443 From 'Electronics – A New Science for a New World', here the Spanish version.

444 Herbert Bayer's exhibition Airways to Peace, Museum of Modern Art, 1943.

445 View of the hollow globe at Airways to Peace.

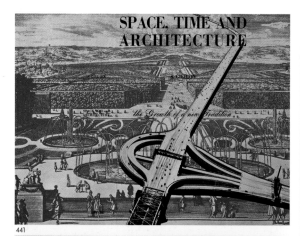

441

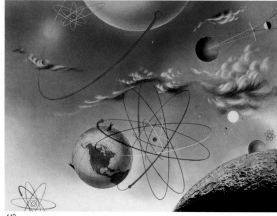

442

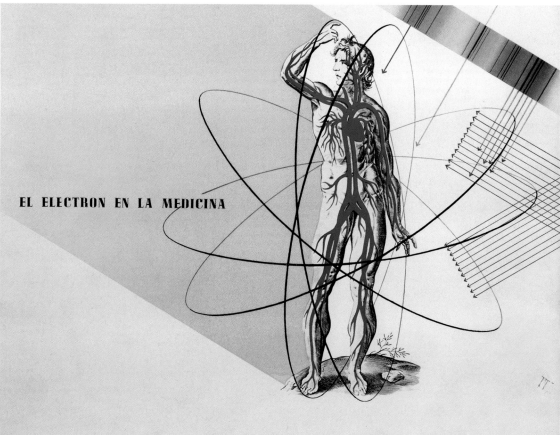

443

444

445

446 Jackson Pollock, working on *Number 32*. Photograph: Hans Namuth, 1950.

447 Mark Tobey, *Aerial City*, 1950.

446

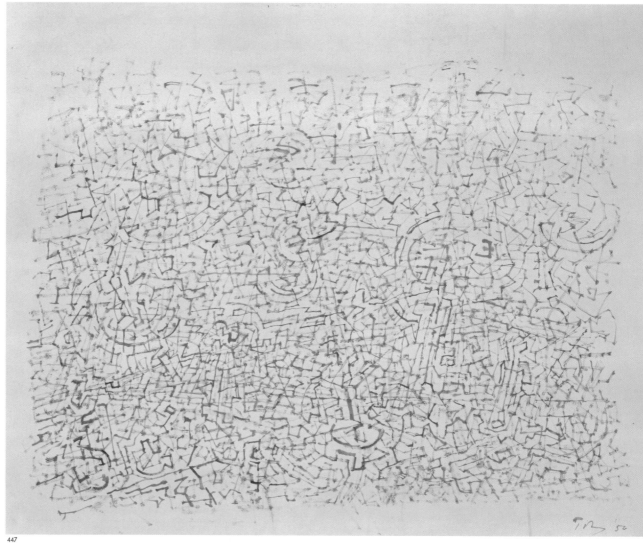

447

Haftmann saw abstract expressionism as an adequate technique for appropriating and administering the world at a time when thinking itself had found itself in 'obscure regions'.[17] This originally American school of painting was dominant during the 1950s, at least west of the Iron Curtain: Haftmann even coined the formula 'abstraction as a universal language'. The artistic strategy of Jackson Pollock in particular would come to epitomise abstract expressionism. Pollock also claimed the representative character of his art as an 'expression of the contemporary aims of the age that we're living in'.[18]

Although the actual feel of the time can only remain somewhat vague, Pollock's work does seem to express a spatial understanding that could only develop in the age of global air travel. Three characteristics mark his painting: the large canvas, an all-over quality, and the use of action painting. A photograph showing him working on Number 32 demonstrates how these three come into interplay with one another (446). The large canvas lies flat on the floor. The posture of the painter is that of a sower, his perspective that of a pilot; he works over the image, throwing the paint down from above. Without touching the base of the painting, his movements are left as traces in the image. Lee Krasner described his procedure as 'Working in the air, [creating] aerial form[s] which then landed',[19] and mentioned at the same time a prerequisite of the suggestive effect caused by Number 32 and related works: when hung on the wall, and thus placed in the usual forces of gravity, these images seem anti-gravitational, de-centred; a notion of above and below is hardly applicable.

A counterpole to Pollock's extensive swinging gestures is Mark Tobey's method: using calligraphic techniques and usually small formats, he created images of objectless worlds saturated with energy. In a work like Aerial City from 1950, which from a distance is reminiscent of an aerial photograph, two levels are superimposed and interpenetrate one another: the lower one implies streets and squares, and the one above it a free web of lines (447). Tobey is concerned with fluctuating spatial relations. With his 'white writing', the webs of lines interact on multiple levels, producing an impression of pulsation, and a 'multiple space' emerges.[20] Despite the different format and intention of Tobey's work, it is linked to Pollock's not only by its contemporaneity and common foundation, but also a light, almost weightless agility.

These aspects of design can also be found in the other arts. For example, when the sculptor Alexander Calder was commissioned to decorate the Aula Magna at Caracas' Universidad Central de Venezuela in the 1950s, he designed a ceiling ornamentation with dark, cloud-like floating sails hung beneath a bright background (448). He thus realised his notion of 'liberated bodies that glide through space',[21] which he had executed in a different way in his mobiles. While Calder used sculptural means to free the ceiling of the impression of being bound by gravity, in the architecture of the period the possibilities of reinforced concrete were taken to their utmost limits to make the buildings seem almost capable of floating. They are elevated from the floor or given flying ceilings; other trademarks include wide arches and thin, freely-formed bowls.

There is certainly no form that expresses lightness and dynamism more fully than the parabola. A parabolic arch is not only the ideal arch form in terms of statics, but also in terms of the use of material. On the symbolic level, it is significant that the words 'parabola' and 'ballistics' derive from the same root (ballein is the Greek for 'to throw'); a ballistic curve is a parabola. Parabolas in architecture can thus symbolically refer to the trajectory of a bullet or missile as well as the overcoming of gravity in general. The small, elegant, and energetically swung parabolic arch that Oscar Niemeyer placed directly before Brasilia's Quartel General do Exército [Army General Headquarters] can be read as a monument to the ballistic curve (449). Probably the most important project of this kind, however, was created by Eero Saarinen: the St. Louis Gateway Arch (450). At first sight, its form seems to approach that of a parabola, but in fact it traces out a catenary, or the curve marked by a hanging chain. Designed in 1948 and completed in 1964, the arch became the model for a large number

17 Werner Haftmann, Malerei im 20. Jahrhundert, Munich, 1976, pp. 464, 518 ff.
18 Quoted in Thomas Kelle, Sputnik-Schock und Mondlandung, Stuttgart, 1989, p. 123.
19 Steven Naifeh and Gregory White Smith, Jackson Pollock, New York, 1991, p. 539.
20 Wieland Schmied, Mark Tobey, Stuttgart, 1966, pp. 8, 13.
21 Akademie der Künste Berlin, Alexander Calder, 1967, p. 17. (Calder's text dates from 1952.)

448 Carlos Raul Villanueva's Magna Aula at the Univerisdad Central de Venezuela, Caracas. The ceiling décor was designed by Alexander Calder, 1952–53.

449 Oscar Niemeyer's Monument to Caxias, placed before Army General Headquarters, Brasilia.

450 Eero Saarinen's Gateway Arch, St. Louis, 1948–64.

448

449

450

451

451 Sky House, Tokyo, 1958. Designed by Kiyonori Kikutake.

452 Philips Pavilion, World Exposition Brussels, 1958. Designed by Le Corbusier.

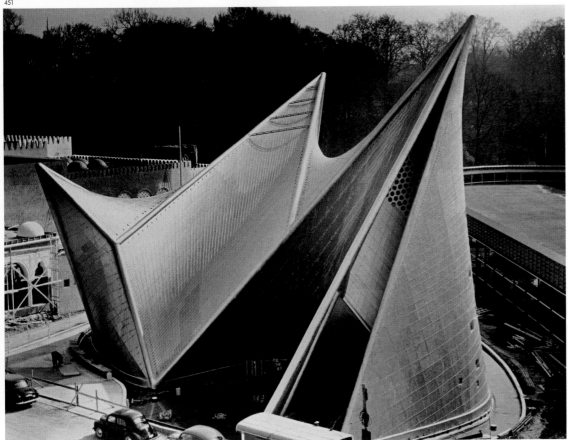

452

22 See *Eero Saarinen on His Work*, ed. Aline B. Saarinen, New Haven, 1968.
23 Jürgen Joedicke, *Schalenbau*, Stuttgart, 1962, pp. 10 ff.
24 A foundational text on this is Bart Lootsma, ‚Poème Electronique', *Le Corbusier. Synthèse des Arts*, Karlsruhe, 1986.
25 Frank Jackson, 'The New Air Age. BOAC and Design Policy 1945–60', *Journal of Design History*, 4.3 (1991), p. 167.
26 John Neuhart, Marylin Neuhart, and Ray Eames, *Eames Design. The Work of the Office of Ray and Charles Eames*, Berlin, 1989, pp. 28 ff., 42 f., 139 f.
27 Ibid., pp. 274 f., 226 ff.
28 See Charles Jencks, *Spätmoderne Architektur*, Stuttgart, 1981, pp. 100 f.

of curved and especially parabolic forms in 1950s architecture. For this monument to the Western expansion of the United States, Saarinen sought a form that did not seem earthbound, but rather strove upwards;[22] he thus modified the form of the dynamically swung curve until the energy that the arch was to develop in space seemed to him truly aesthetically complete.

The drive towards dynamic design culminated in the architecture of the time in the complex construction form of the hyperbolic paraboloid, which up until then had almost only been used in engineering constructions.[23] The fact that the saddle surface of a hyperbolic paraboloid is doubly ruled makes it relatively easy to adapt to various constructions. A highpoint of the architecture of hyperbolic paraboloids, which always seems quite corporeal and sculptural, was set by Le Corbusier's Philips Pavilion at the Brussels World Fair in 1958 (452).[24] Here, interior and exterior blur into one another, flowing, curved surfaces abolish the difference between wall and ceiling. As the Philips pavilion, this construction, the inside of which was resonated with Varèse's *Poème electronique,* is a striking sign of modern information technology. Considering its design quality alone, its hyperbolic paraboloid skin, built a year after the first takeoff of Sputnik, the pavilion represents a kind of an energetic image of space that does without a single stabilising coordinate system.

Historians consider 'air-mindedness' one of the central characteristics of the years following World War II.[25] Social scientists as much as doctors or urban planners concerned themselves with the effects of flight. In design as well, this can be observed, and perhaps nowhere as markedly and complexly as in the work of Charles and Ray Eames. This applies (beside their films and exhibitions, which represented in many ways the effects of advanced technology on civilisation) in particular to the materials with which they worked, often materials that owed their development directly or indirectly to air travel.[26] Plywood, for example, was attractive during the Second World War due to metal rationing. In the production of aeroplane components,

the Eames' developed refined wood treating techniques that helped them in the shaping of their plywood furniture. When he began studies on the Plastic Armchair in 1950, Charles Eames contacted a company that was experienced with fibreglass-enforced plastic in the production of radar dishes.

This orientation towards aeroplane technology was particularly apparent in the Aluminium Group, an ensemble of chairs that Charles Eames first presented in 1958. There is almost no material so closely linked to the history of air travel as aluminium. Because of its light weight and high degree of solidity it was used from the very beginning in zeppelin construction and after the introduction of all-metal aeroplanes took on an outstanding significance in aeroplane construction. In the Aluminium Group, the single surface used for seat and armrests, made of leather, cloth, or plastic, is stretched completely without supports between two slender aluminium supports. In their detailed design and reduced elegance, the chairs embody the quintessence of lightweight construction. A commission of Eero Saarinen[27] returned them to the sphere from which they derived their material and economy of form. For the waiting areas of Washington D.C.'s Dulles Airport, the flying roof of which is held between supports like the seating surface of the chairs, he had a variant of the Aluminium Group made: tandem seating (✈054).

In the 1960s, in many areas the interest in air travel shifted towards an interest in space travel. Because it encompasses large areas of science and technology, this interest also spread to other areas of life; it could perhaps be said that space travel generated the notion of a world regulated by immense technological systems. This had an impact not least on architectural and urban visions. A taste of the future was already offered in 1960 by the Japanese 'metabolists'. The biological sound of this group's name was no accident: they sought to organise modern civilisation's 'metabolism' in the form of megastructures.[28] A model of their conception was Kikutake's Sky House: a square room, supported in

453

454 Fountain, Expo '70, Osaka.
Designed by Isamu Noguchi.

455 Interior, Soviet Pavilion, Expo '70, Osaka.
Designed by Konstantin Roshdestwenski.

456 A photograph of a rocket launching ramp, from René
Burri's *Ein amerikanischer Traum* [*An American Dream*].

454

455

457 Madrid Airport, photographed by Martha Rosler, 1990.

458 TWA Terminal, John F. Kennedy International Airport,
photographed by Martha Rosler, 1990.

457

458

space by four pylons, is supplied by modular elements, aggregates of building technology that are simple to remove and modernise (451).

This group's grand vision, however, came from Kenzo Tange. His Tokaido Megapolis project was conceived as a living space for 10 million people. The entire Tokyo Bay area was to be overlaid with a grid as a movement structure, in order to connect it to the individual complexes of living, production, and administration. Streets were designed as assembly lines of accelerated circulation. Tange speaks of an age of organisation, when cities must connect their traffic and information systems in new ways. The goal of such considerations is no longer a certain kind of space, but – at a time humanity is about to 'free itself from the chains of the earth and push out into space'[29] – potentially every space that is reachable. Thus, in its technical artificiality his mega-structure is difficult to distinguish from the utopian projects of extended space colonies.

Similar notions can also be found elsewhere. For example, R. Buckminster Fuller built a geodesic dome as the United States Pavilion at the 1967 World Exposition (453): he dreamt of a 'Spaceship Earth',[30] which as a kind of mothership would be surrounded by small spherical satellites that would be inhabitable. The highpoint of the technological fantasies of the Space Age would prove to be the Expo '70 in Osaka. The Soviet Union, just beaten in the race to the moon, showed in its pavilion all the recently returned capsules from Soyuz, in a way reminiscent of Malevitch's cosmism: the exhibition design by Roshdestvenksi,[31] an earlier collaborator of the Malevitch student Suyetin, used suprematist motifs as a decorative background for Lenin images and Sputniks (455). However, the all-dominating building at the exposition was Tange's theme pavilion. Conceived as a small part of a potentially infinite structure, this was an accessible spatial structure of 108 by 292 m that floated 30 metres high over a fixed position and was closed at the top by transparent air cushions. It was complemented by Noguchi's over-sized fountains: large cubes sitting on narrow supports that

reverse the principle of the fountain, in that the streams of water, although directed downward, seem to leave the earth (454).

After the moon landing, the Age of Discovery's centuries' old interest in opening real space slowly began to shift towards a virtual 'data space'. The status of air and space travel, undeniably the most advanced traffic technologies, changed with the enormous progress in information technology, which now became the dominant technology, bundling the potentials of the time. Even if the economic significance of air travel continues to grow, and technological development progresses, this sphere no longer exudes the idea of emancipation from all spatial limitations, and perhaps also no longer the same glamour, that it did in the years between 1930 and 1970. This is also indicated by changing artistic perspectives, as shown by *In the Place of the Public*, the title of a 1998 book and exhibition project by Martha Rosler. With an almost sociological interest (that is reminiscent of the thoughts of Marc Auge on 'non-places' of modernity)[32] the American artist photographed the world of airports over a span of 20 years: the photographs show an endless series of neutralised spaces that have lost all expression or intention towards self-expression (457, 458).[33]

In the same way, a book like René Burri's *Ein amerikanischer Traum – Photographien aus der Welt der NASA und des Pentagon [An American Dream: Photographs from the World of NASA and the Pentagon]* could never have been possible before 1970, since it shows abandoned and slowly decaying rocket launch pads, now more reminiscent of Egyptian necropolises than the shiny world of high-technology (456). Even individual military aeroplane types are taken by artists as the object of their ruminations on the status of technological civilisation in general. James Rosenquist's work *F-111* is a 26 meter long painting that shows a then current fighter plane intersecting with images of the American way of life: hair dryers, spaghetti, and automobile tyres (459). War technology and consumer culture here appear as if they inseparably interlinked with

29 *Kenzo Tange*, ed. H. R. von der Mühll, Zurich and Munich, 1978, p. 203.
30 R. Buckminster Fuller, *Bedienungsanleitung für das Raumschiff Erde*, ed. Joachim Krausse, Reinbek 1973, p. 177.
31 On Roshdestvenski, see Larissa Shadowa, *Kasimir Malewitsch und sein Kreis*, Munich, 1982.
32 Marc Augé, *Non-Places. Introduction to an Anthropology of Supermodernity*, London and New York, 1995.
33 Martha Rosler, *In the Place of the Public*, Ostfildern-Ruit, 1998; See Martha Rosler, 'In the Place of the Public. Observations of a Frequent Flyer', Airport, eds. Steven Bode and Jeremy Millar, London, 1997, pp. 90 ff.

459 James Rosenquist, *F-111*, 1964–65. Oil on canvas with aluminium (3.05 x 26.21 m). The Museum of Modern Art, New York. Gift of Mr. and Mrs. Alex L. Hillman and Lillie P. Bliss Bequest.

459

460, 461 Interior, Health Pavilion, Expo 2000, Hanover.
Designed by Toyo Ito.

462 Mediatheque in Sendai, 2001. Designed by Toyo Ito.

460

461

462

34 Martina Knoben, 'Höchste Potenz', *Süddeutsche Zeitung*, 25 October 2002, p. 14.
35 Frank R. Werner, 'Die ganze Welt als Videoclip', *Bauwelt* 24 (2000), p. 76.

one another. Hartmut Bitomsky's 2000 documentary film *B-52* deals with an eight-jet long distance bomber that, developed in the 1950s, was still used in the 2003 Gulf War as a carrier of cruise missiles. This aeroplane, in which technology and the power of destruction amalgamate, is for Bitomsky, as he explains with a fascinated horror, the 'pinnacle of Western civilisation'.[34]

But the emphasis on flying that found such diverse forms of expression in the heroic era of classical modernism has not entirely disappeared. Interestingly, it is the technologies of the Age of Information that give these ideas a new life. The Japanese architect Toyo Ito uses two different strategies: at exhibitions, he often stages spaces in which an experience of floating is suggested through visual means. This was demonstrated in an especially impressive way in his Health Pavilion at the Expo 2000 (**460, 461**). Patterns of light and films projections on the walls and floor overplay the space limitations and the visitors who, according to the specialist journal *Bauwelt*, stand before the flow of images 'as if in a hypnotic trance',[35] and find themselves on their softly vibrating massage lounges in a subjective loss of gravity.

The means used in the Mediatheque, opened in 2001 in Japan, are quite different (**462**). A highly filigreed supporting system that seems to emerge slightly off the vertical from a river stabilises a glass construction, the essential characteristic suggested is permeability. It seems weightless and polymorphous; clever lighting makes the Mediatheque into a transformable appearance of colourful light. Here, a new modus of symbolisation for a new cultural pull becomes visible: the external, that is, corporeal representation of lightness, openness, and free possibilities of movement in space, qualities that were at issue in classical modernism and which earlier for example were provided by flying roofs have now in the architecture of the Age of Information been replaced by the presentation of inner transformability, as if light phenomena or data streams might serve as substitutes for the desired characteristics.

Christoph Asendorf is professor for art and art theory at the Europa-Universität Viadrina in Frankfurt (Oder), and the author of *Super Constellation – Flugzeug und Raumrevolution. Die Wirkung der Luftfahrt auf Kunst und Kultur der Moderne.*

Koos Bosma is an architectural historian and associate professor at the Vrije Universiteit in Amsterdam. His recent publications include the recent coedited volume *Mastering the City: North European City Planning, 1900–2000.*

Jochen Eisenbrand is a cultural historian and curator at Vitra Design Museum.

Joanne Entwistle is lecturer in Sociology at the University of Essex. She has published numerous articles on fashion, gender, and the body, including *The Fashioned Body: Fashion, Dress and Modern Social Theory.*

Barbara Fitton Hauß completed degrees in art history, English literature, and linguistics at Amherst College and the Universität Freiburg, and works as a freelance translator and art historian in Lörrach. She has published articles on a wide range of topics, including Norman Bel Geddes and streamlining.

Mathias Remmele teaches design and architectural history at Basle's Hochschule für Gestaltung und Kunst. As a guest curator at the Vitra Design Museum, he has organised exhibitions on Verner Panton and Marcel Breuer.

Hasso Spode is a historian and sociologist and teaches in Berlin and Hanover. He is director of the Historical Tourism Archive at the Willy-Scharnow-Institut of the Freie Universität Berlin and coeditor of *Voyage: Jahrbuch für Reise- & Tourismusforschung* and *Tourismus-Journal.* His most recent publication is *TraumZeitReise: Geschichte und Philosophie des Tourismus.*

Index

Aerial Express: 88, 90,
Aeroflot: 18, 24, 32
Aerospatiale France: 114
Aida Group: 138, 140
Aicher, Otl: 150, 159, 160, 225
Airbus: 32, 34
- A300: 31, 116
- A330: 116
- A340: 116
- A380: 119
Air France: 18, 19, 23, 24, 28, 106, 107, 109, 110, 114, 115, 116, 130, 132, 135, 146, 147, 150, 152, 154, 155, 168, 178, 181, 182, 188, 189, 228, 227, 231, 233, 244, 249, 258, 262
Air India: 26
Airliner Number 4: 89, 91
Air Orient: 146, 147
Air Union: 18
Albatross L73: 85, 87
Albers, Josef: 155
Alitalia: 26, 150, 154, 155, 174, 186, 190, 191, 223
All Nippon Airways: 141, 142
American Airlines: 16, 24, 25, 95, 100, 113, 133, 137, 146, 150, 168, 169, 185, 192, 193, 213, 221
Amies, Hardy: 197
Amsterdam Schiphol Airport: 37, 44, 45, 59
Andreu, Paul: 49, 51, 52, 60
Anttinen: 237
AOA/American Overseas Airlines: 25, 239, 241
Armani, Giorgio: 190, 191
Asaka, Michiko: 226
Avro
- Tudor: 150
- York: 99

BA/British Airways: 116, 119, 138, 140, 142, 151, 168, 174, 186, 196, 197, 216
Balenciaga, Christobal: 181, 188
Balmain, Pierre: 204, 207
Barnes, Edward Larabee: 156, 157, 160
Baumann, Hans Theo: 225, 227
Bayer, Herbert: 271, 272, 273
BEA/British European Airways: 24, 26, 28, 106, 150, 151, 171, 196, 197, 234, 236
Bel Geddes, Norman: 89, 91, 95, 96, 97, 100, 268, 269
Berlin Tegel Airport: 48, 50

Berlin Tempelhof Airport: 19, 21, 22, 26, 28
Bernadotte, Sigvard: 220, 221
Bezombes, Roger: 258, 260, 261, 262
Bingler, Manfred: 235, 237, 253, 254, 257
Bircher, Rudolf: 152, 153, 160
Bird, Cyril Kenneth: 242, 243
Bitomsky, Hartmut: 288
Blass, Bill: 182, 185
BOAC/British Overseas Airways Corporation: 100, 107, 109, 145, 146, 150, 151, 152, 163, 164, 168, 196, 215
Boeing: 24, 32, 112, 119
- Boeing Air Transport: 181, 208
- B 17:
- B 247: 92, 93, 129, 241
- B 307 Stratoliner: 13, 17, 21, 97, 99, 100
- B 314: 95, 97, 107, 213
- B 377 Stratocruiser/C-97: 100, 103, 106, 214, 215
- B 707: 29, 32, 107, 108, 109, 137, 157, 160, 215, 216, 221
- B 727: 109, 225
- B 730: 172
- B 747 (Jumbo): 31, 32, 91, 111, 112, 114, 137, 142, 215, 216
- B 757: 116
- B 767: 116
- B 777: 116, 117, 119, 120, 142
- Model 80: 86, 87
- Sonic Cruiser: 119
- SST 2707: 114, 115, 116
- 7E7 Dreamliner: 118, 119
Bonfils, Bo: 228
Bourke-White, Margaret: 270
Braniff International: 145, 164, 165, 166, 181, 183, 185, 194, 195
Brauer, Klaus: 119
Breda-Zappata: 215
Breuer, Marcel: 85, 86
Breuhaus de Groot, Fritz: 20
British Aircraft Corporation: 114
Brûlé, Tyler: 173, 174
Brun, Donald: 249, 250
Brunhes, Jean: 13
Brunswick, Charles: 235
Bruun, Rolf Erik: 250
Bühler, Fritz: 249, 250
Burnelli, Vincent: 88, 91
Burri, René: 280, 283
Butler, Charles: 106, 116, 120
BWB/Blended Wing Body A20.30: 119, 121

Capital Airlines: 106
Calder, Alexander: 275, 276
Carlu, Jean: 258
Carr, J. Gordon: 269
Carven: 181, 182, 188, 204
Cavallero, Steph.: 241, 243
Chadwick, Hulme: 120
Chicago O'Hare International Airport: 45, 57
Christmas, William Whitney: 88, 91
Clivio, Franco: 226
Colin, Jean: 235, 237, 258
Colombo, Joe: 222, 223
Concorde: 34, 114, 115, 116, 235, 241, 249
Condor: 26, 32
Conran Design Group: 38, 57
Consolidated Vultee
- Convair 37/XC 99: 99, 100, 102
- Convair 39: 99
- Convair 440 Metropolitan: 172
- Convair 880: 107, 109
- Convair 990 Coronado: 235, 236
Cook, Thomas: 28, 34
Copier, Andries: 217, 221
Couallier: 146, 147
Court Line: 32
Cyrén, Gunnar: 228

Dallas-Fort Worth International Airport: 50, 53
Davies, R. E. G.: 150
Day, Robin: 163, 164, 215, 221
De Havilland Comet: 29, 32, 107, 108, 164
Delagrange, Ferdinand Léon: 83
Delaunay
- Robert: 265, 268
- Sonia: 265
Del Guidice, Frank: 100, 112
Deruluft: 18
Deutsche Aero Lloyd: 16
Deutsche Luft-Reederei: 13, 14, 145, 146
Deutsche Luftschiffahrts AG: 13
Deutscher Flugdienst: 26
Deutsche Verkehrsflug AG: 18
Dewey, John: 268, 271
Dior, Christian: 182, 188, 203
van Doren, Nowland & Schladermundt: 214
Dorner, Alexander: 271
Dornier
- Claude: 146
- Marcel: 146

- Do X: 92, 94, 95, 99
- Superwal: 125, 126
- Wal: 19
Douglas:
- C54: 128
- DC-1: 92
- DC-2: 17, 92, 93, 95, 130, 131
- DC-3/DST/Douglas Sleeper Transport: 17, 18, 95, 98, 99, 103, 129, 135, 146, 149, 161, 163, 215, 221, 233, 235, 265, 268, 270
- DC-4: 20, 27, 99, 100, 112, 215
- DC-6: 104, 106
- DC-7: 163, 235
- DC-8: 107, 109, 110, 153, 160, 161, 163, 164, 215, 218, 221
- DC-10: 113, 114
Dreyfuss, Henry: 95, 98, 99, 100, 102, 105, 106, 107, 109, 115, 120, 157, 168, 169, 215, 216, 221
Drömmer, Friedrich Peter: 146, 148
Duintjer: 44, 45
Dunton, George: 57

Eames
- Charles: 46, 57, 278
- Ray: 57, 278
Earl, Harley: 109, 110, 114
Eastern Air Lines: 16, 24, 106, 110, 146, 168, 169
Edwards, George R.: 106
Egtvedt, Claire: 86, 100
El Al: 26, 249, 252
Erkelens, Paul: 245, 246
Excoffon, Roger: 168,

Farman: 83, 145
- F-60 Goliath: 83, 84
Ferraud, Louis: 188, 189
Finnair: 150, 164, 218, 221, 235, 249, 251
Fiore, Amleto: 248
Firle, Otto: 144, 147, 160
Fischer von Poturzyn, Friedrich A.: 16, 23
Flueler, Caroline: 173
Focke-Wulf Fw 200 Condor: 20, 22, 99, 101, 109
Fokker:
- F.III: 83
- F.VII/3m: 85
- F.XII: 87

- F.27 Friendship: 161, 163
- F. 32: 17
Forberg, Charles: 156, 157, 158
Ford Tri-Motor: 85, 92, 125, 126, 127, 129, 130, 213
Foster, Norman: 46, 60, 62
Frankfurt Airport: 27, 28, 32, 54, 55
Frei, Hans: 253, 256, 257
Fuller, Richard Buckminster: 23, 279, 283
Fuss, Albert: 238

Gautier-Delaye, Pierre: 116
Georget, Guy: 249, 250, 258
Gerkan, Meinhard von: 48, 60, 61
Gerster, Georg: 253, 256, 257
Gerstner, Karl: 151, 152, 168
Gibberd, Frederick: 38, 57
Giedion, Sigfried: 271, 272
Giefer, Mäckler & Kosina: 54, 55
Girard, Alexander: 164, 166, 167
GMP/von Gerkan, Marg und Partner: 60, 61
Gonda, Tomàs: 160
Göring, Hermann: 18, 20, 21, 23
Graves, J. A.: 109, 110
Gruen, Victor: 45, 46

Haftmann, Werner: 275
Halston: 195
Hamburg Airport: 60, 61
Handel-Mazetti, Eduard Freiherr von: 232
Handley-Page HP 42: 90, 91, 213
Hannoversche Waggonfabrik Hawa F 10: 83
Harrison, Wallace K.: 42
Heinkel
- He 70: 18, 19
- He 178: 23
Hellmuth, Yamasaki & Leinweber: 56
Henrion, F. H. K.: 145, 150, 151, 168, 171
Him, George: 238, 241
Hoar, Marlow & Lovett: 43, 45
Hochschild, Arlie: 178
HOK/Hellmuth, Obata & Kassabaum: 50, 53

IATA/International Air Transport Association: 16, 18, 24, 28, 32, 107, 145, 174
Ie, Kho Liang: 44, 59
Immermann, Milton: 120

Imperial Airways: 18, 85, 91, 146, 150, 151, 213, 235, 238, 240, 241, 242
Industrial Design Studio: 121
Interflug: 26, 27, 28
Ito, Toyo: 286, 287, 288

Jacobsen, Arne: 155
JAL/Japan Airlines: 26, 139, 142, 152, 154
Jobis: 201
John F. Kennedy International Airport/Idlewild: 40, 41, 42, 56, 282
J. S. K./Joos, Schulze, Krüger-Heyden: 54, 55
Juhl, Finn: 110, 155, 163, 164
Junkers: 16, 85, 86, 129, 133, 135, 146, 148
- Hugo: 86
- Luftverkehr AG: 16, 146
- EF 100: 100
- F 13: 13, 14, 83, 84, 129
- G 24: 85
- G 31: 86, 87
- G 38: 88, 91
- G 39: 88
- J 1000: 86, 88
- Ju 1: 85
- Ju 52: 15, 18
- Ju 90: 21, 22, 99, 101, 135
- Junkerissime: 86

Kahn, Albert: 269
Kansas City International Airport: 50, 53
Karnagel, Wolf: 225, 227
Kepes, Gyorgy: 155
Kern, Alfred: 160
Ketcham, Howard: 100
Kikutake, Kiyonori: 277, 278
Kivett & Myers: 50, 53
Klein, Calvin: 182, 203
KLM/Koninklijke Luchtvaart Maatschappij voor Nederland en Kolonien: 16, 17, 18, 24, 26, 83, 85, 87, 105, 106, 131, 145, 146, 147, 150, 152, 155, 161, 163, 168, 170, 198, 199, 217, 221, 244, 245, 247
Koller, Otto: 91
Kracauer, Siegfried: 34

Lacroix, Christian: 177, 181, 189
Laker, Freddy: 32

Lambert St. Louis International Airport: 45, 56
Landor Associates: 116, 174
Lantal Textiles: 139, 142
Larsen, Jack Lenor: 157
Lauren, Ralph: 185, 207
Lawler, Paul: 232
Le Corbusier: 265, 267, 268, 277, 278
Lee-Elliot, Theyre: 146, 150, 151, 238
Lepistö, Kari: 164
Lescaze, William: 269
Lévi-Strauss, Claude: 34
Lewitt, Jan: 238, 239
Lindon, Patrick: 173
Lippincott & Margulies: 168, 169
List, Friedrich: 23
Lockheed: 135
- L-10 Electra: 92, 95
- L-188 Electra: 106, 107, 109, 136, 137, 161, 163, 215
- L-1011 Tri Star: 113, 114, 215
- L-2000 SST: 114, 115
- Constellation: 21, 99, 112
- Super Constellation: 24, 27, 32, 34, 105, 106, 134, 135
Loewy, Raymond: 56, 100, 115, 116, 155, 160, 169, 182, 183, 207, 209, 265
- Loewy, Raymond/William Snaith Inc.: 56
Loftleidir: 32
London Gatwick Airport: 43, 45, 59
London Heathrow International Airport/Central: 38, 42, 45, 59
London Stansted Airport: 60, 62, 63
Loper, Don: 183, 207
Lorenz, Anton: 130, 133, 134, 135, 137
Louis, Jean: 209, 210
Lovegrove, Ross: 139, 142
Luce, H. R.: 24
Luckhardt, Hans: 130, 131, 132, 133, 135, 137
Luftag/Aktiengesellschaft für Luftverkehrsbedarf: 26
Luftfartselskab: 18
Lufthansa: 18, 19, 21, 22, 23, 24, 26, 27, 28, 31, 32, 87, 91, 93, 99, 101, 106, 113, 119, 130, 134, 135, 142, 145, 152, 155, 159, 160, 168, 178, 182, 200, 201, 223, 224, 225, 226, 227, 228, 231, 235, 238, 240, 241, 243, 253, 257
- Deutsche Luft Hansa AG: 15, 16, 85, 86, 87, 90, 91, 146, 147
Lufthansa of GDR: 26

LTU: 26
L'viv: 56

MacDonald, Julien: 186, 197
Machnik, Werner: 201
Madrid Barajas International Airport: 282
Marg, Volkwin: 48, 60, 61
Martin M 130 China Clipper: 94, 95, 96, 97, 233
Mason, E. Gilbert: 104, 106, 107, 136, 140
Mathieu, Georges: 258, 259, 262
Matter, Herbert: 249, 253, 254
McArthur, Warren: 128, 129, 130
Messerschmitt: 32
- Me 262: 23
Milch, Erhard: 18
Moholy-Nagy, Lázló: 271
Molloy, John T.: 186
Monö, Rune: 163, 168, 172
Möller-Brockmann, Josef: 235, 237
Munch-Petersen, Ursula: 228

NACO/Netherlands Airport Consultancy: 44, 45
Namuth, Hans: 274, 276
Nathan, Jacques: 244, 258
Nelson, George: 56
Newson, Marc: 138, 142
Nickels, Klaus: 48
Niemeyer, Oscar: 275, 276
Noguchi, Isamu: 280, 283

Odermatt und Tissi: 253
Odermatt, Siegfried: 257
Oeschger
- Alfred: 39, 42
- Heinrich: 39, 42
Ott, Henri: 249, 250
Overseas National Airways: 30

PAA/Pan Am/Pan American: 16, 18, 24, 28, 32, 95, 96, 97, 100, 112, 125, 135, 140, 145, 146, 150, 152, 155, 156, 157, 160, 168, 182, 183, 217, 232, 233, 235, 248, 249
Pagès, Raymond: 258, 260, 262
Panair do Brasil: 235, 237
Paris Orly Airport: 58, 59

Patou, Jean: 189
People's Express: 32
Perceval: 244, 246
Perriand, Charlotte: 154, 155
PIA/Pakistan International Airlines: 202
Plesman, Albert: 146
Pollock, Jackson: 274, 275
Ponti, Gio: 154, 155
Product Design Factory: 116
Prokosch, Walther: 106
Prouvé, Jean: 58, 155
Pucci, Emilio: 164, 165, 181, 183, 185, 194, 195
Purcell, William: 106
Putman, Andrée: 116

Qantas: 138, 142
Querengässer, Fritz: 160

Radi Designers: 227, 228
Rado, L. L.: 154, 155
Rau, Emil: 92
Raymond
- Antonin: 154, 155
- Arthur E.: 125
Reisinger, Dan: 249, 252
Rellstab, Ludwig: 23
Ricci, Nina: 181, 188, 189
Rietveld, Gerrit: 161, 163
Robillard, R. J.: 113, 114
Roericht, Hans Nick: 160, 224, 225, 226
Roissy Charles de Gaulle Airport: 49, 50, 51, 52, 60
Roosenburg, Dirk: 146, 147
Rosenquist, James: 283, 284, 285
Roshdestwenski, Konstantin: 280
Rosler, Martha: 282, 283
Royal Airship Works R 101: 21
Rumpler, Edmund: 91

Saarinen, Eero: 40, 41, 42, 46, 56, 57, 275, 276, 278
Sabena: 18, 26
Sagebiel, Ernst: 21, 22
SAS/Scandinavian Airlines System: 100, 110, 145, 150, 154, 155, 163, 168, 171, 174, 182, 203, 220, 221, 228, 243
Satre, Pierre: 109, 110
Savignac, Raymond: 244, 246, 258, 262

Schneider, Uwe: 116
Schön, Mila: 190
Schulthess, Emil: 253, 257
SIA/Singapore Airlines: 186, 204
Sikorsky
- Bolshoi Bal'tiskii: 83
- Igor: 83
- Ilya Muromez: 86
- S-40: 150
- S-42: 129
SISA: 18
Skytrain: 32
Smith, Zay: 146, 149
SOM/Skidmore, Owings & Merrill: 42
Sommerlatte, Horst: 116
Southwest Airlines: 185, 205
Stam, Mart: 86, 130, 133, 135
Steinbüchel, Rambald von: 155
Stockholm Design Lab: 173, 174
Strenesse: 201
Sud-Est Aviation/Sud Aviation: 114
- S.E. Caravelle: 31, 32, 109, 110, 160, 164
Sundberg-Ferar: 113, 114
Swissair: 17, 18, 23, 32, 144, 150, 152, 153, 160, 168, 206, 218, 219, 221, 231, 233, 234, 235, 249, 250, 253, 254, 255, 256, 257
Swiss International Air Lines: 173, 174
Syndicato Condor: 19

Tange, Kenzo: 283
Tangerine: 119, 138, 142
Tapiovaara, Ilmari: 164
Tautz, Ursula: 182, 200, 201
Teague/Walter Dorwin Teague Associates: 100, 103, 106, 107, 108, 109, 111, 112, 115, 116, 117, 120, 137, 268, 270
Tippetts-Abbett-McCarthy-Stratton: 50, 53
Tobey, Mark: 274, 275
Tola Design: 141, 142
Topel und Pauser Industrial Design: 225, 227
Trans Canada Airlines: 106
Transcontinental Air Transport: 126, 127, 213
Tréze, de Georgette: 188
Tscherny, George: 30
Tupolev
- Tu 104: 31, 32
- Tu 144: 33, 34, 114
TWA/Trans World Airlines: 16, 24, 40, 41, 42, 45, 56, 100, 109, 135, 136, 140, 146, 150, 155, 168, 169, 182, 185, 207

Ungers, Oswald Mathias: 54, 55
United Airlines: 16, 17, 18, 24, 95, 98, 99, 100, 146, 149, 150, 181, 182, 208, 209, 210, 213, 215, 221, 248
USAir: 120

Valentino: 207
van Naess and Murphy: 45, 57
Varig: 183, 184
Vicariot, Henry: 58, 59
Vickers:
- Super VC-10: 163, 164
- Vimy: 125
- Viscount: 106, 108, 215, 223
Vieira, Mary: 235, 237
Villanueva, Carlos Raúl: 276
Virgin Atlantic Airways: 139, 142
Vogel, Hans: 231, 232, 240, 241

Wagenfeld, Wilhelm: 223
Walther, Jean: 233
Warhol, Andy: 145
Washington Dulles International Airport: 45, 46, 47, 56, 57
Weiss, Jürgen: 201
Wells, Mary: 164, 165, 183
Welsh, Robert: 116
Willkie, Wendell: 268
Wirkkala, Tapio: 218, 221
Wirth, Kurt: 234, 235
Wissing, Benno: 44
Wöhler, Karlheinz: 34
Wright, Wilbur: 83
Wronsky, Martin: 16

Yorke, Rosenberg & Mardall: 43, 45

Zeppelin: 18, 21
- LZ 6: 83
- LZ 7: 83
- LZ 127: 18
- LZ 129 (Hindenburg): 18, 20, 21
- LZ 130: 21
- LZ 131: 21
Zholtowsky, Ivan: 56
Zindel, Ernst: 86, 91, 99
Zurich Kloten Airport/Unique: 39, 42, 58

Illustration Credits

AIDA Development GmbH, Schwäbisch Hall: 189
©Airbus S.A.S 2003: 156, 157
Air France Museum Collection. Department of Cultural and Historic Heritage: 253, 254, 255, 257, 258, 259, 260, 261, 262, 263, 382, 394, 396, 407, 408, 423, 424, 425, 426, 427, 428
Air France Museum Collection. Department of Cultural and Historic Heritage/©VG Bild-Kunst, Bonn 2004: 397, 429, 430
Allen, Roy: Große Flughäfen der Welt. Zurich 1968, S. 15: 050
All Nippon Airways/TOLA Design, Sammamish/Designer: Wallace A. Peltola: 196
American Airlines C.R. Smith Museum, Fort Worth: 268, 269, 270, 272, 273, 276, 321
Paul Andreu architecte, Paris: 060, 064, 065, 066
Paul Andreu architecte, Paris/©ADP: 062, 063 (Photograph: B. Bienaimé)
Paul Andreu architecte, Paris/©IGN/ADP: 067
Paul Andreu architecte, Paris/©Paul Maurer: 061
Architectural Design 7/1969, S. 391, Abb. 4: 038; S. 396, Abb. 19: 039
The Architectural Review, October 1958, S. 252/©VG Bild-Kunst, Bonn 2004: 211
L' Architecture d'Aujourd'hui. June-July 1971. "Aéroports," p. 11: 049, 057, 071, 073
Architekten von Gerkan, Marg und Partner, Hamburg: 058, 077(Photograph: Christoph Gebler), 078 (Photograph: Klaus Frahm)
Architekten von Gerkan, Marg und Partner, Hamburg/Landesbildstelle Berlin: 059
Archiv der Luftschiffbau Zeppelin GmbH, Friedrichshafen: 013, 014
Archive, Verkehrshaus der Schweiz, Lucerne: 030, 087, 104, 145, 316, 317, 372, 377, 379, 405

Bauhaus Archiv Berlin/©VG Bild-Kunst, Bonn 2004: 441 (Photograph: Markus Hawlik), 442, 443 (Photograph: Markus Hawlik), 445 (Photograph: Gottscho-Schleisner, New York)
©Bildarchiv Preußischer Kulturbesitz (bpk), Berlin, 2004: 018
Rudolf Bircher, Zurich: 207, 208
Bluequest, Darmstadt: 370
Boeing: 159, 160
Photograph ©Margaret Bourke-White Estate: 440
British Airways: 284, 287, 288, 289
Courtesy of Nicholas and Shaunna Brown, Camden, Maine: 172, 173, 174, 175
©René Burri/Magnum Photos: 456

Studio Joe Colombo, Milan: 357, 358, 359, 360
Cooper-Hewitt, National Design Museum, Smithsonian Inst.: 118, 125, 126, 149, 150, 186, 187, 238, 347

Courtesy Dallas Historical Society: 277, 278, 279, 281
Robin Day, Chichester: 226
Department of Special Collections, Stanford University Libraries/The Estate of R. Buckminster Fuller, Santa Barbara: 453
Designmuseo, Helsinki: 353, 354
Deutsche Lufthansa AG: 001, 002, 003, 004, 010, 011, 012, 015, 016, 021, 022, 024, 086, 088, 089, 098, 099, 102, 105, 107, 108, 123, 124, 144, 166, 185, 197, 214, 297, 298, 299, 300 (Photograph: Gundlach), 301, 302, 303, 304, 305 (Photograph: Claus Freytag), 306 (Photograph: Wolfgang Fritz), 340 (Photograph: Peter Pfander), 362, 364, 369, 373, 384, 387, 391, p. 296
Deutsche Lufthansa AG/Boeing: 032

Deutsche Lufthansa AG/Deutsches Plakat Museum Essen: 421
Deutsches Filminstitut-DIF, Frankfurt: 247, 248, 249
Deutsches Filmmuseum, Frankfurt am Main: 250, 251
Deutsches Museum, Munich: 005, 028, 083, 084, 085, 093, 094, 106, 113, 120, 122, 148 ,152, 252, 274, 275, 280, 285, 290, 319, 342,
Donne, Michael, *Above Us the Skies.* Whitley 1991, p. 35: 035, 047

EADS Deutschland: 158
Ezra Stoller ©Esto: 044, 045, 046, 053, 054, 056

©Fondation Le Corbusier/VG Bild-Kunst, Bonn 2004: 434 (Le Corbusier, *Aircraft*, figs. 111-112, 1935 A3 (18) 98 and 99 Rio de Janeiro: urbanisme), 435 (Le Corbusier, *Aircraft* fig 43-46, 1935), 452 (Archive FLC L1 (3) 32)
Foster and Partners, London: 079, 081
©Lee Funnell/Graphicphoto: 194
Fraport AG, Frankfurt am Main: 070, 072
Fundação Oscar Niemeyer, Rio de Janeiro: 449
Fundación Villanueva, Caracas ©VG Bild-Kunst, Bonn 2004: 448

General Motors Corp. Used with permission, GM Media Archives, Detroit: 437, 439

Ludo van Halem/Fokker/©VG Bild-Kunst, Bonn 2004: 222
Harry Ransom Humanities Research Center/The University of Texas at Austin: 095, 096, 097, 110, 111, 112, 438
Hellmuth, Obata + Kassabaum, Inc., St. Louis/Photograph: George Silk: 068
F H K Henrion Archive, Faculty of Arts and Architecture, University of Brighton: 239, 240, 241, 242, 291
HfG-Archiv Ulm: 215, 216, 217, 218
Hochschule für angewandte Wissenschaften Hamburg/Technische Universität München: 161

Kho Liang le Associates, Amsterdam/Photograph: Jan Versnel: 051, 052
Industrial Design Studio, Hamburg: 162, 163
Industrial Design, February 1961, S. 59: 188; March 1959, pp. 34-35: 213; November 1966, p. 45: 236
Interiors, June 1957, p. 108: 209
Toyo Ito & Associates, Architects, Tokyo: 460, 461, 462 (Photograph: Naoya Hatakeyama)

Jefferson National Expansion Memorial/National Park Service, St. Louis: 450

Kansas City Aviation Department: 069
Kiyonori Kikutake, Tokyo/Photograph: Yukio Futagawa: 451
Kunstindustrimuseet, Copenhagen/© Photograph: Pernille Klemp: 212, 224, 225

Lantal Textiles, Langenthal, Switzerland: 192, 193
Lexel Electric Oy, Stomfors: 355
©L & M SERVICES B. V. Amsterdam 20031014: 431, 432, 433
Luftbild Schweiz, Sammlung 'Photoswissair', Dübendorf: 040, 041

Maria Austria Instituut, Amsterdam: 199
Collection Achim Moeller, New York: 447
Münchner Stadtmuseum B(SF) 17.4/1: 409
©Musée de l'Air et de l'Espace/Le Bourget: 286, 309,
©Musée de l'Air et de l'Espace/Le Bourget/Air France: 256, 264

©Musée de l'Air et de l'Espace/Le Bourget/American Airlines: 318, 320, 323
©Musée de l'Air et de l'Espace/Le Bourget/Boeing: 139
Cliff Muskiet Collection, Amsterdam, www.uniformfreak.com/Photograph: Andreas Sütterlin: 266, 267, 282, 283, 292, 293, 294, 295, 296, 310, 311, 312, 322, 324, 334
Museum für Gestaltung, Zurich, Poster collection: 029, 205, 374, 376, 378, 380, 381, 383, 385, 386, 388, 393, 399, 401, 402, 403, 404, 406, 410, 411, 412, 413, 414, 415, 416, 417, 418, 419, 420, 422
Digital Image ©2004 The Museum of Modern Art, New York/VG Bild-Kunst, Bonn 2004: 444, 459

©Hans Namuth Estate/Collection Center for Creative Photography 1991, University of Arizona/©Pollock-Krasner Foundation/VG Bild-Kunst, Bonn 2004: 446
National Air and Space Museum, Smithsonian Institution: 006 (SI 89-20588), 007 (NASM 00134226), 101 (SI 75-12144), 109 (SI 88-17652), 114 (SI 75-219), 115 (NASM 00014319), 117 (SI 89-4024), 119 (SI 77-5844), 133 (NASM 00039304), 138 (NASM 00023524), 140 (NASM 00092395), 141 (NASM 00092388),146 (NASM 00063955), 147 (NASM 00063943), 165 (NASM 00133887), 168 (SI 78-1485), 201 (SI 87-10380), 326 (SI 88-18945), 330 (SI 88-18946),
National Air and Space Museum, Smithsonian Institution/Alitalia/Photograph: Ivo Meldolesi, Rom: 265 (NASM 00130752)
National Air and Space Museum, Smithsonian Institution/Boeing: 090 (photo no. 2571-B, dated 8-14-29), 091(SI 91-207), 103 (photo no. 9378-B), 132 (Douglas ref. no. 58-31-9), 134 (Douglas photo no. 58-31-6), 142 (photo no. P-41082)
National Air and Space Museum, Smithsonian Institution/Estate of Clayton Knight: 092 (SI 89-8109)
National Air and Space Museum, Smithsonian Institution/The Port Authority of New York and New Jersey: 042(NASM 9A01579), 043 (The Port of New York Authority, negative no. IA 11804, 5/17/61)
Nederlands Architectuurinstituut, Rotterdam/©VG Bild-Kunst, Bonn 2004: 219, 220, 221, 223
Isamu Noguchi Foundation, Inc., New York: 454

Orly. 600 Tonnes d'aluminium. Paris, no date, p. 15: 076; p. 42: 074; p. 5: 075

Gio Ponti Archiv, Milan/Photograph: S. Licitra, Milan: 210
Poster Collection, National Air and Space Museum, Smithsonian Institution: 400 (SI 98-20065)
Poster Collection, National Air and Space Museum, Smithsonian Institution/British Airways: 389 (SI 98-20520), 390 (SI 98-20435), 395 (SI 98-20238)
Poster Collection, National Air and Space Museum, Smithsonian Institution/KLM: 135 (SI 98-20317)
Poster Collection, National Air and Space Museum, Smithsonian Institution/SAS: 392 (SI 98-20618)

Qantas: 191

Radi Designers, Paris: 371
RIBA Library Photographs Collection, London: 037, 048, 080, 082
Nick Roericht, Ulm: 363, 365, 366
Martha Rosler, New York: 457, 458

Shadowa, Larissa A.: Malewitsch. Kasimir Malewitsch und sein Kreis. Munich 1982, Fig. 286: 455
Singapore Airlines Ltd.: 313
Southwest Airlines: 314, 315
Stiftung Archiv der Akademie der Künste, Berlin,

Abteilung Baukunst, Gebrüder Luckhardt: 176, 177, 178, 181, 182, 183
Stockholm Design Lab: 244
Swiss International Air Lines: 245, 246
Syracuse University Library, Department of Special Collections: 436

Tangerine, London: 190
Teague, Seattle: 027, 116, 128, 129, 130, 131, 137, 143, 155, 341, 343, 344, 346
©Photo: Hans Thorwid Nationalmuseum, Stockholm: 243, 356
Tupolev Public Stock Company, Moscow: 031, 034

United Airlines Archives, Chicago: 325, 327, 328, 329, 331, 332, 333, 335, 336, 337, 338, 339

Virgin Atlantic Airways Ltd.: 195
Vitra Design Museum: 008, 017, 023, 025, 026, 036, 121, 179, 200, 227, 228, 229, 230, 231, 232, 235, 375
Vitra Design Museum/Photograph: Andreas Sütterlin: 170, 348, 349, 350, 352, 367, 368, 164, 167, 169, 171, 180, 351
Vitra Design Museum/Airbus: 033, 154
Vitra Design Museum/Air France: 153, 198
Vitra Design Museum/American Airlines: 019, 020, 184, 233, 234, 237, 271
Vitra Design Museum/Boeing: 151
Vitra Design Museum/British Airways: 100, 127, 136, 203, 204, 206 (Photograph: Andreas Sütterlin), 345 (Photograph: Adrian Meredith)
Vitra Design Museum/KLM: 009, 398
Vitra Design Museum/Pakistan International Airlines: 308
Vitra Design Museum/United Airlines: 202

Wilhelm Wagenfeld Stiftung, Bremen/©VG Bild-Kunst, Bonn 2004: 361